In Defense of a Nation
Servicewomen in World War II

In Defense of a Nation
Servicewomen in World War II

EDITOR
Major General Jeanne M. Holm
USAF (Ret.)

EXECUTIVE EDITOR
Judith Bellafaire, Ph.D.

VANDAMERE
PRESS

This edition published by special arrangement with Military Women's Press

Dedicated to the women and men
who served America
in
World War II

Acknowledgements

Jeanne M. Holm
Major General
USAF (Ret.)
Editor

From start to finish this book has been a collaborative effort and a labor of love for the many individuals involved. Motivated by a belief that the contributions of America's women to our nation's defense during World War II was a story that needed to be told, they wanted to help in its telling without personal gain or remuneration.

The idea for this project emerged from a brainstorming session of interested individuals gathered in the offices of the Women In Military Service For America Foundation, Inc. in October, 1996. From this and subsequent meetings a core group evolved that became the editorial advisory board comprised of Brigadier General Margaret Brewer, USMC (Ret.); Jean Ebbert, Author; Colonel Bettie J. Morden, USA (Ret.); Brigadier General Connie Slewitzke, USA (Ret.); Bettie Splaine, CWO4, USCG (Ret.); Dr. Judith Bellafaire, Foundation Curator; and myself. This board developed the concept, organization, guidelines, and parameters of the publication and reviewed each input to ensure continuity and historical accuracy. Their knowledge of the subject, active participation and thoughtful advice were essential to the process at every phase.

At the heart of this book are the chapters devoted to the patriotic women who served in the various components organized for war. The content and views expressed in each chapter are those of the individual authors based upon their own research and knowledge of the subject. While editing and advice were provided by the advisory board, final decisions on content and style rested with the authors. It is they who deserve the credit for the substance of this work. Without their enthusiasm for telling this important story and their dedication to historical accuracy this volume would not have been possible.

We are deeply indebted to Brigadier General Wilma L. Vaught, President of the Foundation, for her total support and enthusiasm for this project from the outset and to her excellent and devoted staff: Britta Granrud, Marlene Reckling Murty, Jan Shaw, Jennifer Finstein and others who provided vital assistance when needed. But it is Dr. Judith Bellafaire who bears a lion's share of the credit for this publication. Performing the painstaking and often frustrating tasks of executive editor, Dr. Bellafaire reviewed manuscripts submitted by the authors and worked with them to finalize the text of each chapter. Using her many skills as an historian, writer and editor, she did yeoman service in pulling together the various elements of the publication. We are all in her debt.

Contents

Acknowledgements   vii

Foreword   Brigadier General Wilma L. Vaught, USAF (Ret.)   xi

1   **America Goes to War**   1
Major General Jeanne M. Holm, USAF (Ret.)

2   **Army Nurse Corps**   9
Colonel Mary T. Sarnecky, USA (Ret.), RN, DNSc

3   **Navy Nurse Corps**   29
Susan Godson, Ph.D.

4   **Women's Army Corps: WAAC and WAC**   39
Colonel Bettie J. Morden, USA (Ret.)

5   **WAVES: Navy Women's Reserve**   57
Jean Ebbert, M.A. and Marie-Beth Hall, B.A.

6   **Marine Corps Women's Reserve**   77
Colonel Mary V. Stremlow, USMCR (Ret.)

7   **Coast Guard Women Reserves: SPARs**   97
Captain Mary E. McWilliams, USCGR (Ret.)

8   **Women Airforce Service Pilots: WASP**   111
Lieutenant Colonel Yvonne C. Pateman, USAF (Ret.)

9   **Army Dietitians, Physical Therapists and Occupational Therapists**   123
Colonel Ann M. Ritchie Hartwick, USA (Ret.)

10 | **We Also Served**   133
Judith Bellafaire, Ph.D.

11 | **The Legacy**   143
Major General Jeanne M. Holm, USAF (Ret.)

About the Authors | 151

Chronology | 157

Cover Key | 166

Abbreviations | 169

Chapter Notes and Sources | 171

Selected Bibliography | 181

Index | 185

Foreword

Wilma L. Vaught
Brigadier General
USAF (Ret.)
Foundation President

As I look back upon my entry into the Air Force in 1957, I realize anew how very fortunate I was to have been taken under the wing of two women who had served in World War II. One was Lieutenant Colonel Ruth L. Blind, Deputy Director of Personnel for the bomb wing to which I was assigned. The other was Captain Marian Hand, a nurse at the Barksdale Air Force Base hospital.

These two women gave me an education about the history, service, and accomplishments of the women who served during that critical period for our nation that few could have given, because they had lived it from the very beginning of the war.

As I listened, hour after hour, to their "war" stories, and those they recounted of other women they had known, I kept wishing it were all written down some place, never to be forgotten. From such a record, those of us following could have known of their experiences and challenges, and it might have made it easier as we built on what they had accomplished.

Most people do not realize that when World War II ended, women were in every service branch and were assigned around the globe. Thousands were in countries they never expected to be in and, in most cases, would never see again. It wasn't always easy for our World War II women. There were many barriers, but they overcame most of them, one by one. Nothing ever dimmed their enthusiasm.

It is only fitting that in this first book published by the Women In Military Service For America Memorial Foundation, we should record the story of these women, one-fifth of all the women who have served in over 220 years of American history, and pay a special tribute to them in this way. They changed the world—not only with respect to women in the military but women in the workforce in general. They performed jobs women had not done before and did them well. Their service proved a catalyst for expanding women's roles and opportunities throughout the world.

It should be no surprise that at the June 22nd, 1995 groundbreaking ceremony for the Memorial, Colonel Mary A. Hallaren, USA, Retired, the third Director of the Women's Army Corps, would sum up the contributions of the World War II women as follows: "Almost 400,000 women served in that war, at home and overseas. They served in Europe, in North Africa, and the Far East. They island-hopped in the Pacific—strafed by Japanese planes. They served in England under the buzz bombs. The quality of their work is on record in the unit citations, Purple Hearts, Bronze Stars, and Legions of Merit that were awarded them. All these women truly have earned their place on the roll of the Women's Memorial."

We at the Foundation feel honored to have provided a forum for the very talented women who have come together under retired Major General Jeanne M. Holm's leadership to put together this brief history of women's service in World War II. Each author worked hard to portray the many aspects of service of our stalwart, adventuresome World War II women.

We only wish that we could have mentioned by name and told the story of each woman, but that could never be. It is our hope, however, that some day the name and record of service of each one will be included in the Memorial computer register. For most, World War II was the defining moment of their lives. Still today, more than fifty years later, they say, "It was the best time in my life. I would do it all over again if my country needed me."

It wasn't just my brother's country, or my husband's country, it was my country as well. And so this war wasn't just their war, it was my war, and I needed to serve in it.

Major Beatrice Hood Stroup
WAC, World War II

In Defense of a Nation
Servicewomen in World War II

1

America Goes to War

Major General
Jeanne M. Holm
USAF (Ret.)

More than any other event in this century, World War II transformed the United States from an isolationist country with a small military establishment designed primarily for self-defense into a leading military power with forces stationed around the globe. In the process, the U.S. Armed Services were transformed from essentially all-male to mixed-gender forces.

From the birth of the nation until well into the twentieth century, American women struggled with only limited success for the right to serve in their country's defense. The United States came to the reluctant realization that women had important contributions to make to the armed forces at the turn of the century and took a limited first step by officially accepting military nurses into the Army and Navy. A second step forward was taken by the Navy, Coast Guard, and Marine Corps during World War I when they recruited women into their enlisted ranks. The first step had long-term implications reaching in an unbroken line to the modern military. The second was a temporary manpower expediency which was abandoned at war's end. But the concept of having women in the military ranks would not die, and by 1942 it was an idea whose time had truly come. Women were desperately needed, and they were ready and willing to serve.

World War II was the major turning point in the relationship of women to the armed forces. For the first time in our history, the military services set out to recruit large numbers of women to fill not only essential nursing positions, but to meet military requirements across a vast array of officer and enlisted skills. Before it was over, some 400,000 American women had answered the call of the Army, Navy, Marines and Coast Guard. This great endeavor exceeded all but the most optimistic expectations, and paved the way for women's permanent integration into the U.S. Armed Forces.

At the outset, it was intended that, in addition to the nurses, women would be recruited to provide traditional administrative skills for military units in the United States, thereby releasing men from desk jobs for reassignment to combat duties at the front and at sea. But within months, women were being trained to assume a great variety of nontraditional, noncombat duties at bases in the U.S. and in combat theaters all over the world. Also, it was soon clear that the influx of women service members helped alleviate military manpower shortages which had been growing more critical by the day.

In the industrial sector, civilian women also broke new ground by filling jobs previously held only by men. Additionally, many thousands of patriotic civilian women served their country during the emergency as volunteer members of national organizations which provided much needed support to the military troops at home and overseas.

The Gathering Storm

For most Americans, World War II started on 7 December 1941 when the Japanese attacked Pearl Harbor. For most Europeans, the war began on 1 September 1939 when the German Army smashed across the Polish border despite international guarantees protecting Polish territory. By the time the United States entered the war on the Allied side, most of Europe was under German domination, Great Britain had been driven from the European mainland and was fighting for her very survival, and the armed forces of the Japanese Empire had taken control of most of Southeast Asia and were advancing into the Southwest Pacific.

Until the attack on U.S. territory, most Americans remained relatively indifferent to the catastrophe befalling the rest of the world. They were determined to remain aloof from foreign entanglements, and felt secure behind Congressional declarations of neutrality. But as tensions mounted in Europe, the posture of U.S. neutrality became increasingly difficult to sustain. In September 1939, President Franklin Roosevelt proclaimed a limited national emergency and authorized small increases in the armed forces. Less than a year later, Italy attacked France and the U.S. President declared that the Allied powers had the nation's full support. In August, Congress authorized the President to call the National Guard and Reserves to federal service, and one month later passed legislation authorizing the first peacetime draft in American history. During the ensuing months, the United States moved gradually yet inexorably toward a wartime footing.

Mobilization for War

The military manpower challenges involved in preparing for a global war were staggering. After the rapid demobilization at the end of World War I, the U.S. Armed Forces had remained small. America's armed forces were at a peacetime level of less than 350,000 men in 1939. The military services were undermanned, under-funded, poorly trained, and ill equipped. When America finally entered the war in December 1941, there were slightly more than one million men in arms and a few thousand female military nurses. By the summer of 1945, there would be more than 12 million men and women on active duty in the Army, Navy, Marines and Coast Guard, deployed all over the world.

As the armed forces gradually built up in 1940 and 1941, the only military women to be mobilized were nurses. The all-female

Army and Navy Nurse Corps had been established in 1901 and 1908. They were called up in 1917 and served honorably and effectively throughout World War I, both stateside and with General John J. Pershing's American Expeditionary Force in Europe. When the war ended, both nurse corps were reduced to their small peacetime authorizations. Many of the nurses became reservists to be ready for the call to duty in the event of another emergency. As expected, in the force buildup preceding World War II, nurses again answered the call. When the Japanese attacked U.S. bases in the Western Pacific, Army and Navy nurses were among the first Americans to face enemy fire and the prospect of death or imprisonment.

During the early period of the new military buildup, however, there were no plans for mobilizing women for duties other than nursing. This attitude was curious, considering that there were many other skills required by the military that in the civilian workplace were almost totally dominated by women, to the extent that they had come to be referred to as "women's jobs"—typists, clerical workers and telephone switchboard operators, for example. Yet in the armed forces these jobs were routinely performed by enlisted men who often lacked the training, motivation and skills required. The notion seemed to prevail that there was something inherently masculine about performing these same tasks in the military environment—even in the safety of a headquarters at a stateside base.

The concept of recruiting women to fill clerical and similar jobs in the military was not without precedent. During WWI, the Navy and Marines, on orders from the Secretary of the Navy, recruited women into their enlisted ranks as a means of

acquiring the _____ duty in stateside headquarters an___ ___its. A few even served in administrative posts overseas with naval units in Europe and in U.S. territories. The intent was to release able-bodied sailors and Marines for duties with the fleet and at the front. Although the women proved to be highly successful, both programs were disbanded in the general demobilization that occurred at the end of the war. Furthermore, the loopholes in the Navy's law under which the women had been recruited were closed to preclude similar occurrences in the future.

The Army, on the other hand, had steadfastly refused to depart so radically from tradition by allowing women to serve in its ranks. Despite entreaties from General Pershing and the known fact that the British army was using enlisted women with great success, the U.S. Army held firm. The idea would not die, however. Various plans were floated within the Army's staff during the interim years, but each met with stiff resistance. Those plans which did surface were kept alive chiefly to placate powerful women's civilian groups and a female member of Congress.

As war clouds gathered once again and the pace of mobilization increased, the pressure on the military mounted. With full military and industrial mobilization, manpower shortages became a reality. Decisions were made at the top levels of the U.S. government to mobilize American womanpower as never before in both the civilian and military sectors. Shortly after Pearl Harbor, at the request of the services, Congress authorized new women's military components for each of the services, and increased the number of active duty slots in the Army and Navy Nurse Corps.

The two nurse corps had the advantage of being well-established components of the Army and Navy. They had the better part of four decades of experience, and an earlier war, to fall back on while organizing for World War II. By contrast, the new women's components would have to be organized and staffed from scratch.

But even before legislation establishing any of the new women's components could be passed by Congress, one central contentious issue had to be resolved—the question of their official status. Would women service members be in the armed services with full military status, or would they serve with the military in quasi-military or auxiliary status? The differences between the two were vast. It was the difference between being full-fledged military personnel, with the privileges, benefits and legal protection provided service personnel on the one hand, or on the other, being an organized part of the armed forces subject to many of the rules and obligations of military service, while legally they were civilians in uniform.

This question had long been a thorny one with the nurses. When the all-female nurse corps were established more than forty years earlier, it is unlikely that either Army or Navy leadership ever seriously considered granting them full military status, or that the women themselves would have expected it. The concept would have been alien to the societal mores of the time. In essence, those early women pioneers volunteered to don uniforms, submit to military rules, and even to risk their lives in order to serve their country in war—all without the benefits and protected status granted to the men with whom they served. Their circumstances were somewhat improved in the early 1920s in recognition of their contribution to World War I. But when the Army and Navy Nurse Corps mobilized for yet another war in the early 1940s, the issue of their military status still had not been resolved, nor would it be until well into the war.

When the subject of organizing new military women's components arose, the question of their status became a major bone of contention, with strong advocates on both sides of Capitol Hill and at the senior levels of the services. On at least one occasion, even the White House became involved. Initially, the Army pulled Congress one way and the Navy the other. Eventually, a single solution was settled on that would ultimately apply to the nurse corps as well.

The Racial Policy Dilemma

Probably the most vexing problem facing all of the women's program planners was how to deal with the issue of race. The military services of the early 1940s reflected the racial attitudes and policies of contemporary society at large. The military, like much of society, operated on a segregated basis. Blacks and whites were trained separately, lived and ate separately, and served in segregated units.[1] In the south, where many military installations were located, the communities surrounding military bases had "Jim Crow laws" relegating blacks to the status of second-class citizens. Civil rights activists and organizations were actively pressing the administration to end racial practices in the military, with a view to eventually desegregating the armed forces. Although the political power of these groups was growing, as of the start of the war, they had been unable to crack the military bastions. The services, convinced of the rightness of their policies, were determined to resist changes in the status quo. That determination soon foundered on the realities of the manpower buildup.

In 1940, the Selective Service and Training Act required that one in ten draftees be black. The impact on the Army was immediate, since it relied heavily on draftees to meet its manpower requirements. But, despite the sudden influx of blacks created by the 10 percent quota, the Army remained committed to racial segregation. Its leaders were convinced that racial problems should not be permitted to complicate the task of fighting a war.

Initially the 10 percent quota on draftees had little impact on the other services, since they were meeting their requirements with male volunteers. Then in 1942, a Presidential Proclamation decreed that the draft would be the sole source of military manpower, which meant that henceforth the 10 percent black quota on male recruits would apply across the board. It would lead to radical changes in the racial composition and policies of the sea services—the Navy, Marine Corps and Coast Guard—during the war.

From the outset, the women's components were required to follow the racial policies of their respective services. But since women were not subject to the draft, there was no legal obligation to recruit black women. Nonetheless, the War Department (Army) informed Congress that it intended to apply the 10 percent quota to female recruiting for both officers and enlisted women. None of the other services followed the Army's lead, nor did they plan to recruit black women. Only late in the war did the Navy and Coast Guard recruit black women in token numbers. The Marine Corps did not accept them at any time during the war.

Ironically, during the war the only service to actively recruit black women from the beginning—the Army—would come under the heaviest scrutiny of civil rights activists.

Getting Organized

Between May, 1942 and the following January, each of the military services organized its new women's components and set out to recruit modest numbers of women for officer and enlisted ranks. On 15 May the Army got the authority to establish the Women's Army Auxiliary Corps (WAAC). The other services followed in quick succession with their own programs, but with an important difference. The Navy, Coast Guard and Marines all rejected the notion of auxiliary status for their women, opting instead to enroll them in the reserves on the same basis as their male counterparts. The members of the Navy Women's Reserve came to be known by the acronym WAVES. Similarly, Coast Guard women were known as SPARs. The Marine Corps alone of the services rejected the use of clever acronyms for its women; they would simply be the Marine Corps Women's Reserve or MCWRs (also WRs). The decisions by the other services to grant women full military status put the Women's Army Auxiliary Corps at a distinct disadvantage, particularly in the recruiting market. Subsequently, the Army sought Congressional authority to redress the imbalance. In September 1943 the WAAC was converted to the WAC—Women's Army Corps, thus putting Army women on an equal footing with their sisters in the other services.

Viewed from the perspective of the 1990s, when the military operates as a gender integrated force, the concept of "women's components" strikes many people as something of a paradox. But in the 1940s it would have been totally unacceptable to even consider integrating women fully into the military. Gender segregation was common practice on college campuses and in many social organizations. It was assumed that the women's programs would be supervised and administered by an all-female support structure headed up by senior women. Although the degree to which these programs would be segregated varied from service to service, each group was set up to maintain its own identity as a women's component.

A precedent had been set forty years earlier with the establishment of the all-female Army and Navy Nurse Corps, but that example was of limited value in planning for these new programs. The nurses had a well-defined mission confined to one function. The functions of these new women's groups were only vaguely understood.

The laws creating the WAAC, WAVES, SPARs and the Marine Corps Women's Reserve provided a general framework and some specific policy requirements, but much was left unsaid. Just how they should be organized, recruited, trained, housed, clothed, assigned and administered, as well as who should set policy remained to be worked out. And all of this would have to be accomplished expeditiously by service staffs already swamped with the more pressing issues of mounting a gigantic force to fight a global war.

The first order of business was to bring in someone of recognized stature with experience in women's matters. Each of the services tapped a woman of exceptional talent and abilities to help design and head up its new women's program. For most of the war, the WAAC/WAC was headed by Oveta Culp Hobby; the WAVES by Mildred McAfee; the SPARs by Dorothy Stratton and the MCWRs by Ruth Cheney Streeter. Designated "directors," each woman held the highest rank authorized by the law which established the component she directed. Although officially their authority was limited to advising the senior service staffs on the women's program, the directors exercised influence far beyond their designated rank and positions in the service hierarchy.

Many of the problems the directors faced were service unique, others were gender specific and shared by all four. In navigating the hostile waters of the male-oriented military, the women directors were mutually supportive—sharing their views and experiences and working out policy issues collectively.

As the new support structures emerged, many similarities in function and organization in the women's service components developed since their missions, or reasons for being, were essentially the same. There was one significant difference, however. The WAAC, and later the WAC, was organized as a separate all-female corps of the Army. None of the other services followed that example. Contrary to a popular misconception (which persists to this day) the WAVES, SPARs and Women Marines were not separate corps. They were more informal and loosely formed with no official organization similar to a corps structure.

By early 1943, the number of official women's military components had expanded from two (the Army and the Navy Nurse Corps) to six. At about that same time another organization of uniformed women emerged under the aegis of the Army: the Women Airforce Service Pilots (WASP) which was formed to perform flying missions for the Army Air Forces within the continental U.S. What distinguished the WASP from the other uniformed women's components was that they were civilians under contract to the Army. Efforts to militarize them failed in Congress even though they had the strong support of Army leaders. However, despite their lack of military status, the WASP added a significant chapter to the history of women's service to America during World War II.

Another group of women serving with the armed forces had more success in gaining military recognition—health professionals trained as dietitians, physical therapists, and occupational therapists. They would eventually succeed and become the Army Women Medical Specialist Corps (WMSC).

Finally, thousands of women volunteered to serve in uniformed civilian service groups which directly supported the military services both at home and overseas. Chapter 10 tells the story of the women who served in such organizations as the Red Cross, the USO, the Public Health Service, and the Cadet Nurse Corps during the war.

The acceptance of women into the United States Armed Forces during World War II opened the door for patriotic women to serve their country in time of national crisis—one of the most important rights and obligations of citizenship. Just where this would lead in the long term would depend on how the women met this new challenge both individually and collectively. Many people saw this venture as a social experiment doomed to fail. Others were convinced that, given the chance, American women would prove up to the challenge.

This book attempts to tell the stories of each of the wartime women's components,

beginning with the already established nurse corps. Each chapter will describe how the services struggled to accommodate the presence of women in its ranks and the women's struggles for acceptance in an alien male-dominated institution which was initially skeptical of the whole idea.

Each author brings considerable experience and background knowledge of her subject to this project, and has drawn extensively on published firsthand accounts of women who served.

It is important for the modern reader to understand that the events described in these chapters did not happen in a vacuum, but were products of the time. These events can only be truly understood within the social-military context of the 1940s, when women's roles in American culture were heavily circumscribed by conventions which were not very far advanced from the Victorian era. The military was barely a generation removed from the days of the horse cavalry. The concept of women in military service was incomprehensible to many Americans. Those women who volunteered for military service took a tremendous risk. Former Lt. Commander Mary Daily of the Navy Reserve said it best.

> Many thousands of women volunteered [to relinquish] secure civilian status to [accept] unknown military experience— some taking substantial salary cuts; each one going into unknown assignments, [and] unknown living conditions—there would be restrictions such as none had ever known. It was...an unchartered course on an unknown sea.[2]

What the military authorities and the women volunteers set out to accomplish together was a remarkable undertaking for its time.

2

Army Nurse Corps

**Colonel
Mary T. Sarnecky**
USA (Ret.), RN, DNSc

The Army Nurse Corps (ANC), established in 1901 and thus the oldest female branch of all the military services in the United States, grew to unprecedented numbers after Japan's attack on Pearl Harbor. To meet the demands of total war, the corps expanded to more than 57,000 Army nurses. Members of the ANC served in almost every corner of the globe, meeting a complex and sometimes bewildering series of challenges. As with most of the World War II generation, Army nurses' contributions spoke of patriotism, sacrifice, and dedicated service.

The Zone of the Interior

Many Army nurses served in the "Zone of the Interior," or the continental United States. Ruth Parks was assigned to Camp Blanding, Florida, a military compound located on a reclaimed swamp. Her sentiments and experiences personified those of Army nurses across the nation as it mobilized for global war.

> An Army nurse, in times like these, does a little for a great many patients rather than a great deal for a few . . . The nurse's objective is to organize the work and run the ward as smoothly and as efficiently as possible . . .
>
> In truth, I can paint no pretty picture of life in the Army during these days of great stress and urgency. In the loneliness and confusion of a chaotic world one finds much hard work and sacrifice and little peace. It takes a few weeks for one to make the necessary adjustments to Army life. There is sadness in leaving home and the sense of security which familiar surroundings give one. In the Army one becomes a member of a systemized force of trained personnel. We act as a united group rather than as individuals . . . Our individual integrity and sense of responsibility is the essence of the success and survival of democracy. Every day we are demonstrating with increasing clarity that we too have that consciousness of the reverence and dignity of human life for which the British and their Allies are so valiantly struggling.[1]

The Attack on Pearl Harbor

The Japanese attack on Pearl Harbor had very real implications for the Army nurses who were in the direct line of fire. Lieutenants Irene Boyd and Monica E. Conter were on duty at Hickam Field on what began as a quiet Sunday morning, 7 December 1941. At 0755 hours, Conter was compiling reports when she heard:

> . . . a roaring of planes very close and remarked, "Sounds like a plane falling." Then came a great explosion. I said "It crashed!" The patients and I ran out on the third floor porch overlooking Pearl Harbor. Numerous planes were diving, an explosion and a great mass of black smoke with each dive . . . One of the patients remarked, it must just be maneuvers. About that time the Japs [sic] were over Hickam Field and had laid the first egg . . . Then we knew.
>
> I rushed downstairs and received permission from our CO to bring the patients down. Some were in the elevator when the electricity was cut off—they used the trap door to get out—and all the electric clocks stopped at exactly eight o'clock. You cannot imagine the noise— aerial torpedoes, bombs, machine gunning, our anti-aircraft . . . In the middle of this, the other ANCs and the doctors reported for duty. Shortly, the first casualties began to come in. Then the work really began.
>
> Everyone was still in somewhat of a daze . . . Phrases registered in my mind, phrases I had never heard used: "All walking casualties in these trucks to Tripler [General Hospital] . . ."
>
> Up to this time we were able to tag all patients, give T.A.T. [tetanus anti-toxin] and M.S. [morphine sulfate]. Then we heard the roaring of planes again . . . one

made a thirty foot crater about twenty feet from the [hospital] wing . . . the next bomb fell across the street near headquarters . . . Smoke and fumes from the bomb came in and someone cried "Gas!" We all thought the same thing: "the bombs didn't get me but the gas will . . . " Soon afterward we had our masks and helmets. More casualties, worse than the first. We didn't even get to tag them. All we could do was give M.S., using 10 c.c. syringes one quarter gr. to each C.C. and send them on to Tripler . . . There are a few cases that are outstanding in my memory . . . the Major who was lying on the floor with a bomb fragment in his collarbone. When I went to give a "shot of M.S." he said "Don't stop to take care of me, I'm alright [sic] give it to the boys who need it" . . . Then the numerous cases who were crying "Water, Water," and there was no water— we heard it had all been poisoned.[2]

Another Army nurse remembered:

> At sunset, directly in front of the hospital "Old Glory" was still flying even tho she had a huge rip completely across, due to machine gunning . . . Then began our first "blackout" night.
>
> The climate, flowers, scenery, nights, et cetera, are still just wonderful but instead of wearing hibiscus and leis, we are wearing little tin hats and gas masks.[3]

The Philippine POWs

Army nurses assigned in the Philippine Islands also came under fire. The advancing Japanese line eventually forced American forces to withdraw to the Bataan peninsula, where conditions became increasingly desperate. Extreme shortages of food and supplies were typical in the open-air military hospitals the nurses established on Bataan. When ordered to retreat further to Corregidor Island, Army nurses reluctantly abandoned their patients. Operating room nurse Lucy Wilson wrote:

[We] took off our gloves and gowns . . . walking out in the middle of an operation with hundreds lined up under the trees waiting for surgery was devastating to me. This I have to live with for the rest of my life.[4]

The "Angels of Bataan" settled in a hospital tunnel carved under Malinta Hill. Dire straits and hopeless conditions worsened. During the month-long siege, ten Army nurses escaped by aircraft and eleven were liberated in a Navy submarine. After General Jonathan M. Wainwright, Commander of American Forces in the Philippines, was finally forced to surrender, the Japanese captured the remaining Army nurses and imprisoned them within the former Santo Tomas University complex in Manila with thousands of other foreigners trapped in the city at the time of the Japanese takeover. The nurses' lives and work at Santo Tomas were difficult. Once again, food was scarce. In their two-and-a-half years' captivity, many nurses became ill with dysentery, jaundice, dengue fever, or malaria. Nevertheless, the sixty-six internees persevered and cared for the sick among the 4,000 inmates.

The Pacific

A multitude of Army nurses served in the Pacific during World War II. As the Allies island hopped toward Japan, Army nurses followed. Major Myrtle E. Arndt succes-

Army nurse POW Rose Reiper at nurses' quarters, General Hospital #2, Bataan, the Philippine Islands, 1942.

ANC Collection, US Army Center of Military History

sively served in a number of settings such as Hollandia and Biak in the Netherlands East Indies, and eventually in Japan. She reflected on the Army nurse's life in New Guinea:

The "jungle" uniform consisted of khaki slacks, mud, shirts, mud, field shoes, mud, and fatigues. Many girls seemed more feet than anything else because they wore men's shoes . . . add leggings . . . and you have a picture of what the well dressed nurse wore . . .

Living in a barracks full of women was part of overseas life accepted by all of us. It was like nothing we'd ever done before and like nothing we'll ever do again.

Thirty beds lined up in rows—eight feet of space reflecting individual taste—a minimum of space, a maximum of gear—mosquito nets rolled nearby—rain dripping from the eaves—limp raincoats hanging from mosquito bars—clots of mud—heavy, soggy shoes—the smell of mildew—coffee can wastebaskets—irons cooling on the floor—waiting lines at the ironing boards and washing machines—percolators, gasoline stoves, electric grills—onion sandwiches at night—warm beer—whispered confidences at midnight—home permanents—rumor, rumors, rumors—yellow skins in the shower—the community latrines—mail time—rows of mosquito nets in the moonlight like so many cages—what memories![5]

The 12th Station Hospital, in the Townsville area of Queensland on Halifax Bay, Australia, cared for casualties from the campaign in Papua, New Guinea. Major Edna Mahar, the Base Chief Section Nurse, wrote of the unit's unusual Christmas celebrations:

I will never forget the Christmas season of 1942 . . . On December 23, a field

artillery band played Christmas carols in front of the hospital . . . the sun was so hot, the band could only play for fifteen minutes . . . The Red Cross workers decorated the street in front of the hospital, using large silver bells and branches of a shrub which had bright glossy leaves . . . after midnight, the Red Cross workers and nurses hung a Christmas stocking on the mosquito bar at the foot of each patient's bed. Christmas day dawned with the rain pouring in torrents and the temperature at 110 degrees. The patients were wakened by carols sung by the nurses; . . . about ten o'clock a convoy of patients which we had expected the previous day arrived from New Guinea. After holiday greetings were exchanged, the nurses set about bathing dirty, sick bodies, dressing wounds, and feeding hungry men. Red Cross workers soon found boxes containing candy, cigarettes, toilet articles, and V-mail forms for our new patients. After a big Christmas dinner,

Army nurses stationed at the 12th Station Hospital, Townsville, Australia, 1942.   The Women's Memorial

Army nurses assigned to the 153d Station Hospital, New Guinea, November 1942.

ANC Collection, US Army Center of Military History

many were happily puffing away on their new pipes . . . Many patients expressed their keen enjoyment of Christmas. It was the first time in months that many had been clean and in comfortable beds, with plenty of fresh milk, green vegetables, and meat to satisfy their hunger. One patient remarked, "Take your time, boys, take your time. They have plenty of food; I've had seven glasses of milk." Soon he had a stomach ache . . . the mess officer went into the country to purchase turkeys and chickens. When he reached town the poultry was dead from suffocation and the heat . . . though this country was unseasonable for Christmas, it was Christmas for us for the true spirit of Christmas was in our hearts.[6]

Army nurses served on board hospital ships as well. The Navy supplied the crew for the 700-bed USS *Mercy*, but the staff were Army medical officers and corpsmen and thirty-eight Army nurses. In October 1944, the vessel supported the invasion force during the air-sea battle in the Philippines' Leyte Gulf. Several weeks later, USS *Comfort* and USS *Hope*, both staffed by Army nurses, joined the *Mercy* off Leyte, where they too provided nursing care for enormous numbers of casualties. Tragedy struck the *Comfort* in April 1945 in the waters off Okinawa. A Japanese suicide plane dived into the vessel, killing six Army nurses.

China, Burma, and India

Army nurses stationed in the China-Burma-India Theater cared for Allied troops attempting to stop Japanese soldiers advanc-

Army nurses view damage to the USS Comfort, 1945. The Women's Memorial

ing through China. Lieutenant Margaret Grace was a member of the 112th Station Hospital in Calcutta, India. The hospital's various wards were located in a Rajah's house; in a private residence dubbed the "Buffalo Flats" where animals roamed free in the grounds; and at a "Pink Palace," an elaborate, rose-colored domicile. During the eight-month long season of enervating heat and high humidity, tropical ailments such as malaria, dengue, diarrheal diseases, and dermatological conditions flourished and a surfeit of patients overwhelmed the luxurious accommodations. Grace reminisced:

A large number of patients with tropical diseases were admitted faster than facili-

ties permitted . . . a few hours overtime meant nothing . . . each nurse tried . . . to give the best she had . . . tents were placed between wards to take care of the overflow. During the monsoon season these tents leaked like sieves and the patients would have to be temporarily transferred into the wards . . . One day it became necessary to admit patients into an unfinished ward that had neither doors nor windows and that night after lights were out and everything peaceful, an ungodly shriek was heard. There in the middle of the ward stood a water buffalo who had been trying to lick the feet of one of the patients.[7]

Many patriotic black nurses wished to join the ANC. However, most were denied the privilege of service. Neither regulation nor legislation justified this ostracism. Rather, prejudicial customs and social barriers prevented their full integration into the U.S. Army. Nonetheless, a few circumvented the ban.

A number of black nurses who began their service at Fort Huachuca, Arizona, and Camp Livingstone, Louisiana, arrived in Burma in September 1944. Their ultimate destination was Tagap, "near the top of a 4,500-foot peak of the Patkai Range" where they opened a "sky top hospital"—the 383d Station Hospital.[8] Their patients were " . . . colored and white Americans, Indian and Burmese laborers, [and] Chinese soldiers"

engaged in building a road through the Himalayan Mountains which would be used to send Allied supplies to China. They were afflicted with "the usual things . . . colds, malaria, pneumonia, broken bones, [and] sprained backs."[9] Mabel Keaton Staupers summarized the black nurses' experiences:

> . . . these nurses, although finding the terrain quite rough, enjoyed their new association with British and Indian nurses and medical officers. They learned that even other American nurses, when away from home, did not find race a barrier to understanding and friendship. This was a new experience for the young Negroes since most of them had been sta-

Army nurses, Tagap, Burma, April 1945.

National Archives

tioned in southern camps in the United States where they found race prejudice most harassing.[10]

Alaska

Other nurses served closer to home in the territory of Alaska, where U.S. soldiers were building the ALCAN Highway through the wilderness. One hallmark of the Army nurse, her ability to adapt to harsh environmental conditions, was illustrated in a letter from Viola Boosalis, Chief Nurse of the 206th Station Hospital located in Yakutat.

> Morale among nurses is very high here. Many have become expert skiers. Some are excellent mushers, in that we have our own hospital rescue dog teams to practice with, and no terrain is too difficult for them on snow shoes. When the thermometer drops to 70 below and the sun never shines, they just put on an extra coat . . . We are located directly under the North Star. Many of us have been swimming just recently on the Arctic Circle where there is a lake fed by hot springs. We are all ardent gardeners and this summer the nurses' flower bed and gardens were the envy of the base . . . We planted lettuce seed on Saturday evening, Monday morning it was up, the reason being the sun shines twenty-four hours a day.[11]

The Atlantic

The north and south Atlantic served as another duty setting for Army nurses. The United States sent troops to Iceland to guard the North Atlantic from German submarines. Soon after their arrival in Iceland in 1941, the women were caring for patients with respiratory diseases and accident victims. They also trained for the eventuali-

ties of gas warfare, air raids, patient evacuation, and fire emergencies. The nurses used their sewing and carpentry skills to cope with the deficiencies of the supply lines. They cut and sewed operating room drapes, stitched bed pan covers, and made surgical dressings. Packing boxes were fashioned into furniture. Lieutenant Edna Umbach, Chief Nurse of the 168th Station Hospital, wrote advising a nurse on orders to include "a hammer, small box of assorted nails, thumb tacks, screw driver," and "even a small saw," in her baggage.[12]

Nurses were also sent to the 200th Station Hospital in Recife, Brazil, to support U.S. troops stationed in South America. The pavilion-style stucco hospital with red tile roofs was situated in a coconut grove on a beach with palm trees, green grass, and sea breezes. However, despite outward appearances, all was not perfect in paradise. Until a water line connected the hospital with the city reservoir in 1943, stringent water rationing restricted showers for staff to one per week and two baths per week for patients.

Flight Nursing

During World War II, the women of the United States Army Nurse Corps pioneered and participated in many progressive enterprises. Flight nursing was one of the most intriguing of these endeavors. The trail-blazing women who provided nursing care to the sick and wounded on air evacuation missions defied conventions to take to the air. As volunteers, they underwent rigorous training and endured harrowing experiences.

Approximately 1,500 Army nurses attended various iterations of the flight nurse school during World War II at Bowman Field,

Army flight nurses of the 803d M.A.E.T.S.

The Women's Memorial

Kentucky, or as the war progressed at Randolph Field, Texas. The school prepared these nurses to assume advanced medical responsibilities which included "administering emergency medical treatment, classifying patients, and treatment while in the air."[13]

The skills and knowledge garnered at the School of Air Evacuation prepared one particular group of thirteen flight nurses to survive a two-month-long endurance test when their plane went down in enemy-held Albania. Partisans sheltered the flight crew and guided their 850-mile escape through the treacherous Balkan mountains. Garbed as Albanian peasants, the nurses and their fellow crew members endured a blizzard, fleas and body lice, dysentery, jaundice, and pneumonia. They dodged bullets from Germans, partisans, and guerillas. On one happy occasion, they dined on water buffalo paid for with a GI watch. After so many arduous miles, some of the trekkers' feet ultimately wore holes through their shoes. The journey concluded with a "27-hour forced march, ending with a stumbling descent in pitch darkness down the last snowy mountain to the rocky Adriatic coast." There a British officer welcomed each with a chocolate bar and brandy. They finally boarded a launch and chugged away to freedom in the direction of Allied-occupied Italy.[14]

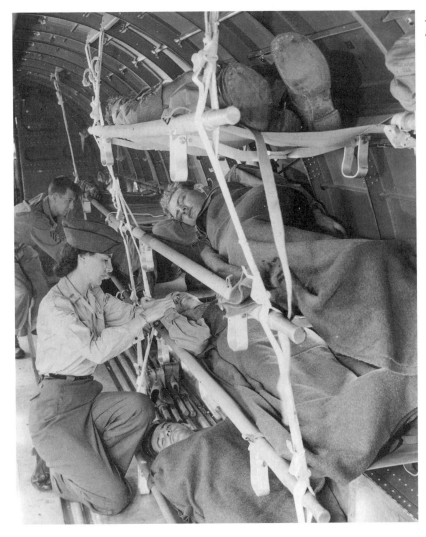

Army flight nurse cares for patients on an evacuation airplane.
ANC Collection, US Army Center
of Military History

The story of Lieutenant Wilma Weatherford's usual sortie from her base in Karachi, India, provides details about the frequently protracted missions and explains some of the difficulties encountered:

Karachi was our introduction to the C-46 (Curtis Time Bomb). Our flights left Karachi between midnight and 2 am, so we could reach Abadan [an island west of Iran] before the heat melted the asphalt runways. The flight to Abadan was seven and a half to nine hours depending on the winds and weather. Abadan was a crew change and a refueling stop. The Red Cross fed our patients and entertained them so we could have a short break. The flight nurse and medical technician went on to Cairo another six and a half to eight hours. Due to time change we were always eating breakfast . . . On arrival in

Cairo you returned on the first available plane sleeping on the cargo or if lucky a passenger plane . . .

The flights were long and tiresome. I think I remained overnight at every airfield from Casablanca to Karachi with engine trouble or weather . . . .

My roommate and I returned to Cairo so many times with engine trouble, the Sgt. in charge of passenger manifests would tell the passengers that if we were on the plane they would be back. One night we returned to Cairo three times.[15]

Seventeen flight nurses made the supreme sacrifice during World War II. Most fatalities resulted not from enemy fire but from crashes during poor weather conditions or inadequate landing fields. The first flight nurse to lose her life in the line of duty was Lieutenant Ruth M. Gardiner, who perished in a plane crash at Naknek, Alaska. Lieutenant Thelma LaFave was reported missing in action after her flight bound from Peleliu in the Palau Islands to Leyte in the Philippines never arrived. Lieutenant Aleda Lutz perished when her aircraft crashed into a mountain in bad weather on a return flight to a base near Marseilles. Without question, the flight nurse's role was hazardous duty.

Maxine Davis, a journalist who had extensive experience with the Army Air Forces, extolled the virtues of the World War II flight nurse:

I cannot seem to speak of flight nurses without sounding like a blurb for a flock of movie stars. Frankly, I found the Army Air Force flight nurses tops. They were gay, friendly, loved their jobs and performed them efficiently, and they were beautiful. I am convinced the officials of the School of Aviation Medicine mea-

sured them, photographed them, and voted on them as for "Miss America." They were, incidentally, healthy, courageous, and stout of heart.[16]

Many of the World War II flight nurses became charter members of the Air Force Nurse Corps which organized in 1949.

The War Against Germany

While some Army nurses supported U.S. troops fighting Japanese forces in the Pacific, many others were sent to Great Britain, North Africa and Europe to take part in the Allied effort against Germany. Army nurses participated in the invasions of North Africa, Sicily, Italy and Normandy.

Most of the Army nurses destined for the European and Mediterranean Theaters went first to staging areas in Great Britain, where instantaneous and drastic adjustments in lifestyle were immediately necessary. Lieutenant Marjorie Peto chronicled her arrival with the 2d General Hospital in Litchfield, England:

Women were not expected . . . the tin huts hastily assigned to them were cold, disgustingly dirty, dismal—a prison-like set-up. The sandwiches given to the nurses . . . proved to be full of worms and were thrown away . . . At the camp there was supper of boiled ham, boiled potatoes and cabbage; it failed to raise spirits . . . the sudden change from comfort, tasty food, lights at night, plenty of soap and hot water, central heating, private baths and familiar surroundings to one of bombed out buildings, scant food, no soap or hot water, black paint on windows, coal stoves, community baths with old-fashioned plumbing, store windows bare or with tragically poor merchandise on display, shabbily dressed people—this was the sharpest adjustment the group ever had to make.[17]

In the years spent waiting for the invasion of the continent, leaders recognized that a need existed to educate hospital chief nurses in matters of military science. In May 1942, the first class of thirty officers arrived at a newly established ANC school at the American School Center, Shrivenham, Berkshire, England. Peto was a member of that first class. Her journal provided a humorous but realistic picture of a student's life.

Drilled in cold rain and sat in class four hours with wet feet. Learning how to cook a chicken (I've seen three since coming over here). ..Yesterday I learned to climb a tree and cross a river on two ropes strung twenty feet above the water; the trick is to hold on one rope and walk on the other. By putting a stretcher on a pulley a patient was pulled over. I was the patient. Then a lecture on booby traps, how to detect them and how to neutralize them; the instructor had me walk into one, a torture thing. Of course this one was a "blank" but it went off with a realistic bang . . .

Up at 4 am to scrub my floor with scouring powder, polish my shoes, then dress for Inspection. Some of the students got demerits for dull buttons but to my eyes they were bright. I have a demerit for having my helmet strap inside instead of outside and I got three demerits the other day for something my shoes did. The rooms were microscoped; everything must be in proper place and folded as directed. Then drill for an hour, an exam on gases and how to inspect a mess. I've just learned, too, how to wash dishes. At one time I thought I was a nurse. Col.

Crawford [Peto's unit commander] wants to come to my graduation, hope I am not in the guardhouse, demerits seem so easy to get. Had an alert last night; we had to get up, dress, and sit in the Hall. The English stay in bed until the bombs fall about their ears—we do things the hard way.[18]

North Africa

After what seemed to be an interminable wait in England, a group of Army nurses from the 48th Surgical Hospital arrived on the coast of Algeria on 8 November 1942, just hours after the first officers and men trudged ashore and began Operation TORCH. One of the group, Lieutenant Theresa Archard, related her experiences as she hit the beach:

. . . Boat by boat we were taken off the ship. It was horrible gazing down at that swaying ladder, our helmets like iron on our heads, full packs on our backs, our shoes untied, and the roar of guns all around us. Suddenly there was an especially heavy explosion and then somehow with the help of that Providence that watches over us all, we were in the commando boat. If Florence Nightingale could see us now!

Toward the shore we raced, but the boat didn't quite make it. We had to wade in—some of the good-looking girls were carried in by the enlisted men. The thought passed through my mind that men were the same the world over—a pretty smile could get you anywhere, even off a commando boat during an invasion. Wet to our waists we floundered up on the beach.

A new land—but what a landing.[19]

Teams of surgeons and nurses set to work through the night with flashlights as their

Army nurses arrive in North Africa, 1943.

National Archives

only illumination. At the time, they occupied a French midwife's abandoned obstetrical home in Arzew. Lieutenant Ruth Haskell described the scene awaiting her in the makeshift hospital:

> . . . I shall never forget the sight that spread out before my eyes in that room. Rows upon rows of American boys lay upon litters all over the floor . . . There were pools of blood beside some of them, where dressings had not been changed since the first shock dressing was applied in the field . . . I experienced at once a violent anger—bitter, surging anger—against a people that, out of greed and power and lust, would cause such things to happen to young manhood.

> . . . As I straddled a litter to continue across the hall, a boy looked up at me and asked "Please, is there water anywhere? I'm terribly thirsty."

> Now we had been told the quart of water we had in our canteen was all we would get until a water point had been established. But what nurse could refuse such a request? Without a moment's hesitation, I bent down and, supporting the boy's head in my hand, helped him to drink from my canteen . . . I asked, "Is that better, sonny? Where do you hurt?"

> There was a moment's silence and then: "My God! A woman, an *American* woman! Where in heaven's name did you come from?" He was almost sobbing when he finished.

There has never been a time in my life
that I have been so proud to be a nurse,
to be able to help.

"Yes sonny," I said. "An American
woman, a nurse. And there are sixty of us
from home over here to take care of you,
get you well, so you'll be able to get back
out there and beat the pants off the guy
that got you—and hundreds like you."[20]

Sicily

Before long, more Army nurses saw action.
Those of the 10th Field Hospital arrived at
Licata two days after the initial invasion of
Sicily and began caring for casualties almost
immediately. The patients were cheered by
the nurses' interest and presence:

While assisting the doctors, the nurses
joked with the patients. Although the
nurse in the shock ward was very busy,
she was usually interested in each of the
boys—asking or guessing where each was
from. The nurses were working twelve
hours, and then hesitated to go off duty
to get rest. They offered the excuse that
"There's a lot of work to be done." or
"Wait until I finish this case."[21]

Italy

Army nurses were among the first wave of
American women to serve in Italy during
World War II. One group of nurses who
were scheduled to arrive during the Salerno
landings on D + 2 on the British Hospital Ship
Newfoundland had their voyage interrupted.
On the night of 12 September 1943, German
planes bombed and sank the hospital ship.
Six British nurses lost their lives in the dis-
aster, but British ships rescued all of the
American Army nurses who returned to
Bizerte, North Africa clad only in their night-
gowns. Many of the survivors sustained

minor injuries, and all lost their personal
effects.

One of the most tragic events, yet a proud
and noble saga in the heritage of the ANC,
was the story of the Army nurses at Anzio
and Nettuno during Operation SHINGLE
early in 1944. Bill Mauldin, the renowned
World War II political cartoonist, provided
a verbal description of the battle area:

Anzio was unique.

It was the only place in Europe which
held an entire corps of infantry, a British
division, all kinds of artillery and special
units and maintained an immense supply
and administrative setup without a rear
echelon . . . there wasn't any rear; there
was no place . . . where enemy shells
couldn't seek you out.

Sometimes it was worse at the front;
sometimes worse at the harbor.
Quartermasters buried their dead and
amphibious truck drivers went down with
their craft. Infantry men dug into the
Mussolini Canal, had the Canal pushed in
on top of them by armor piercing shells,
and Jerry bombers circled as they directed
glider bombs into LSTs [Landing Ship
Tank] and Liberty Ships. Wounded men
got oak leaf clusters on their Purple Hearts
when shell fragments riddled them as they
lay on hospital beds. Nurses died. Planes
crash landed on the single air strip . . .

This wasn't a beachhead that was
secured and enlarged until it eventually
became a port for supplies coming in . . . as
the troops pushed inland. Everything was
expended right here. It was a constant hell-
ish nightmare, because when you weren't
getting something you were expecting
something, and it lasted five months.[22]

Six Army nurses were killed in action at
Anzio. One of those was Lieutenant Blanche
Sigman. In May, 1944 a United States Army

Army nurses wade ashore from a landing craft in Naples, Italy, 1943.   National Archives

Hospital Ship was named for Sigman. Several months later, in October 1944 while en route with casualties from Leghorn, Italy, USAHS *Blanche F. Sigman* sailed past Anzio. At that time, the ship's chaplain lowered the vessel's flag to half mast and spoke over the public address system, saying:

> At this time we ask all aboard to pause for a moment. We are off the coast of Anzio, Italy. It was there on the 7th day of February 1944 that Lieutenant Blanche Faye Sigman ANC was killed by enemy bombs. Wrapped in Old Glory she lies buried over there in a valley. It is an inspiration to all that this Ship, named in her honor, should be transporting others who have fought for the same purpose for which she died. This morning, as we pass close to Anzio, it would seem that Lieutenant Sigman has risen—not merely in the man-made monument of this ship, but especially in the grateful memories of those who owe her and others like her their lives, their liberty and their peace. The loving memory of her heroic death should make us all live better lives and serve more faithfully.

Lieutenant Sigman, we salute you—we salute you and your fellow fighting, serving Americans. Your bodies have stood between us and a relentless enemy. You served faithfully and fought bravely. We are grateful and proud. May God be with you—may God reward you. In your honor we of this hospital ship humbly and reflectfully bow our heads for a minute of respectful silence.[23]

Iran

The environment exerted an adverse impact on those nurses serving in the Persian Gulf Service Command where troop concentrations were widely dispersed. A difficult terrain, harsh climate, and primitive conditions made living and working formidable for the nurses assigned to Iran. The mountains, desert, and coastal areas all presented unique challenges. Dust storms; air temperatures of 150 to 160 degrees; flies, mosquitoes and other insects; and crude sanitation were commonplace. Nonetheless, Army nurses stationed in that corner of the world carried on and zealously performed their assigned duties.

USSR

Duty in the USSR, one of the Allied countries during World War II, was similarly arduous. Soon after three small groups of ANC arrived at their duty stations in the Ukraine, German bombers attacked the hospitals at Poltava, Mirgorod, and Piryatin. The women quickly learned to provide nursing care under fire. Lieutenant Anna Moline, the chief nurse, remembered:

. . . at 1:00 a.m. Luftwaffe planes were overhead, bombing our airfield. We hastily carried non-ambulatory patients

by stretcher to the nearby trenches . . . I hurried to the Russian women's tent . . . and I raced for the trenches . . . We tried to console the patients and watch the intravenous needles inserted into the arms of the critically ill. As we pressed our bodies against the side of the trenches, the earth from the nearby bombing flew over us and into the trenches. I thought "Thank God. I've got my helmet on"—but then remembered that my dogtags were back in the tent! . . . [24]

The bombing ceased at 3:00 a.m. and the nurses' work then began in earnest. Moline wrote:

. . . Patients were returned to the wards that were in great disorder and confusion. Great holes were torn in the top of the tents . . . there were patients on the shock tables, fracture table, x-ray table, and on stretchers on the floor. Plasma and blood transfusions were given, instruments boiled and trays set up . . . the nurses went continuously from one patient to the next, never stopping . . . more patients were brought in, the chaplain came to surgery to see the seriously wounded. Dawn finally came. The nurses washed their faces, had a cup of coffee, and started again.[25]

The Normandy Invasion

By June 1944, all elements were poised for the invasion of Normandy. On 10 June 1944, only four days after that momentous D-Day, the first Army nurses arrived in Normandy. On 22 June 1944, Lieutenant Mary Louise Carpenter wrote to her family sharing her impressions:

. . . I suppose it really was a great event; it certainly seems so from a distance and

Army nurse pauses for a drink in the Ukraine.
The Women's Memorial

viewed in historic perspective, but when you actually see some of the remains of it—the blasted-to-hell farms and villages, a few burnt-out or overturned vehicles, and the face piece of a gas-mask trod into the mud were some of the poignant reminders of death I saw on the first day here—it all seems merely disgusting. Of course, we never see the actual immediate destruction of war as it occurs, but . . .

we see some of the grimmest results of war. Back at the Massachusetts General one has just as seriously ill patients, but by and large they were either oldish or chronically poorly constituted. I can't get used to the way here strong, healthy young men in the course of two days or so turn into those old specters. They're so good, these boys, they bear so much pain and misery without a murmur . . .

Some of the first Army nurses to land at Normandy outside a field hospital between the beach and the front lines, 1944.   National Archives

We work 7 to 7 (so do the day people), which leaves little time for anything else, but one's glad to do it and only wishes that the effort were helping still more than it does.[26]

Soon, the evacuation hospitals were on the move keeping pace with the advancing troops. They would stay in place for several weeks, and then leapfrog one another to maintain short interior evacuation lines. In the cold, snowy month of December 1944, the Germans began their last major offensive against the western Allied advance. The cam-

paign became known as the Battle of the Bulge. Members of the ANC served there in support of Allied operations. Captain Beth Veley was the chief nurse of the 103d Evacuation Hospital which was situated south of Bastogne at Longuyon in crude barracks buildings. The cold was penetrating. The small stoves did little to keep the building's pipes from freezing. Lister (potable water) bags were kept inside to prevent their contents from becoming solid ice. The staff admitted over 500 casualties, many from the 101st Airborne Division, in its first 24 hours of operation. A war correspondent recounted an interaction between Veley and one of her paratrooper patients who voiced his opinion that:

> They shouldn't be up this far. It's too dangerous for a woman. It's good to see them, though, when you come into a hospital. You get a feeling that everything's going to be all right.

The correspondent wrote that in response, Veley:

> . . . lifted a trim eyebrow and smiled. These experienced and battle-scarred fighters didn't know they were talking to a veteran of two sieges; that she was one of the last nurses off Bataan; that a month later she was on the last plane to leave Corregidor; that she wonders daily about the welfare of the sixty-six who were left behind; that the letters "B.B.B." on her gold identification bracelet signify membership in that closed and select corporation "The Battling Bastards of Bataan."
>   They didn't know. She didn't tell them.[27]

December 1944 was another shining moment in the history of the ANC. During the Battle of the Bulge, many Army nurses lost all their clothing and personal property. They endured frigid cold, worked long hours under enemy attack, frequently pulled up stakes in retreat and advance, and ultimately followed the troops into Germany as Victory in Europe was achieved.

Other Concerns

A number of administrative issues which impacted on the ANC surfaced during World War II. Their resolution laid the foundation for the effective, equitable force of women in the Army which would emerge after the war. ANC pay and rank were among these issues. In 1942, the newly formed WAVES and SPARs had rank and remuneration identical to their male counterparts. In contrast, members of the ANC had relative rank and lesser compensation. On 16 June 1942 Congress passed the Pay Adjustment Act of 1942. The legislation provided for higher salaries for Army nurses across all pay grades. However, the nurses' pay still was not equal to that received by the men. The nurses finally were accorded commissioned officer rank, albeit on a temporary basis, on 22 June 1944. The law authorized temporary Army of the United States (AUS) commissions for Army nurses for the duration of the emergency plus six months, along with all the benefits of rank. The next step, the securing of permanent, regular commissions for Army nurses, would not be achieved until after the war with the passage of the Army-Navy Nurses Act of 1947.

Rarely in times of war are numbers of Army nurses perceived as adequate. This discrepancy between projected requirements and actual numbers certainly held true during the course of World War II. Although over 100,000 registered nurses in the United States volunteered for military service in Army and Navy Hospitals and approximately 75,000 actually provided care in military hospitals, continual pressures for more nursing support prevailed.

In 1944, with U.S. military forces engaged on battle fronts around the globe and with military manpower requirements being revised upwards once again, the demand for military nurses increased. In 1945, President Roosevelt requested a nurse draft bill, embarrassing nurses because it seemed to confirm a public perception that American nurses were shirking their patriotic duty by not volunteering for war service.

The entire nurse draft controversy was a result of misinformation, ever-changing military manpower requirements, and innate prejudices regarding the "type" of nurse desired. Had the War Department been willing to accept the services of many qualified black female and/or male nurses who continued to volunteer to serve throughout the war, the question of drafting nurses might have been avoided.

An investigation by Colonel Florence Blanchfield, the Chief of the Army Nurse Corps, concluded that all Army hospitals were adequately staffed. In fact, Blanchfield could not demonstrate any grassroots need for additional nurses. In the final analysis American nurses did react impressively to the threat of legislation and to a stepped up recruitment campaign. A tidal wave of white female nurses did volunteer to serve.

This, coupled with the advent of the end of the war in Europe, ultimately put an end to any more efforts to draft nurses in World War II.

Conclusion

Throughout the epoch of World War II, Army nurses coped with extremes of climatic conditions in deserts, jungles, and the arctic. They lived with rain, mud, cold, snow, heat, sand and flies. Army nurses cared for badly wounded and severely ill soldiers as a matter of course. They suffered illnesses and sustained combat injuries. A total of 215 of these brave women died from a myriad of causes. Members of the Army Nurse Corps endured rudimentary housing and inadequate food, complained, but never faltered on the front lines with the soldiers in every theater. The contributions of the women who served during World War II will remain forever as proud chapters in the history of the United States Army Nurse Corps.

3

Navy Nurse Corps

Susan H. Godson
Ph.D.

Navy nurses were there when the Japanese bombed Pearl Harbor on 7 December 1941, and they were there when the victorious American fleet steamed into Tokyo Bay to accept the Japanese surrender on 2 September 1945. For nearly four years, Navy nurses played a vital role in America's successful war against the Axis forces in Europe and in the Pacific.

Early in the morning of 7 December, Japanese carrier planes swarmed over the island of Oahu and destroyed about 265 military aircraft on the ground. Next, the attackers zoomed in on the ships moored at Pearl Harbor and sank or damaged nineteen vessels of the U.S. Pacific Fleet. The planes flew so low that Nurse Ruth Erickson easily saw the red rising sun on the underside of the wings. Cries rang out, "This is the real thing!" and "Air raid! This is no drill!" The carnage was great: 2,403 Americans killed and 1,178 wounded. The Navy took the most casualties—2,008 killed and 710 injured.

Even before the bombing ended, Navy nurses sprang into action at the Pearl Harbor Naval Hospital. Chief Nurse Gertrude B. Arnest directed thirty other nurses in caring for an endless stream—452 in three hours with many more following—of wounded or burned victims. Many of the burned had jumped from their sinking ships into the water, which had a burning film of oil that engulfed the hapless sailors.[1]

Navy nurses aboard the hospital ship *Solace*, moored at Pearl Harbor, took on casualties even as the bombs fell. Chief Nurse Grace B. Lally and her eleven nurses worked feverishly to alleviate the suffering of several hundred injured. They worked around the clock for days. "Our job was inside the ship," recalled Lally.[2]

On 8 December, the Japanese carried their bombing campaign to other American stations. Enemy aircraft attacked Guam, and two days later Japanese troops captured the island. Five Navy nurses, who had run the training school for native nurses, were among those taken prisoner. Moved first to Zentsuji, and then to Kobe, Japan, the nurses remained prisoners of war until June, 1942, when they returned home as part of an exchange of prisoners.

The list of Japanese targets on 8 December included the Philippine Islands, where the aggressors first launched a systematic bombing campaign before invading the islands on 10 December. Twelve Navy nurses at the Canacao Naval Hospital, led by Chief Nurse Laura M. Cobb, moved their patients to the Army's Sternberg General Hospital, soon to be renamed the Manila Hospital Center. The nurses then served at emergency medical units around Manila. That city fell to the Japanese in early January 1942, and

within days eleven Navy nurses became prisoners of war.

First held in a camp at the University of Santo Tomas, the nurses set up a primitive hospital for fellow internees. When the camp became overcrowded, the Japanese established another facility at Los Banos in May 1943, and the Navy nurses were part of the medical team sent there. Conditions rapidly deteriorated; malnutrition set in; prisoners died. The nurses steadfastly ministered to the sick and injured until American forces recaptured the Philippines and freed the prisoners of war in February 1945. The eleven nurses endured thirty-seven months of captivity, and attributed their survival to

Navy nurse POWs just after their release from Los Banos Camp, February 1945.

US Navy Bureau of Medicine and Surgery Archives

staying busy in their chosen profession and maintaining their dignity and sense of humor. Each received the Bronze Star for their bravery and dedication to duty.[3]

The twelfth Navy nurse, Ann A. Bernatitus, had gone with an Army medical group that set up a hospital on the Bataan peninsula. When the Japanese drew closer, the nurses moved to the island of Corregidor where a series of tunnels housing the Malinta Hospital provided shelter from the endless bombing. On 3 May, three days before Corregidor fell to enemy forces, the U.S. Navy submarine *Spearfish* slipped through Japanese patrols, evacuated twenty-five individuals including Bernatitus, and carried them to safety. When she returned to the United States, Bernatitus became the first recipient of the Navy's new medal, the Legion of Merit.[4]

After an inauspicious entry into World War II, the United States swung into a rapid mobilization of its people and resources. The Navy's Bureau of Medicine and Surgery, charged with caring for the country's naval forces as they fought a two-ocean war, expanded health care facilities at home and overseas. The numbers of all medical professionals—physicians, dentists, hospital corpsmen, and nurses—soared.

The Navy Nurse Corps, so essential to wartime medical service, was fortunate in its leadership. Superintendent Sue S. Dauser joined the Corps during World War I and had served as chief nurse at a variety of hospitals and overseas stations as well as in three ships prior to her appointment as superintendent in 1939. Charged with recruiting, examining, and assigning nurses, Dauser brought warmth, charm, and humor to her post. She would need these traits during the difficult years ahead.[5]

Dauser's most immediate problem was recruiting enough nurses to meet the Navy's needs. As early as 1939, Dauser had foreseen the potential demand for nurses and had begun building a reserve force of Navy nurses that could be quickly called to active duty. When the war began in December 1941, there were 787 Navy nurses on active duty and another 966 inactive Naval Reserve nurses.[6]

The superintendent and her staff used every recruiting means available—the American Red Cross, the War Manpower Commission Procurement and Assignment Service, direct applications to the Bureau of Medicine and Surgery, and finally the Offices of Naval Officer Procurement. A few nurses entered through the federally

Navy nurse Ann Bernatitus, the first recipient of the US Navy's Legion of Merit.

US Navy Bureau of Medicine and Surgery Archives

Captain Sue Dauser, Superintendent of the Navy Nurse Corps from 1939-1946.

US Navy

sponsored Cadet Nurse program. In early 1945, the Secretary of the Navy also lifted the ban on retaining nurses who married while in the Corps and invited back women who had recently left the Corps because of marriage. So successful were these recruiting methods that the Navy Nurse Corps reached its peak strength of 11,086 by June 1945. A total of 14,178 women served in the Corps during the war.[7]

Although there was a chronic nationwide shortage of nurses, the Navy maintained its high standards. Its entering nurses had to be between 22 and 30 years old for Regulars, and between 21 and 40 for reservists. They must have graduated from high school and an approved school of nursing and have qualified as registered nurses. They had to be

unmarried and U.S. citizens. The next hurdles were professional, mental, and physical examinations.[8]

Navy nurses were predominantly white, middle-class women. A majority of volunteers came from New York, California, Pennsylvania, Illinois, and Michigan. Some had attended college or taken postgraduate nursing courses after they had finished training school, and the majority had worked in civilian hospitals. In early 1945, the Nurse Corps accepted five black nurses on a fully integrated basis.[9]

Patriotism motivated most women to join the Navy Nurse Corps. They wanted to help their country win the war and serve a "cause above self," recalled one chief nurse. They came "not for personal gain or glory but to give the very best" that they could. The prospects of foreign travel, more education and training, and diversified experience attracted others.

After new nurses entered the corps, they went right to work. "We had no introduction to Navy nursing or life," remembered Alene Duerk, who later became director of the corps. "We went straight to the wards."[10] In late 1943, recruits began attending a two-week indoctrination course at Portsmouth, Virginia, to learn naval vocabulary, customs, medical practices, and military drill.[11]

When the war began, Navy nurses had no kind of military rank; they were, quite simply, nurses or chief nurses. To make naval service more attractive, Congress in July 1942 granted the nurses relative rank, a status that Army nurses had had since 1920. Their highest rank was lieutenant commander, a slot filled by the superintendent until December 1942, when a new law raised the superintendent to captain, and her assistants to commander. Dauser became the first woman captain in the U.S. Navy and in the Nurse Corps. Finally, in February 1944, Congress granted temporary commissioned rank to Navy nurses for the duration plus six months. The law brought the nurses "honor and dignity . . . and authority consistent with their responsibilities."[12]

Nurses could display their rank on their uniforms, which evolved as the war continued. At first the nurses only had white ward uniforms and caps with blue capes, sweaters, and hats for outdoor wear. In 1942, when they acquired relative rank, a more formal officers uniform became mandatory and consisted of a semi-fitted Navy blue (or white for summer) jacket with gilt buttons and gold stripes signifying rank, an officer's cap, and a corps insignia pin. In 1944 a few minor changes in metal corps insignia and a new gray working uniform completed nurses' outfits.[13]

Navy nurses had always served at a variety of stations in the United States and overseas, and their deployment expanded to meet wartime demands. By June 1945, there were 40 regular hospitals and 176 dispensaries in the United States, with 9,436 of the 11,086 nurses at these facilities. Nurses ministered not only to Navy, Marine, and Coast Guard personnel, but also to their dependents, who had become eligible for naval medical care.[14]

In addition, fourteen special hospitals treated general and surgical convalescents, and neuropsychiatric and orthopedic patients. Navy nurses dispensed reassurance and sensitivity as well as their healing talents at these hospitals, where rehabilitation was the goal. In these hospitals, nurses felt their greatest triumph when "an independent man says good-bye—and walks away."[15]

A vitally important role for Navy nurses was instructing members of the Hospital Corps—those enlisted men who provided most of the actual nursing care in hospitals, ships, aircraft, and on invasion beachheads. Six training schools, staffed by physicians, nurses, and senior hospital corpsmen, taught basic theory to thousands of new recruits. When women became eligible for the corps, they trained at three all-female schools. After the theoretical courses, hospital corpsmen learned the techniques of bedside nursing at naval hospitals under the watchful eye of Navy nurses, who took their teaching responsibilities very seriously. One nurse reflected the sense of urgency: corpsmen must remember their training in the heat of battle, and they must not fail. Corpsmen's failure would be the nurses' failure.[16]

More than 1,200 Navy nurses served overseas in at least forty-one hospitals or dispensaries and in twelve hospital ships. Helping to protect the western approaches to the United States, nurses went to the naval hospital at Kodiak, Alaska, in June 1941. Others saw duty at even more remote hospitals in Dutch Harbor, Adak, and Attu in the Aleutian Islands. These outposts shared common relentless weather—snow, ice, fog, rain, and sudden wind gusts called "williwaws." In spite of the hardships, nurses such as Margaret Allen felt it a privilege to have served in Alaska.[17]

The Navy protected the southern approaches to the United States, and the requirements of an enlarged force brought medical facilities and Navy nurses to the Caribbean. Nurses were at naval hospitals at Guantanamo Bay, Cuba; St. Thomas, Virgin Islands; and Coco Solo and Balboa, Canal Zone. Still others served at San Juan, Puerto Rico; Trinidad, British West Indies; Bermuda; and Curacao, Dutch West Indies. To the north, Navy nurses became part of the medical staff at the naval hospital at Argentia, Newfoundland, in early 1943.[18]

A more unusual assignment fell to Lieutenants (junior grade) Stephany J. Kozak and Dymphna Van Gorp, the Navy's first flight nurses. In January 1944, they went to Rio de Janeiro and established an air evacuation training program for Brazilian Air Force nurses. The Brazilian nurses, noted Van Gorp, were enthusiastic students and liked "combining service to country with a grand new adventure."[19]

To roll back Adolph Hitler's Nazi forces in North Africa and Europe, the Allies launched a series of amphibious operations, and naval medical care followed the fighting. Twenty-five Navy nurses, led by chief nurse Lieutenant (junior grade) Clyde E. Pennington, reached the large base hospital in Oran, Algeria, in March 1944. Soon some of these nurses went to dispensaries in Palermo, Sicily; Naples, Italy; and then Bizerte, Tunisia. Still other Navy nurses had duty on the hospital ship *Refuge* as it shuttled casualties from Italy, from the hospital in Oran, and from the British Isles back to the United States.[20]

The largest contingent of Navy nurses in the European Theater served in England. Anticipating heavy casualties from an invasion of Europe through France, the Navy had established a series of dispensaries throughout the United Kingdom. In March 1944, the Navy commissioned a base hospital at a British military hospital built at Netley in 1862. Lieutenant Commander Mary Martha Heck supervised ninety-eight Navy nurses in preparing for the influx of wounded, all the time watching the damage caused by German V-bombs. Within days of the Normandy invasion of 6 June 1944, casualties poured into the hospital, and

nurses joined the frenetic pace to save lives. "There was no time for meals or rest," recalled one nurse. In only four months, the medical staff treated 7,877 patients with the astonishingly low mortality rate of only 0.26 percent for battle casualties.[21]

The island-hopping campaign in the Pacific required a large number of Navy nurses, and they served with distinction in far-flung hospitals and in hospital ships. After the ignominious disasters at Pearl Harbor, the Philippines, and Guam in 1941, the Nurse Corps, like the rest of the Navy, regrouped and prepared for the sustained effort to push the Japanese back to their home islands. One spot in the Pacific had come through relatively unscathed—Samoa. Although the Japanese had, in passing, shelled the island in January 1942, they caused no major damage, and the Nurse Corps continued to operate the training school for natives which it had begun in 1911.

In late 1942, Navy nurses arrived at Efate, then Espiritu Santo, New Hebrides. When the Navy built a string of hospitals the next year, the nurses were there—in New Zealand, Australia, the Solomons, New Georgia, New Guinea, and New Caledonia. As American forces advanced, larger base hospitals spread from New Guinea to the Admiralties, the Schoutens, the Marianas, and the Marshalls. Fleet hospitals operated at Samar, the Philippine Islands, and at Guam.[22]

Each of these hospitals had around forty Navy nurses, usually more, and many described their unique experiences. Lieutenant Sarah O'Toole wrote of being in the first group to reach Tinian, in the Marianas. "We are pioneers, the first white women, as well as nurses . . . here." Similarly,

Lieutenant Mary H. Staats and 127 nurses arriving in the Solomons had the same distinction.[23]

A major duty for the nurses at all the island hospitals was continually instructing the hospital corpsmen. These men must become so proficient in patient care that they could independently tend to the sick and wounded on battlefields and in combatant ships where nurses were not allowed to go.[24]

Navy nurses served in hospital ships as well as ashore. By the end of the war, the Navy had fifteen of these floating hospitals in the Pacific, and Navy nurses staffed twelve of them. After her fiery initiation at Pearl Harbor in December 1941, *Solace* accompanied invasion forces in the Solomons, the Marianas, Iwo Jima, and Okinawa. *Relief* joined the Pacific Fleet in 1943 and evacuated wounded from the Solomons, the Marshalls,

the Marianas, and the Palaus. She was hit by enemy aircraft during the Okinawa invasion. By 1945, ten more hospital ships with Navy nurses sailed in the Pacific. When the Japanese surrendered aboard the USS *Missouri* in September 1945, nurses in hospital ships *Rescue, Tranquillity,* and *Benevolence* joined the triumphant force in Tokyo Bay and then began evacuating Allied prisoners from Japan.

New to naval medicine in World War II was the air evacuation of the wounded from combat areas, and this technique created another specialty: flight nursing. In late 1944, training began at Alameda, California, and within months 110 women became Navy flight nurses. Stationed at Guam, part of a squadron of flight nurses went into the combat area at Iwo Jima on 6 March 1945. Ensign Jane Kendeigh was the first Navy

USHS Solace *Navy nurses wearing Army uniforms, 1945.*

US Navy Bureau of Medicine and Surgery Archives

First Navy flight nurse to reach Iwo Jima, Ensign Jane Kendeigh, March 1945.   Naval Historical Center

nurse to land there, and she helped load wounded into the evacuation plane. Although the crew came under mortar attack, Kendeigh recalled that she was too excited, and then too busy, to be afraid. Twelve flight nurses continued the air evacuations from Iwo Jima. Next came Okinawa, and once again Ensign Kendeigh was the first Navy flight nurse to reach the island to airlift the wounded. Such rapid evacuation and prompt medical treatment saved thousands of combat casualties.

Air evacuation coupled with an array of new drugs and treatments led to a lower mortality rate. Sulfa drugs came into use in the 1930s, and the introduction of penicillin provided greater control over infections. Whole blood and plasma, better antimalarial drugs, more effective treatment for shock, and the use of DDT against disease-ridden pests all contributed to higher survival rates.

Although no Navy nurses were combat fatalities during the war, nine died while

Navy flight nurse gives records and reports to physician after air evacuation flight from Okinawa to Guam, 1945.

National Archives

overseas and thirty-one died while on duty in the United States. The valor of these nurses earned them 303 military awards, including the Distinguished Service Medal to Captain Sue Dauser for her superb wartime leadership, and the Legion of Merit to Lieutenant (junior grade) Ann Bernatitus. In tribute to the Nurse Corps, the Navy named the destroyer *Higbee* after the corps' second superintendent, Lenah S. Higbee.

Praise for the nurses' wartime service came from the highest echelons. Admiral William F. Halsey, commander of the Third Fleet, pointed to the nurses' "untiring service, their professional skill, and their ability to sustain the unparalleled morale of the wounded," while Fleet Admiral Chester W. Nimitz noted their knowledge, training, and devotion to duty. For General Jonathan Wainwright, released from a prisoner-of-war camp, "The sight of the beautiful Navy nurses was the best medicine an American could have."[25] Dauser was proud of her

nurses and commended their "ever-ready, unselfish solicitude."[26]

After the war ended, Navy nurses, like all the military, underwent rapid demobilization. By July 1947, their numbers had dropped from the wartime high of 11,086 to 2,100. The Navy tried assorted methods to attract and retain its nurses during the post-war era: raises in pay and allowances, expanded educational opportunities, and vigorous recruiting efforts; but the most obvious enticement—permanent commissioned rank—required Congressional action. Finally, on 16 April 1947, the Army-Navy Nurses Act established the Navy Nurse Corps as a separate staff corps within the Medical Department. Its members held permanent commissioned rank ranging from ensign to commander. The superintendent, now called director, became a captain. Navy nurses finally achieved the pay, benefits, prestige, and status they had long sought and so richly deserved.

4

Women's Army Corps: WAAC and WAC

Colonel
Bettie Morden
USA (Ret.)

They [the WACs] might, like the forty-niners, shrink from thought of repeating such a passage, but it would be the prized memory of any lifetime.

Mattie E. Treadwell

The news on December 7th, 1941, that the Japanese had attacked Pearl Harbor, Hawaii, had the effect of a bolt of lightening. It stunned people around the world. Americans were outraged. The sneak attack had killed 2,400 Americans and injured a thousand more. Clearly, the Japanese intended to conquer and rule all the islands and continents in the Pacific—particularly the U.S. possessions: Hawaii, Guam, American Samoa, Midway Islands, Wake Island, and other small islands. Reaction came quickly. President Franklin D. Roosevelt and Congress declared war against Japan on 8 December.

Meanwhile in Europe, beginning in 1939, Hitler's storm troopers had used a similar method called *blitzkrieg,* to surprise, invade and subjugate Poland, Czechoslovakia, Belgium, Holland, Luxembourg, Yugoslavia, Greece, and France. Starting in late 1940, Germany had begun to concentrate on an invasion of England. To help its European friends, the United States had stretched its neutrality law to the limit, but now the time had come for action.

The Women's Army Auxiliary Corps (WAAC)

Beginning in October 1940, men between 21 and 35 were drafted for military service and on 11 December 1941, the U.S. declared war against Japan's allies—Germany and Italy. As their husbands, sons, and brothers left home, many American women asked, "How about us?" Acting as their spokeswoman,

Representative Edith Nourse Rogers (Massachusetts) introduced a bill in May 1941 calling for the creation of an all-volunteer women's corps in the Army.

Initially, members of Congress, the press, and the military establishment joked about the notion of women serving in the Army. But, as war in Europe deepened, the idea seemed less improbable. It received positive attention after the Japanese bombed Pearl Harbor. Soon thereafter, Mrs. Rogers introduced a new bill that would make the women's corps an integral part of the Army. General George C. Marshall, Army Chief of Staff, put his full support behind the bill. With America facing a war on two fronts,

he realized the nation would soon experience a severe manpower shortage.[1]

This situation and General Marshall's influence led both the House and Senate to approve a bill on 14 May 1942, creating the Women's Army Auxiliary Corps (WAAC). President Roosevelt signed the bill next day. (Several months passed before WAAC headquarters knew it had *not* been signed on the 14th. In the interim, the WAAC staff chose 14 May to celebrate the birthday of the Corps—it was never changed.)

To head the Corps, General Marshall recommended and the Secretary of War appointed Mrs. Oveta Culp Hobby of Houston, Texas. On 16 May 1942, she took

Oveta Culp Hobby is sworn in as Director of the Women's Army Auxiliary Corps, May 1942.

Women's Army Corps Museum

the oath of office as Director of the Women's Army Auxiliary Corps and received the relative rank of colonel but the pay of an Army major. In 1940, Mrs. Hobby had been Chief of the Women's Interest Section in the Public Relations Bureau in the War Department. In this position, she helped develop the plans for the WAAC. Married to a former Governor of Texas, Colonel Hobby had been a parliamentarian in the Texas House of Representatives, a newspaper woman, and a civic and social leader in her community. She and her husband had two children. From the beginning, Colonel Hobby was a charismatic inspiration and role model for the women of the Corps. Her words to the first officer candidate class were never forgotten:

> May fourteenth is a date already written into the history books of tomorrow . . . Long established precedents of military tradition have given way to pressing need. Total war is, by definition, endlessly expansive. You are the first women to serve [in the WAAC] . . . Never forget it.

She continued with the words that became the enduring motto of the Corps: " . . . you have a debt and a date. A debt to democracy, a date with destiny."[2]

The WAAC bill was a disappointment to Mrs. Rogers. It made the corps an auxiliary *to* the Army rather than a part *of* it: "The corps shall not be a part of the Army, but it shall be the only women's organization authorized to serve with the Army, exclusive of the Army Nurse Corps."[3] The bill stated that women would serve in noncombat positions, and the corps would be operated and administered according to normal military procedures of command and perform duties prescribed by the Secretary of War. Though the women considered themselves *in* the Army; technically they were civilians working *with* the Army. The law provided for the enrollment of a maximum of 150,000 women. The Army initially planned to increase WAAC strength from 12,000 in the first year to 25,000 by 1943 and to 63,000 by 1944.[4] Initial WAAC recruiting proved so successful that planners had to go back to their drawing boards.

By the end of June 1943, the WAAC already had over 60,000 women. WAAC members had to be citizens between the ages of 21 and 45. Of course, most American women of those ages had been working for some years, and already had the training and experience necessary for the administrative positions it was assumed they would occupy in order to release Army men to serve in combat units.

The distinctive lapel insignia chosen for the Corps was the head of Pallas Athene, the Greek goddess of victory, peace and prosperity, and the virtuous womanly arts. Enlisted women wore the Pallas Athene insignia on the left lapel of the uniform and the U.S. insignia on the right lapel. Officers wore a Pallas Athene on each lapel. The WAAC hat insignia was not the beautiful eagle worn by male soldiers, but a slightly lop-sided version of it that the WACs affectionately dubbed "the buzzard." The Pallas Athene insignia never lost its place as the revered symbol of the WAAC and WAC. When the Corps was accepted into the Army of the United States (AUS) in 1943, "the buzzard" was replaced by the regulation Army eagle on WAC dress hats with a visor—forever known as the "Hobby Hat."

The Army opened five WAAC Training Centers: Fort Des Moines, Iowa; Daytona Beach, Florida; Fort Oglethorpe, Georgia;

Newly arrived recruits march from the train station to Fort Des Moines, Iowa, 1942.

National Archives

Fort Devens, Massachusetts, and the combined Camps Polk and Ruston in Louisiana. A group of 440 women officer candidates and 330 enlisted women began training at Fort Des Moines in July 1942. Uniform supply was inadequate but it did not deter training. Except for weapons and tactical training, the women's courses paralleled those for Army men, as did their training circumstances. As Gertrude Morris remembered basic training:

> . . . falling out for reveille at 6:00 A.M. in dark, below-zero weather in deep snow . . . the oversized man's GI overcoat which I wore over a thin fatigue dress . . . a typical sad sack GI shivering with a coat dragging in the snow.[5]

Life as an officer candidate wasn't much better. Georgia B. Watson wrote:

> We went through Officer Candidate School in tennis shoes, foundation garments, seersucker dresses with bloomers and gas masks. Apparently there was a supply mix-up somewhere in the pipe line. The overconcern with underwear by the male planners paid dividends. But they were not pink with lace. They were O.D., tannish and awful. Foundation garments such as even our grandmothers would not have worn, did give us moments of hilarious parading in our barracks after the "study hour."[6]

WAAC Ranks

After six weeks in WAAC Officer Candidate School (OCS), the graduates received commissions as a "third officer," the equivalent of second lieutenant. They could progress in rank to "second officer," which was equivalent to an Army first lieutenant and to "first officer," equivalent to captain. Basic training for enlisted recruits, who were called "auxiliaries" lasted for four weeks. At graduation, the women received the title, "auxil-

WAAC Color Guard, First WAAC Training Center,
Fort Des Moines, Iowa, 1942.   National Archives

By September 1942, the first WAAC graduates began to be assigned to Army posts. The enlisted women worked primarily as clerks, drivers, telephone operators, cooks, and bakers. Under the law, the officers were exclusively assigned as administrators or training officers at the WAAC training centers and schools, as WAAC recruiters, or as officers leading WAAC units.

The Antiaircraft Artillery Experiment

"If British women can work in antiaircraft batteries, why not the WAACs?" That was the question General Marshall posed to Colonel Hobby in late December 1942. He had observed women of the Auxiliary Territorial Service (ATS) manning antiaircraft batteries in London and was impressed with their proficiency. In October 1942, Colonel Hobby had been in London and had also observed ATS women on the antiaircraft batteries. Even Prime Minister Winston Churchill's daughter, Mary, was assigned to the battery in Hyde Park in London. Over 56,000 ATS women served in the antiaircraft command.[7] Colonel Hobby agreed to try the WAACs in an antiaircraft experiment—provided the women did not fire the 90 mm guns or handle ammunition. Using top secret orders, she directed fifteen WAAC officers and 450 enlisted women to report to the 36th Coast Artillery, Antiaircraft Brigade, at the Arboretum, Washington, D.C. in January 1943. Top secret orders were necessary because she could not risk publicity that made it appear the WAACs were being assigned to combat duty—the law that created the Corps specified that the women be assigned only noncombatant duties. The WAACs were trained by the men to oper-

iary first class. Thereafter, they could progress in rank to "junior leader," "leader," "staff leader," "technical leader," "first leader" and finally, "chief leader." Those titles were the equivalent of: private first class, corporal, sergeant, staff sergeant, technical sergeant, and master sergeant.

ate the fire control director, the dials that controlled the elevation and the left or right movement of the 90 mm gun. As a matter of orientation, they learned the men's jobs on the search lights, loading ammunition, and firing the gun, but did not occupy these positions.

In April the best qualified women were assigned to Composite Battery X—a unit of men and women who participated in a firing exercise at Bethany Beach, Delaware. It would be the test of women's ability to serve as range crew for 90 mm guns. Battery X would fire at a 40-foot-long red target sleeve, towed behind a B-10 bomber, piloted by a WASP (Women Airforce Service Pilots). Third Officer Georgia Watson, Executive Officer of Composite Battery X, remembered the week-long exercise:

> Firing at a simulated target [in training] was one thing. Having someone out there piloting the real plane being tracked was a whole new ball game . . . In the gun battery set up on the beach, the female range crew, blind tracking with the SCR 268 radar, height finder and director, brought the 90 mm guns on target and without hesitation, I gave the command to fire . . . [before the shoot] one male officer said to me, "If your range crew women let my gun crew men hit that plane, you can take your range crew women, walk toward the Atlantic ocean and keep going until your caps float."[8]

The practice exercise *was* a success as were others that followed. However, in late April, the Army decided that men would handle the antiaircraft mission and the women could be more valuably used in other assignments. The experiment ended in August 1943. The highly secret operation was never revealed by any of the men or women who participated in it. In 1968 the operation was declassified. Though Colonel Hobby wanted it to be a success, she had no intention of letting this experiment prove that women could be used in combat operations.

Another Top Secret Job

The Manhattan Project was the name for the work begun in late 1942 to produce an atomic bomb—before the Germans did—that would end the war quickly. Its development progressed at locations in Chicago; New York; Washington, D.C.; Oak Ridge, Tennessee; Pasco, Washington; and Los Alamos, New Mexico. Over 400 WAAC (later WAC) officers and enlisted women with perfect performance, character, and behavior ratings were selected for assignments on this super secret project.[9] They were stenographers, typists, telephone and teletype operators, cryptographers, chemists, metallurgists, electronics technicians and photographers.

Almost 300 WACs were assigned to the largest and most isolated of the locations—Los Alamos, New Mexico. Eleanor Stone Roensch, a telephone operator, wrote:

> We . . . waited for a promised driver to pick us up . . . a passing soldier, seeing our duffel bags . . . chuckled and warned us to buy lots of souvenirs right away since we were probably going to "The Hill" and would never get back to town [Santa Fe] until the end of the war. Our anxiety increased when a WAC driver finally appeared and crammed us into the back of an official car, telling us to say farewell to civilization. We were off to Los Alamos![10]

The women worked long hours, six days a week. Very few were ever released for overseas duty or to go to OCS because finding, clearing, and training replacements took precious time from the project. Until the implosion test in the Arizona desert in July 1945, few knew the ultimate mission of the project. Of the secrecy, Marian White Campbell said: "I knew far too much and I knew I knew too much. But I *tried* not to know anything."[11]

Eleanor Stone Roensch wrote, that often— "There were also many loud blasts. When the ground shook and the air smelled of firecrackers, we knew the scientists were testing explosives. When I washed my hair, I could smell that firecracker smell."[12]

Later, she wrote:

> . . . in 1945 . . . [a friend] confided his fears about an imminent test to take place in the desert. He was afraid that a chain reaction might take place that could not be controlled. This was the first I had heard about this mysterious weapon and I shared his nightmares until July 16 [1945] when the Trinity test proved successful.[13]

Then, on 6 August, the first atomic bomb fell on Hiroshima. "We were proud that Los Alamos had been able to develop the bomb and happy the secrecy was over. Most of all, we anticipated the war's end."[14]

The WAC unit at Los Alamos received the Meritorious Unit Award. One woman received the Legion of Merit, twenty others, the Army Commendation Medal.

Field Assignments

Some of the first women sent to the field were assigned to the Aircraft Warning Service in 1942 and 1943 in cities on the East coast from Maine to Florida. In December 1942, the first two black WAAC units arrived at Fort Huachuca, Arizona. They worked in administrative jobs (clerks, typists, stenographers) but also as drivers, telephone operators, and medical care and treatment specialists. By March of 1943, other WAAC units had arrived at posts within the United States under the three major commands: the Army Air Forces, the Ground Forces, and the Army Service Forces. To assist in administering the WAAC units and personnel, WAAC officers with the title, "WAAC Staff Director" were assigned to the headquarters of the major commands; the various branches (e.g., Adjutant General, Surgeon General, Quartermaster, Transportation, Signal); ports of embarkation, and to overseas theaters to assist these commands in administering the WAAC units and personnel.

The WAACs Overseas

The WAACs began deploying overseas in December 1942. Five WAAC officers had a harrowing experience en route to reporting for duty at Allied Headquarters in Algiers, North Africa. The troop ship on which they traveled from England to North Africa was torpedoed by a German U-boat in the North Atlantic. A British destroyer came to the rescue and saved the women officers and other survivors of the burning, sinking ship and delivered them safely to the port of Oran, Algeria. It had been an experience to remember—that day in the lifeboat! They lost their uniforms, cosmetics, and other personal items, and were smeared with oil and grit when they debarked at Oran. The welcoming party at the port brought oranges, toothbrushes and emergency items. Within a few days, they were at work in Allied Headquarters.[15]

WACs arrive in North Africa.

National Archives

The next month, the first WAAC unit to serve overseas, the 149th WAAC Post Headquarters Company, arrived—without incident—for duty at General Dwight D. Eisenhower's Allied Forces Headquarters in Algiers. Hand-picked for the assignment, most were bilingual and specialists in telephone operations and communications. Vida M. Gaoni remembers her arrival in Algeria.

The 149th debarked at Oran, Algeria, on the morning of January 27, 1943, and were transported by train and then by military trucks to the Monastery of the Good Shepherd at El Briar. It was dark by the time we reached the convent and after dusk we traveled under blackout conditions. The very first night we were welcomed by an air raid. The eerie sound of the sirens was frightening—then came the sound of the planes; the thunder of bombs exploding; the shrill whistle of bombs being dropped around us; the deafening sound of our huge anti-aircraft guns . . . and, finally, after what seemed forever, the welcome moan of the "all clear" sirens . . . The raids weren't nightly affairs, but frequent enough.

After several months we became so accustomed that we could sleep right through . . . But c'est la guerre![16]

One large platoon, later named the 2666th WAC Wires Company, staffed the command's telephone switchboard system (the Freedom Exchange). Other WAACs were postal directory workers (in the 2664th WAC Postal Company) and succeeded in reducing a mountain of misaddressed mail to zero and in keeping up with the never-ending load of mail and packages needing redirection. Still others worked as motor transport drivers, secretaries, clerks and supply specialists. Most moved from Allied Headquarters in Algiers to Italy in October 1943, where they were part of Lieutenant General Mark Clark's Fifth Army Headquarters, Special Troops.

One platoon of the 6669th WAAC Headquarters Company was assigned to General Clark's Fifth Army as it proceeded up the coast of Italy. About half of the members of this platoon were in the advance party that at times was as close as five or six miles behind the combat troops. Like the men, the women lived in tents that winter of 1943-1944. Commanders welcomed the WAC's skills. They used WAC telephone and telegraph operators to reach commanders and units in the field and WAC clerk-typists "to plot the location and movement of troops and supplies." This platoon received the Fifth Army Plaque with Clasp and the Meritorious Service Unit Plaque.[17]

In July 1943, the 1st WAAC Separate Battalion (555 enlisted women and nineteen officers), arrived in England and was assigned for duty with the Eighth and Ninth Air Forces. The Battalion was commanded by Captain Mary A. Hallaren, who later became the WAC Staff Director for the Army Air Forces in Europe (1943-1945) and eventually became the Third Director of the Women's Army Corps (1947-1952). Praising the Battalion's performance at war's end, Colonel Hallaren told the women:

> You are the pioneers, there were many bets against you when you first came to the ETO [European Theater of Operations]—that you couldn't take it with the boys; that American women couldn't endure Army discipline; that you'd use your femininity when the going got rough; that you'd break within a year. Everyone who bet against you, lost.[18]

General Ira C. Eaker commanded the Army Air Forces in the European Theater of Operations. The women were dispersed to various air force offices and flight control rooms where they were assigned as teletype operators, typists, and switchboard operators. The air forces did not stop there in assigning women. A few, perhaps twenty or more, served as crew mechanics, radio operators, photographers and flight clerks on planes. More often, they served on the ground as administrators, photo interpreters, control tower operators, photo laboratory technicians, weather observers, weather forecasters, Link trainer instructors, and stock record clerks.

The European Theater of Operations (ETO) received the largest number of WACs. Over 8,300 served in England, France, Germany, and Italy. They received eight Legions of Merit, one Soldier's Medal (for bravery), and 305 Bronze Star Medals. At the end of the war, General Dwight D. Eisenhower, the Supreme Allied Commander, said of them:

> During the time I have had WACs under my command, they have met every test and task assigned them. I have seen them at work in . . . England, France, and at Army installations throughout the European Theater. Their contributions in efficiency, skill, spirit, and determination are immeasurable.[19]

Slanderous Rumors

Around the same time that the first WAACs were being sent to England, certain members of the media and some male members of the Army began repeating slanderous, mocking rumors against the Corps that provoked the women, frightened their parents, and damaged the WAAC recruiting effort. British women in two wars had had similar experiences. Unsubstantiated rumors of numerous pregnancies, immoral behavior, and drunkenness ran rampant. They were investigated by Army Military Intelligence with the assistance of the Federal Bureau of Investigation and found to be groundless. The reports of their findings were published but the rumors persisted for more than a year until they had run their course. The slander campaign had the effect of forever making the Corps extremely sensitive about its public image.

The Women's Army Corps

By the Spring of 1943, WAAC strength had increased to 60,000 women and the problems of administering them without full military status had become untenable. The need for separate administration, supply, disciplinary procedures, and command lines both in the United States and overseas caused great confusion.

From the beginning of field duty for the WAACs, male commanders had questions concerning their women's status. Were they or were they not "persons in the military service?" The answer was "yes" for some things and "no" for others. "No" was the answer most often given. WAACs were NOT entitled to the franking privilege on mail; National Service Life Insurance; allotments to dependents; re-employment rights (unless they had previously held Civil Service jobs);

the Good Conduct or other medals; appointment as warrant officers; burial with a flag; military honors and an escort home with the body; nor disability or retirement benefits such as a pension or veterans hospitalization. The WAACs were not subject to the Army's discipline and court system unless they were on duty overseas. They could not be confined in a guardhouse. They *could* shop at the post exchanges and commissaries. Especially irritating was the fact that servicewomen in the Navy, Marine Corps, and Coast Guard had had full military status from the outset even though they weren't allowed to go overseas.

It was clear that the WAACs needed full military status. On 14 January 1943, Congresswoman Rogers introduced a bill that would give Army women military status and a new name, the "Women's Army Corps," or WAC. After months of haggling, Congress passed Rogers' bill and President Roosevelt signed it on 1 July 1943. When the Women's Army Auxiliary Corps went out of existence on 30 September 1943, the

Swearing in of enlisted WAC, Eagle Pass Army Airfield, Texas, August 1943. The Women's Memorial

women who wished to return home were discharged. More than 41,177 enlisted women joined the new Women's Army Corps and some 4600 WAAC officers accepted commissions in the WAC.[20]

Their new status within the Army greatly helped to administer the WACs. Enlisted women and officers now held the same titles of rank as men. Although they could not obtain dependency allowances for their husbands, they could have allotments taken from their pay checks for parents who were more than 50 percent dependent upon them for support. They could not count their WAAC service for longevity or other financial benefits, but they could use their WAAC service for promotions, accrued leave, overseas ribbons and the Good Conduct Medal. A WAAC Service Ribbon was awarded to those who had served in the WAAC and who also served in the Women's Army Corps.

By 1 January 1944, WAC strength (officers and enlisted) totaled 57,500 with 260 units in the field in the continental United States and overseas. A year earlier (1 January 1943), WAAC strength was 12,767 with only two companies in the field (the black units at Fort Huachuca, Arizona) and approximately 4,000 women in the Aircraft Warning Service on the East Coast. Others were at, or preparing to go to, the new training centers.

Segregation

Segregation of blacks and whites was still a way of life in the United States in the 1940s. Life in the military was no exception. The Army had set a ceiling of 10.6 percent on the number of black men who were conscripted for Army duty. Thus WAAC planners set 10.6 percent as the recruiting goal for the officers and enlisted ranks.[21]

Following this guideline, the first WAAC officer candidate class convened with 440 members—forty of whom were black women. As required by Army policy, housing and

WACs of the 6888th Central Postal Directory Battalion parade in Birmingham, England.

The Women's Memorial

dining facilities were segregated for WAAC officers and enlisted women. In OCS the black and white women candidates attended classes and ate together but their housing and recreational activities were segregated.

The NAACP and other black organizations strongly protested segregated treatment of the black WAACs. In November 1942, the War Department relented and integrated women officers' housing and eating facilities at Fort Des Moines. WAAC officer candidate school was desegregated and, thereafter, all the candidates lived in the same barracks, ate at the same tables in the mess hall, marched and attended classes together. These rules were extended to include women officers at all WAAC and WAC training centers but not at other Army posts.

The rules for black enlisted women were stricter and followed exactly the segregation policy for enlisted men. In basic training, black enlisted women trained, lived, and ate apart from the white women. When they went to specialists training schools, they were housed with the black WAAC or WAC unit on post, but went to classes and ate in the same mess halls with white men and women. Often the tables in the mess halls had signs that said "white only." If a post did not have a black women's unit or the number enrolled in the course was small, the women shared a barracks with the white women students.

The Army's system of unit organization and assignment was designed for combat units but not suitable for women's units. Nonetheless, it had to be followed. Accordingly, separate black and white units were formed at the WAAC training centers and given a set number of officers, cadre, and enlisted women who had to fit personnel spaces for cooks, chauffeurs, or typists. Both

black and white women who held expert skills as photographers, dental hygienists, medical technicians, keypunch operators, teachers, or executive secretaries were often retrained as cooks, chauffeurs, or typists to fit the Army mold. Finally, this system was partially discarded in May, 1943, and thereafter commanders requesting women's or men's noncombat units specified only the number and grades allotted to a unit, not the skills. This eliminated many but not all malassignments for both black and white women.

Army commanders had to request WAAC units by race for duty at a specific Army post. Many black women went unassigned because commanders failed to request black WAAC units. For this reason and others (malassignment, segregation, and discrimination) black women comprised only 4 percent of WAC total strength throughout the war.

Commanders in the overseas theaters did not requisition black WAC units through most of the war years. Near the end of 1944, however, the European Theater of Operations commander requested approximately 800 black women for a central postal directory unit. Black women who had been waiting for years for a chance to serve overseas quickly volunteered, and received overseas training and processing for overseas duty at the Third WAC Training Center (Fort Oglethorpe, Georgia). The women, assigned to the 6888th Central Postal Directory Battalion, arrived in England in February 1945 with thirty officers and 800 enlisted women. The unit was commanded by Major Charity Adams, a black officer from South Carolina with troop command experience who was later promoted to lieutenant colonel. As the war progressed, the unit

WACs of the 6888th Central Postal Directory Battalion sort mail at the 17th Base Post Office in France. National Archives

moved from Birmingham, England, to Rouen, France, and to Paris, France—always living, working, and eating separately. But there were some benefits in overseas duty. Accustomed to discrimination at home, the women were accepted socially by the British and French people. The attitude of these white nationals pleased and delighted the members of the unit. According to Brenda Moore:

> The royal treatment members of the 6888th describe receiving from the British not only boosted their morale, but also enhanced the self-concept of individual members . . . In Europe they were no longer treated as second -class citizens. Through this experience members of the 6888th gained a new perspective on themselves.[22]

The unit performed its directory duties with distinction. Its members returned to the states in groups between November 1945 and March 1946.

WACs in the Pacific and the Far East

Over 5,000 WACs served in the Southwest Pacific area and in the China-Burma-India theater of war in World War II. WACs first arrived in New Delhi, India in October 1943. Approximately four WAC officers and sixty-two enlisted women served in Vice-Admiral Lord Louis Mountbatten's headquarters there, along with British servicewomen, members of the Indian WAC, and local civilians. The unit later was moved to Ceylon and remained there until the end of the war. A larger unit of almost 300 "Air WACs" (WACs assigned to an Army Air Forces command) served in Major General George E. Stratemeyer's Air Force Headquarters in Calcutta, India, from July 1944 until August 1945 when the unit moved to Chungking, China. Women in this unit worked as stenographers, typists, clerks, draftsmen, radar specialists, medical specialists, telephone operators, and in the intelligence field.

Even larger WAC units began serving in the Southwest Pacific Area beginning in May 1944. Eventually 5,000 women served in this area that included Australia, New Guinea, the Philippine Islands, Hawaii, Guam, and other U.S. possessions in the Pacific. The major commander was General Douglas MacArthur. Women served in units of General Headquarters, U.S. Army Forces Far East, the Far East Air Forces, Services of Supply, Army Forces in the West Pacific, and other related commands. The WACs followed in the footsteps of the U.S. Army as it drove the Japanese from New Guinea and up the island chain to the Philippines. Living and working conditions were as deplorable for the women as for the men in the

Southwest Pacific Area. Mary Blakemore Johnson describes it best:

Hollandia was a very busy place when we arrived. The harbor was a mass of ships arriving for the push north to the Philippines . . . Jeeps and trucks plowed up a windy, twisty road to the top of the big hill that overlooked the harbor where General MacArthur had his headquarters and where the WAC camp was located . . . We were warned to keep our sleeves down, wear our wool socks, take Atabrine daily and watch out for wallabies (small rodent- like kangaroos that bumped under our cots at night), tarantulas (dump boots every morning), and snakes . . . The tents were hot during the

WACs arrive in Australia, 1944.

National Archives

day and cold at night because we were sitting right on the Equator. We had cold showers, mail call, regular meals, and dust everywhere.[23]

Despite the unhealthy and uncomfortable living conditions, the women performed their duties like seasoned troopers. Most of the enlisted women were stenographers, clerks, and typists but others served as postal directory clerks, intelligence analysts, stock record clerks, cryptographers, translators, keypunch operators, telephone and teletype operators, and photographers. Women officers served as unit commanders and company officers, administrative and finance officers, mail censors, interpreters, supply officers, training officers, personnel officers, communications officers, and in other supervisory positions. The WACs reached Manila in March 1945 and did not leave until December 1945 under demobilization rules.

When in Japan in October 1945, Colonel Boyce, the Director of the WAC, asked General Douglas MacArthur, the Supreme Allied Commander, about the women's performance. The General:

Air WACs repair airplane.   US Army Air Forces

> . . . praised the WACs highly, calling them "my best soldiers," and alleged that they worked harder than men, complained less, and were better disciplined. He informed Colonel Boyce [then Director, WAC] that he would take any number of the WACs the War Department would give him in any future command he might ever have.[24]

WACs in the Army Air Forces ("Air WACs")

The biggest user of WACs during World War II was the United States Army Air Forces. Designated "Air WACs," more than 40,000 of over 100,000 WACs who served in World War II were assigned for duty with Army Air Forces commands at headquarters and air bases throughout the continental United States and overseas. In many instances the Air Forces Commanders interpreted Army regulations issued by the Pentagon more liberally than the Army Service Forces and Army Ground Commanders. For example, the Air Forces was first to assign WAC officers in "non-WAC" jobs, to permit women to replace their Pallas Athene lapel insignia with the Air Force insignia, to recommend redesign of the WAC uniforms, and to enroll women on a coeducational basis in all of its noncombat technical schools. It even assigned several dozen women as crew on scheduled flights. The Air Forces trained and assigned women as radio operators and mechanics, code instructors, cryptographers, control tower operations keypunch operators and airplane mechanics.

The WAC Staff Director for the Air WACs throughout the war was Lieutenant Colonel Betty Bandel. She also held the title of Chief of the Air WAC Division in the office of the Air Staff Personnel Officer at the Pentagon. The WAC Staff Directors for the Army Ground Forces (Lieutenant Colonel Katherine R. Goodwin) and the Army Service Forces (Lieutenant Colonel Emily C. Davis) also operated from their Chief of Personnel's office at the Pentagon. Colonel Bandel was the first WAC officer to be promoted to the rank of lieutenant colonel in November 1943. The other major command WAC Staff Directors were promoted to lieutenant colonel the following month.

Colonel Hobby Departs

On 1 January 1945, General Marshall, the Army Chief of Staff, awarded Colonel Hobby the Distinguished Service Medal. She was the first WAC officer to receive this award. Colonel Hobby's health had become impaired through long stressful hours for almost three years at her job. Soon after V-E Day (Victory in Europe) was proclaimed on 8 May 1945, she submitted her resignation in order to return to her home and family and regain her strength. She recommended her Deputy Director, Lieutenant Colonel Westray Battle Boyce replace her. The Chief of Staff agreed with her choice, and Colonel Boyce was sworn in as the second Director of the Women's Army Corps on 12 July 1945.

World War II Ends

Victory in Europe was still being celebrated when rumors began that the war in the Pacific would also be ending soon. In August, after the atomic bombs fell, the rumors came true when the Japanese Emperor agreed to an unconditional surrender. The terms of the surrender were signed on USS *Missouri* on 2 September 1945. World War II was over.

The Army began to return its male soldiers and WACs to their homes and to wind down its wartime activities. Since the WAC had no peacetime role, it was scheduled to be disbanded six months after the war was declared over. Hence, enlistments in the Women's Army Corps were closed in late August 1945. By then all but one of the training centers had been closed. The final WAC officer candidate class graduated in November and, in December, the last WAC Training Center at Fort Des Moines shut its doors.

The WACs had "paid their dues" and had won the respect of the male officers and enlisted men with whom they had served. Major Army commanders like Generals Eisenhower, MacArthur, Arnold, Eaker and Clark praised their efficiency, endurance and adaptability. But the future of the WAC as part of the Army was unclear and demobilization was taking its toll in reducing WAC strength. Meanwhile, male draftees were leaving the Army by the thousands.

A New Role for the WACs

Then, in January 1946, General Eisenhower, now Chief of Staff of the Army, announced that he would seek both Regular Army and reserve status for the Women's Army Corps. He asked WACs still on duty to stay and

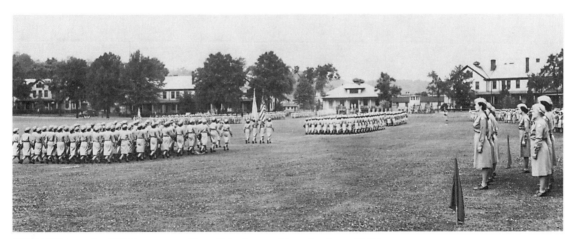

WAC NCOs review WAC troops at Fort Oglethorpe, Georgia, June 1945.   US Army

those who had been demobilized to return. The Army needed the women's experience and skills at separation centers, hospitals, and headquarters at home; and to staff occupation forces in Europe and Japan. This slowed discharges of WACs. Many of them took over administrative, medical and communications jobs formerly held by men. The women who stayed did not expect a three-year wait, but their patience was rewarded. In June 1948, Congress passed the law authorizing the Women's Army Corps in the Regular Army and the Organized Reserve Corps. WACs were in the Army to stay.

5

Navy Women's Reserve: WAVES

**Jean Ebbert
and
Marie-Beth Hall**

*At 9 AM on 30 July 1942 I had a phone call from 9th Naval
District headquarters and was greeted with, "Good morning, Lt.
Daily." I was in the Navy!! I was told to report immediately to be
sworn in. Naively, I asked if I could give my employer two weeks'
notice. The caller said, "This is war. Report immediately." Right
then I learned "Yes, sir."*

—former Lieutenant Commander Mary Daily, one of
the first eleven women commissioned in the USNR,
speaking to group of Navy women in Seattle, 1983.

The Navy Struggles To Accept Women

Women's first struggle with the Navy in World War II was simply to be allowed into it. The Navy Department had enrolled
women in both the Navy and Marine Corps Reserves in World War
I, but post-war legislation had specifically barred all women except
nurses from serving. As it was, in 1942 the Army led the way;
a bill to create the Women's Army Auxiliary Corps (WAAC) pre-
ceded a similar Navy bill by six months.

Prior to the attack on Pearl Harbor in December 1941, few Navy
officials had any idea of the vast manpower shortage facing
them. Most believed that Civil Service would be able to take
care of additional personnel for the shore establishment. But
two key groups believed otherwise. The Office of the Chief of
Naval Operations (CNO) needed a hugely expanded wartime communications network that civilian workers could not fill. Because
of the hours they worked and the secrecy of the messages they
handled, communications personnel *had* to be under military
discipline and control. The Bureau of Aeronautics already had
a detailed plan to employ women in technical work in naval

aviation. It even suggested policies that anticipated most of the subsequent organization
of the Women's Reserve. Although outside
Washington, D.C., most offices and districts
showed little interest, a few readily saw ways
to use both enlisted and commissioned
women in communications, specifically in
coding. By late spring, the Navy had identified more than 1,000 enlisted and 150 officer billets (Navy term for jobs or positions)
that could be filled by women.[1]

Within itself, the Navy was struggling to
accept an unwelcome reality—it *needed*
women in uniform. Moreover, it began to
accept that it would need not only enlisted
women, but women officers as well to lead
and manage the enlisted women.

"In" or "With"

Navy officials wished to tailor the women's
component to their own requirements. If
they must do this thing, then they wanted
to do it right—or at least, their way. They convened a group of distinguished women educators—deans and presidents of women's
colleges—to form an Advisory Council. One
of the Council's earliest and most important acts was to recommend Mildred
McAfee, President of Wellesley, a highly
prestigious women's college, to head the
Women's Reserve. She had an impeccable
personal and professional reputation and
was a proven leader and administrator much
admired for her quick wit. Her maturity
and dignity could command respect from
both men and women, and at age forty-two
she was sufficiently trim and vigorous to
wear a Navy uniform with style and distinction.

Still to be resolved was the crucial issue
of whether women should serve *in* the Navy
or *with* it. The Senate wanted the legislation establishing the Navy Women's Reserve

*Lieutenant Commander
Mildred H. McAfee takes
oath as Director, WAVES,
August 1942.*

National Archives

to follow the pattern of that for the WAAC. But the Navy insisted that for reasons of security and discipline its women should be in the Navy, rather than organized in a separate, auxiliary corps. The Navy view prevailed: the legislation signed into law on 30 July 1942, specified that Navy women were to be in the Naval Reserve, not serving with it. This emphatic inclusion assured them equal pay for equal rank, something WAAC members did not have. The women reservists were to be at least twenty years old and to perform shore duty only within the continental United States, releasing men for combat duty. They were not to be assigned to Navy ships or to combat aircraft.

The Navy's newest group of members was ready to be launched, but first it had to be christened. Already the press had coined some atrocious nicknames—"Goblettes" and "Sailorettes." Former Barnard College professor and soon-to-be Lieutenant Elizabeth Reynard struggled to comply with Navy officials' orders to come up immediately (preferably yesterday) with something that was:

> . . . nautical, suitable, fool-proof and attractive. I realized that . . . two letters . . . had to be in it: *W* for women and *V* for volunteer, because the Navy wants to make it clear that this is a voluntary and not a drafted service. So I . . . finally came up with "Women Accepted for Volunteer Emergency Service"— W.A.V.E.S. I figure the word "Emergency" will comfort the older admirals, because it implies that we're only a temporary crisis and won't be around for keeps.[2]

The Navy's First Women Officers

The Navy immediately commissioned McAfee a lieutenant commander, its first

Lieutenant Joy Bright Hancock christens the destroyer, USS Lewis Hancock, *August 1943.*

woman officer. She later said, "My first assignment was just getting enough women there to start doing something, and what they were to do was as vague to me as it was to all the rest of the Navy at that time."[3] Almost without exception, the first women officers knew little or nothing about the Navy. To accept commissions they left responsible positions and leaped into an unknown world. The greatest unknown was what they might be doing in that world. Yet these women had to persuade others to make the same leap. As one of them later said, "It was indeed an uncharted course on an unknown sea."[4]

Many excellent candidates came from the upper echelons of women educators, while many more came from business and professions. These women had made their way up steep ladders, often in highly competitive and/or male-dominated environments. Joy Bright Hancock was a shining example. She lacked a college degree but was nonetheless well educated. She had been a World War I Yeoman (F), was the widow of two naval aviators, and had worked for many years in the Bureau of Aeronautics as an editor, writer, and researcher. McAfee, long accustomed to evaluating women, immediately recognized that Lieutenant Hancock had a remarkable gift: she could "speak Navy." Her knowledge of the Navy Department enabled her to suggest very useful shortcuts and end runs, while her innumerable friends in naval aviation often helped her to deal with the naval bureaucracy.

The Navy commissioned about one hundred and fifty women officers directly from civilian life. It assigned about twenty of them to its Washington, D.C. headquarters to get the Women's Reserve program underway. Another eleven were placed on duty immediately at the various Naval District Headquarters around the country to recruit other women.

Initiative and gumption were the order of the day. Lieutenant Jean Palmer, one of McAfee's assistants, later recalled:

> Here was this stack of mail, and I began looking at it and I said, "Well, who's answering this?" . . . nobody knew . . . . I said, "I know the answers to these questions and I'm going to answer this mail." I had nothing else to do . . . I had Navy stationery [and] . . . I wasn't doing all this fancy Navy lingo, I just gave them the answers . . . about 50 people got told in one day what they wanted to know.[5]

Similarly, the first women officers out in the Naval Districts, without benefit of any naval indoctrination whatever, had precious little to guide them other than their own good sense. While McAfee and her crew were hammering out policy as fast as they could—sometimes in concert with other Navy Department planners, but more often not—the District WAVES often had to make local policy on the spot. They met some resentment from Navy men, although to many field commanders who had to meet recruiting quotas, they looked like rescuing angels—*they* could deal with the women who wanted to join the Navy. Civilians usually reacted with amiable curiosity; in Seattle, Lieutenant Etta Belle Kitchen considered hanging around her neck a sign that read, "Yes, I'm a WAVE. Yes, I like it. I joined because . . . "[6]

A critical difficulty was that the Navy's overall mobilization plans were inadequate. In January 1941, the Bureau of Naval Personnel assumed it would need no more than 10,000 reservists. Within months, it quadrupled that estimate—and not for the last time. Into this inevitable havoc and confusion came the first women officers, who achieved some notable successes. One was the important matter of uniforms, a matter in which the Navy was willing to seek the best. A famous American designer named Mainbocher created a uniform for the WAVES so attractive and classic that some uniforms worn by today's Navy women closely resemble it.

Women Officers' Training

Greatly encouraged by the first women officers' steady progress in establishing the program, the Navy nonetheless saw that women subsequently commissioned must be given some basic training in the ways of the Navy. Where should this training take place?

Again, women's colleges played a leading role. Smith College in Northampton, Massachusetts, volunteered a generous portion of its campus for a training unit for women officers. Soon thereafter Mount Holyoke College, eight miles southeast of Northampton, agreed to handle any overflow. The Navy recalled to active duty a recently retired captain, whose distinguished record included being awarded the Navy Cross, to command the unit. Lieutenant Elizabeth Crandall was ordered to be the regimental commander, accountable to the commanding officer for the trainees' uniforms, quarters, and performance. The training staff, including those serving at Mount Holyoke, eventually consisted of 112 officers (seventy-five of whom were women) and thirty-seven enlisted personnel.[7]

In August 1942, 120 women officers reported to the school, soon dubbed "USS Northampton." They included engineers, radio operators, meteorologists, and other technical specialists, as well as teachers, lawyers, and administrators.[8] Their course was accelerated, for they were to become instructors and administrators themselves early in October, when the next class would report as midshipmen. Within one month these women, most of them in their thirties and forties, many of them used to giving orders, had to accustom themselves to taking orders, marching in squads, undergoing rigorous physical conditioning, and absorbing large amounts of unfamiliar material. They studied naval organization, history, protocol, personnel administration, ships and aircraft, correspondence, communications, and law.

Learning how to drill was particularly challenging. However, once conditioned, they took to it with verve. Three times each day they marched down the street from the campus to the local hotel for meals and back again. Crandall, having only two more weeks' practice in drill than her trainees, soon learned that directing efficient movement of troops is a skill that no one acquires immediately. The first time she led the women back to classes after lunch, she discovered too late that she had headed them directly toward a parked car. In that instant, she could not recall a command that would remedy the situation. She called out, "Ladies, use your judgment!" No one was more gratified than she when they did just that, swerving the line of march around the car.[9]

The training program soon settled into a form much like that employed to train male reserve officers. Directly under Crandall were other women officers responsible for military performance, drills, discipline, and administration. Similarly, each of the regiment's battalions had a commander and an adjutant. A parallel structure of student officers from the battalion and company levels downward gave each student "hands on" experience in accepting specific responsibilities within a naval unit. Students learned how to stand watches and to be prepared for daily inspections of their quarters, uniforms, and grooming. In all, more than 10,500 women officers were trained on the Smith and Mount Holyoke campuses.[10]

In November 1942, the Coast Guard became the next service to establish a women's component. McAfee recommended Lieutenant Dorothy Stratton, then in training in Northampton, to be appointed its director. In December, eleven Navy women graduating from Northampton agreed to accept Coast Guard commissions, thus forming the initial cadre of SPAR officers. Similarly, in February 1943, when the Marines established their women's component, its initial cadre of women officers was also drawn from women then in training in Northampton.

Specialized Training

Navy planners had first assumed that the greatest need for specialized training for women officers would be as communications watch officers, and trained more than 1,700 in the required skills. So great was the need for officers who could speak Japanese that the Navy opened its very rigorous and selective 13-month course to eighty-eight women who met the same high qualifications as the men chosen. Most of those women served in communications units in Washington, D.C., where one of them discovered a description of an enemy aircraft previously unknown to U.S. intelligence agencies.[11]

The Bureau of Aeronautics quickly requested specialized training for women officers in aviation. Some women took a nine-month meteorology course given at the Massachusetts Institute of Technology in Cambridge, Massachusetts, or at the University of California in Los Angeles. At the University of Chicago, 113 women officers began a nine-month course in aerological engineering and then went on to take complete charge of aerological operations at various naval facilities. As the need to train aviators rapidly expanded, the Navy met a critical shortage of air navigation instructors by training 121 women officers for such duties. In order to comply with legislative restrictions, the women's required fifty flight hours had to be made in noncombatant aircraft. In 1945 the Navy designated eighty of these women as naval air navigators, proudly noting them as the "first women to perform duties as part of a United States military air crew."[12]

Fifty-two women served in the Naval Air Transport Service, completely responsible for planning and supervising the fueling, loading of cargo, mail, passengers, and baggage, plus all the administrative details connected with each NATS flight. Another substantial number were trained to administer the rapidly expanding radio-radar program, while still others trained as specialists in air combat information, air combat communication procedures, photographic interpretation, aircraft recognition, and aviation gunnery instruction.

The Navy's Supply Corps replaced many of its male officers in shore billets with women. Nearly 800 women officers served at Navy commissaries, supply depots, disbursing offices, and transportation centers. They managed inventories, shipping, salvage conservation, and materiel catalogs, assigned stock numbers, and monitored contracts. Some delivered payrolls; one woman delivered hers by jeep, with a pistol on her hip.[13]

By December 1944, nearly 3,200 women officers had been specially trained in one of the areas already mentioned, or in others such as astronomy, radar operations and maintenance, ship design, and intelligence.[14] In training so large a number of women in so many different technical fields in so short a time, the Navy gave an impressive performance. Equally impressive were the women themselves, who proficiently accomplished tasks many of them had never even heard of before they volunteered for the Navy.

Enlisted WAVES Come On Board

The growth of the Navy's enlisted force during World War II, from not quite 250,000 to nearly three million was a staggering expansion for which the Navy was quite unprepared. It had initially assumed that most of the men to be replaced by enlisted women would be clerks and communications technicians, and instructed recruiters to find women able to fill such jobs. Other than that, plus a few guidelines about age, health, and weight, recruiters had little idea of what to look for. One male recruiter took quite literally the rationale that the WAVES were to replace men, and so insisted that women recruited meet the height and weight requirements established for men. He could find only a few such women, but those few were, according to McAfee, "amazons, superb-looking women."[15]

It turned out that many high-quality women were eager to enlist in the Navy. Many women qualified to receive commissions could not do so because the law severely restricted the numbers of women officers; a good percentage of these college graduates enlisted instead. Moreover, because the public viewed the Women's Reserve so favorably, the Navy could be highly selective as to which women it accepted.

Not that the Navy attracted only privileged and well-educated women. As Commander Mary Jo Shelly (later Director of the Women in the Air Force) explained to an interviewer:

> We didn't get all the snobbish, effete elite. We had some pretty plain youngsters . . . some from the country and some that saw no prospect of college. . . . We had every kind of girl, from debutantes to little peasants, some with extraordinary motivation, some partly self-interested. But if you did the job you got on in the Navy, you got a better rating and you got more pay.[16]

The Navy first thought its women enlistees would need only a modicum of boot training (Navy term for recruit training) and, again looking to colleges, set up training units for women radiomen at the University of Wisconsin in Madison; for storekeepers at the University of Indiana in Bloomington; and for yeomen (Navy clerks) at Oklahoma A&M College in Stillwater. Hardly had these units begun their work than the Navy realized that women recruits needed a stronger boot training program, one much like that given to men. But its "boot camps" were already stretched to the limit by the vast numbers of men being

WAVES check inventory in the Supply Department, Naval Air Station, Livermore, California, June 1944. Naval Historical Center

mobilized, so the Navy set up its first women's basic recruit training unit at the University of Iowa's campus at Cedar Falls, which could accommodate about 1,600 recruits at one time.

A woman ensign explained to an audience of high school girls what to expect if they were to become "one of us":

> After a long tiring train trip, the double deck bunks you'll find in your [room] will be most inviting, but don't think you can just flop down. You can't. Nor can you run out to the corner for a "coke." Somehow the Navy manages to budget time thoroughly and you as part of the Navy will be falling into line pronto. The Uniform Officers will undoubtedly have you standing for hours that first day, being fitted, and perhaps the Medical Department had agreed to give you the first of your "shots" the very minute you arrive and in addition, the Instruction Department will certainly decide to issue books right then and there. After about the tenth time up and down the ladder another call comes to get your linen and immediately make up your bed. Be sure you make "square corners." The Mess bell finally rings and although you don't care whether you eat or not by that time, the sight of the tin tray filled to the brim with the best food you ever saw changes your mind. After mess, you are really exhausted and a hot shower and that flannel nightie you brought were never more appealing—but this is the Navy now and one doesn't go to bed until taps.[17]

Even before the first class at Cedar Falls graduated in January 1943, more changes took place. First, the Navy was realizing how many different kinds of jobs it needed women to do. Consequently, just before their brief Christmas leave, women who had enlisted believing that they would become yeomen, storekeepers, or radiomen learned that they would instead become metalsmiths, pigeon trainers, or aviation machinist mates. Most had never even heard of such jobs, much less dreamed they'd be doing them.

Second, the Navy drastically raised to 75,000 its estimate of how many women it would need. That rise owed much to the excellent reports being received about the first groups of WAVES now working at naval installations all across the country. Now the Navy needed a larger boot camp where it could train 4,000 to 5,000 women at one time.[18]

WAVE Recruit Training at Hunter College

In February 1943, barely two months after the Navy had first inspected the site, it formally commissioned the U.S. Naval Training School (WR), The Bronx, New York, at Hunter College, which the city had turned over completely for the war's duration. The first recruits arrived nine days later.

From then until October 1945, every two weeks 1,680 women recruits arrived at Hunter for the six-week course. On board at any one time were 5,040 boots, plus 1,000 staff members. The operation's logistics were gargantuan. Every breakfast required 10,000 eggs. A meal of baked beans used half a ton of beans. Recruits and staff consumed one and a half tons of salt each month. The laundry handled 25,000 items of clothing each week. Every day 260 recruits got complete physical examinations. Uniforming the recruits required the resources of six New York department stores.[19]

WAVE in the Assembly and Repair Department, Naval Air Station, Seattle, Washington, 1943.

National Archives

Recruits found the boot camp experience bewildering, exhausting, and finally exhilarating. In March 1943 the first women's troop train to cross the country to Hunter was assembled, with bunks stacked three deep and Lieutenant Mary Daily in charge. Trains from the West joined up at Chicago, and all proceeded eastward together. On one of those trains, coming from Portland, Oregon, was Patricia G. Morgan, who arrived at New York's Grand Central Station four days after leaving the West Coast.

> We had been told to bring no more luggage than we could carry, that we would have to carry it when we arrived and to have our orders with us, on our persons. As we staggered off the train, a Red Cross

worker grabbed our bags and took off with them . . . what confusion as we scrambled . . . to find and claim the right one![20]

A few weeks later Marie Bennett arrived by train from her home in Texas and found that boot camp consisted of:

> Muster. Line up. Wait. Hurry up and wait . . . .We marched to breakfast. Marched to class. Marched to lunch. Marched for the nice sergeant. Marched to testing and lectures and marched to gym. Marched to see film on hygiene and marched to barracks. We marched to the head [Navy term for bathroom] and marched our sheep into the night as we slept.[21]

Graduation ceremonies, with nearly 4,000 women marching past the reviewing stand, climaxed the weeks of training. A total of nearly 81,000 WAVES, 1,900 Coast Guard SPARs, and 3,200 women Marines successfully completed the course between February 1943 and October 1945.[22]

Specialized Enlisted Training

Three different Navy Bureaus handled the specialized training of enlisted women, and each did it differently. The Bureau of Naval Personnel continued establishing separate facilities for the women at college campuses, while both the Bureau of Medicine and Surgery and the Bureau of Aeronautics sent their enlisted women to train right alongside their enlisted men.

The Bureau of Naval Personnel's schools graduated 735 yeomen every three weeks, 220 radiomen every four weeks, and 1,120 storekeepers every two weeks. Other specialized courses trained enlisted women as cooks and bakers, mail clerks, and personnel clerks. At any given moment during the operation of these schools, 6,380 WAVES were under instruction.[23]

At seventeen naval hospitals throughout the country, the Bureau of Medicine and Surgery sponsored the training of the approximately 13,000 women who served in the Hospital Corps. Some of these women thereafter received instruction for general duties in naval hospitals, or for more specialized duties as occupational and physical therapists; as X-ray, laboratory and dental technicians; and as pharmacist's mates. They studied anatomy, physiology, sanitation, and numerous other subjects contained in the 1,000-plus pages of the *Handbook of the Hospital Corps*. In mid-1945, as more and more war-wounded returned to the United States, the Bureau established a 16-week Rehabilitation School. One hundred thirty-two Hospital Corps women completed the course, for which they received sixteen college credits.[24]

The Bureau of Aeronautics also trained its women in the same schools as men—not only to save time and money, but also to enhance the women's credibility as they worked alongside men in non-traditional jobs. WAVES subsequently proved themselves as aerographers, parachute riggers, control tower operators, aviation metal-smiths and aviation machinist mates. One visitor to a training center reported on the women preparing to become aviation machinist mates. She observed them:

> . . . bending over lathes, doping airplane wings, dissecting engines . . . "How good are they?" I asked a head mechanic supervising machine-shop work. "Magnificent. Ducks to water." . . . .In the engine shop, former schoolteachers, shopgirls, and debutantes learn to tear down a giant airplane engine of about 3,000 parts and put it back together again. With engines roaring and props spinning, a harassed student may suddenly hear an offbeat, and it's up to her to find its ailment. Frequently it is a wad of chewing gum purposely stuck over a fuel vent by an instructor.[25]

Women who became instructors in celestial navigation, gunnery, and simulated flight in Link trainers were very rigorously screened; for example, only 1 percent of all WAVES qualified to enter the Link trainer instructors course, and sometimes only three out of every four candidates graduated. During the war's two final years, every naval aviator going into combat had received some part of his training from a WAVE.[26]

WAVES at Work: The Challenges

By 1943 women reservists were not only in jobs previously held by Navy men, they were

WAVE studies specimens under microscope at the dispensary, Naval Air Station, Seattle, Washington, July 1943.   National Archives

WAVES at the Naval Training School, Norman, Oklahoma, lower an airplane engine onto a block, July 1943.

Naval Historical Center

in hundreds of jobs never done before by any Navy man, chiefly because warfare and weapons were rapidly becoming far more sophisticated, and the Navy now needed more people capable of learning the continually emerging technical skills. Also, Navy women were filling numerous jobs normally held by civil servants, because there weren't enough civil servants to go around.

By mid-1943 nearly 4,000 women were already serving as officers, and more than 21,000 enlisted women had completed their initial training.[27] Their morale was high, they were performing well, and the general public viewed them favorably. Now they and the Navy had to pull together successfully for the war's duration, which might be for years.

For the Navy, the challenge was to keep on adjusting to new ideas about women's capabilities and to assign them to a far wider range of jobs than it had originally envisioned. As the number of women grew, the Navy also struggled to use them as efficiently as possible and to maintain their initial enthusiasm. Sometimes this meant developing formal policies for their administration, sometimes it meant *ad hoc* accommodation of their needs. The difficulties lay in determining when to treat them the same as men and when not to. The senior women officers who advised the Chief of Naval Personnel in Washington and those who advised commanding officers in the field had to discover how to integrate themselves into the Navy's systems and make those systems work for women. For *all* the women, the challenge was simply to do whatever the Navy asked of them and to keep on doing it until the war was won. That challenge is captured by the lyrics of the song written in 1943 by Ensigns Elizabeth Ender and Betty St. Clair, which can be sung in harmony with "Anchor's Aweigh."

WAVE telegrapher checks monitor tape at the Navy's communications center, Washington, D.C., July 1945.   Naval Historical Center

WAVES of the Navy, there's a ship sailing
   down the bay,
And she won't come into port again until
   that vict'ry day.
Carry on for that gallant ship and for
   every hero brave
Who will find ashore his man-sized chore
   was done by a Navy WAVE.

The WAVES' enthusiasm, devotion, and abundant success have to some degree obscured the difficulties they faced in "carrying on" with their "man-sized chores."

Working hours were always long and conditions often very difficult. For example, it was not unusual for some hospital corps women to work 70 hours a week. Also, the women who constituted 80 percent of all personnel in the Washington Communications Office and did *all* encoding and decoding faced particular challenges. The need for absolute secrecy required that each woman work on only one small portion of the process, repeating the same few tasks day after day for the eight hours of her watch. Veronica Mackey recalled her job as:

> . . . dull, and anyone could have done it. We were given a graph, which told us to set the dials and rotors on certain numbers. Then we punched a switch and the machine would print out a piece of paper. We took the paper to a room down the hall and knocked. The door would open, someone would take the paper from us, and then we'd return to reset the dials and rotors from yet another graph.[28]

Some other women's sole duty was to stare at TV-like screens, reporting to a supervisor whenever a blip appeared. The deadly monotony became more bearable only when some astute women officers explained how each woman's task fit into the larger process.

WAVE makes celluloid transparencies for a deep-sea diving training film, Naval Photographic Laboratory, Anacostia, Maryland. National Archives

Some women were not assigned to jobs for which they'd been trained. For instance, at one station women who'd been trained as machinist's mates were used instead as clerks—a waste of resources that the women resented. Hancock discovered the cause of the situation, which was trivial but had significant consequences.

There were no toilet facilities for the women in the hangars, so they weren't assigning the women there . . . I talked to the leading chief and he said he didn't particularly want the women aviation machinist's mates to come in. However, he'd never worked with them. His was a part of that feeling . . . particularly on the part of the old-time chiefs, that women couldn't do the jobs properly . . . one chief . . . said to me, "Well, I guess we're going to have to have them. And here's what I'd do. Put a peg outside the door of the head, and when a man goes in he hangs his hat on the peg and no women go in. When a WAVE goes in let her hang her hat on the peg and the men will stay out."[29]

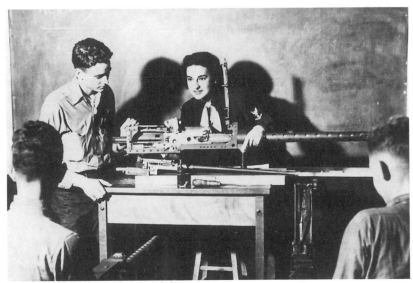

Underlying all other difficulties was the fact that the men with and for whom the WAVES worked had differing, inconsistent, and often contradictory attitudes. Many Navy men at all levels put aside their doubts and reservations, welcomed the women's contributions, and treated them fairly. Some were downright hostile, and others were resentful because the women's arrival meant that the men would be sent to sea. As one woman officer observed, "that meant to go out and get killed and that wasn't very popular."[30] Some men dealt too leniently with the women who worked for them. They had to be reminded that if women weren't treated as firmly as their male counterparts, then they just weren't part of the team.

When all was said and done, both men and women were in the same Navy fighting the same war, and loyalty to one's shipmates is fundamental in the Navy. McAfee concluded that "what saved the life and reputation of the women in the Navy in the earliest days was the tradition that, if he's on my ship, he's all right. And we got women on so many 'ships' [i.e., stations and units] the Navy loved us dearly!"[31]

Policy Development—Wives, Discharges, Transfers, Promotions, and Benefits

Originally, the wife of a man serving in any armed force could not enter the Women's Reserve, and a woman could not marry during indoctrination. The Navy gradually relaxed this impractical policy; by 1943 it abandoned all attempts to make its women choose between continued service or marriage to a serviceman. However, the wife of a Navy, Marine Corps, or Coast Guard officer could not *enter* the Women's Reserve; the concern was that she might carry undue influence flowing from her husband's rank.[32]

WAVES presented very few disciplinary problems, which boosted their popularity among their supervisors. Restriction to quarters was the usual punishment given to women. The rare woman who could not or would not adjust to the Navy was discharged rather than being subjected to repeated punishment. Few women had to be discharged. As of June 1943, only 469, or less than 3 percent of the enlisted women, had been separated from the service, for reasons of inaptitude, physical disability, undesirability, or unsuitability. These numbers included women who had married during indoctrination and who presumably knew that such action would lead to a discharge. They also included pregnant women, Navy policy being that pregnancy was a medical condition that rendered a woman ineligible to serve; having a child under the age of eighteen also precluded eligibility. Of the 10,000 women appointed as officers during the war, only four were discharged for disciplinary reasons. The comparable number of male officers was four out of 1,000, or ten times greater.[33]

Initially, women were discouraged from applying for transfers, the Navy's stated policy being that they would be allowed to transfer "only for the good of the service." After late 1944, transfers were considered and permitted for enlisted women for certified reasons of health, and if they had served at least eighteen months in their current duty station. A woman could also request transfer to reduce hardship to her family.

Because the number of women officers was limited by law, promotions were stifled. This discouraged some very qualified women from applying for commissions. Congress relaxed the restrictions in 1943, allowing the Navy to promote McAfee to the rank of captain and to advance other women officers. Congress had set no limits on the rates of enlisted women, and they were promoted in roughly the same way as enlisted men. However, Navy policy allowed

very few women to rise to the level of chief petty officer; by the war's end in 1945, only about 100 had been promoted to chief.[34]

Originally, women reservists could receive allowances for their dependents, just as male reservists could. But Congress later declared that no allowance could be authorized for a woman's husband, even if he did in fact depend on her for his support.

WAVES Pioneer for the Navy

The growing presence of women pushed the Navy to cross certain frontiers. The first was in housing. Barracks built or modified to house women had cubicles that two or four women could share and decorate. Showers were partitioned, and doors hung on toilet stalls. For some years, the Bureau of Medicine and Surgery had in vain urged cubicles for all barracks in order to contain the spread of communicable diseases. The Navy acquiesced only when it had to set up women's housing. After experience showed that epidemics did in fact run more slowly through the women's barracks, cubicles became standard in all barracks. Also, women's barracks had lounges and laundry facilities. Most bases with WAVES aboard provided more and sometimes better recreational facilities, which of course benefitted the men as well. Everyone from chaplains to chief masters-at-arms at these bases noted that the men had fewer disciplinary problems, groomed themselves better, spoke less coarsely, and attended church more often. In one naval district, chapel facilities had to be tripled after the WAVES arrived.[35]

Navy chow was undeniably good, but it was notably high in calories—suitable for an all-male population, many of them in their late teens. But all WAVES were past their teens and had little appetite for such menu items as beans for breakfast. Women on a Navy diet gained too much weight. At a training station in Idaho, the senior woman officer discovered that the 200 women assigned there had gained an average of about ten pounds each, for a total weight gain of one ton—a provocative statistic. The local commander promptly ordered salads and other lower-calorie items for the mess hall, a move soon imitated at many Navy bases. Not only did the women find the new offerings more appealing, so did many men.[36]

Black women were excluded from the WAVES for more than two years. From the Navy's point of view, the question of accepting black women was complex, chiefly because racial discrimination and segregation were common throughout the country, in some areas undergirded by strict laws. But McAfee, the Women's Advisory Council, and black women leaders all kept pressure on the Navy Department to accept black women on a fully integrated basis. Finally, in October 1944, the Navy announced plans to commission especially qualified black women, and to put the first enlisted black women in training by 1 January. Two black women, Harriet Ida Pickens and Frances Wills, were sworn in and rushed up to Northampton, arriving a week after the current class convened. Both women were generously welcomed, and at graduation in December, Pickens stood third among her classmates. Seventy-two black women enlisted; their integration at Hunter was largely uneventful. As the recruits assembled, a white woman told one of her superiors that there must be some mistake, "My roommate is a Negro girl." The reply was, "Well, we're in the Navy now, and we're all citizens," whereupon the woman returned to her room and helped her roommate make up her bunk.[37] From a longer historical perspective, the smooth incorporation of black women into the Navy set a precedent for later successful integration of black men.[38]

WAVES in Hawaii

Late in 1944, the Navy persuaded Congress to allow WAVES to serve outside the conti-

Lieutenant (j.g.) Harriet Ida Pickens and Ensign Frances Wills were the first black WAVES commissioned, November 1944.   National Archives

The first contingent of WAVES arrives at Pearl Harbor, Hawaii, for duty at the Headquarters of the 14th Naval District, January 1945.   US Navy

nental United States. The Fourteenth Naval District in Hawaii had the greatest need, with more than 6,000 billets that women could fill, as well as sufficient suitable housing. The women assigned were all volunteers highly recommended by their commanding officers. They were sent overseas for at least eighteen months, with no leave back to the United States. They were to expect little glamour: all enlisted personnel in Hawaii had curfew at 6 p.m., officers and civilians at 10 p.m. After a rough sea voyage from San Francisco, 203 enlisted women and ten women officers arrived in Honolulu in January 1945 to a tumultuous welcome.[39]

Then suddenly the war was over. The speed of Japan's surrender on 14 August took most people, including Navy planners, by surprise.

WAVES' Contributions

By the war's end, women constituted roughly 2 percent of the Navy, but in certain critical areas, they were majorities.

- At the Navy Department, 55 percent of the uniformed personnel were WAVES, and within the Bureau of Naval Personnel, 70 percent.
- WAVES did about 80 percent of the administrative and supervisory work of the Navy's mail service for the entire Navy.
- WAVES filled 75 percent of the jobs in Radio Washington, nerve-center of the Navy's entire communications system.
- 1,000 WAVES taught instrument flying in Link trainers to 4,000 men a day.
- At the Indian Head powder plant, which tested about 70 percent of all U.S.

WAVE Link trainer operator uses a radio range chart, Naval Air Station, St. Louis, Missouri, November 1943.

National Archives

rocket propellant, WAVES performed about half of the ballistic calculations, "manned" one of the two firing bays, and completely operated the plant's laboratory.[40]

The number of WAVES on duty in 1944 equaled the number of men needed in peacetime to man ten battleships, ten aircraft carriers, twenty-eight cruisers, and fifty destroyers. France considered the services of three WAVES so important in training French pilots that it awarded them the Cross of Lorraine.[41]

The WAVES' contribution was not without cost. Between 7 December 1941, and 31 August 1945, seven women officers and sixty-two enlisted women died while on active duty, many in the line of duty. For example, Seaman Second Class Elizabeth Kerensky died instantly when a series of depth charges exploded at the Naval Air Station in Norfolk, Virginia.[42]

Demobilization

When the war ended, the Navy faced the task of releasing about 265,000 officers and 2,500,000 enlisted people—roughly 85 percent of its members—as quickly as possible.[43] But it still had many remaining missions. First, vast numbers of American servicemen and women, together with equipment and supplies, had to be brought home. The Navy's so-called "Magic Carpet," which included battleships, cruisers, and aircraft carriers, brought back the men and women of all the armed services. These same ships would then return, maintaining a continuing stream of supplies needed for the occupation forces overseas. Second, the Navy faced a gigantic task in caring for and reha-bilitating large numbers of wounded sailors and Marines. Even before the war ended, the Bureau of Medicine and Surgery had asked that an additional 1,000 enlisted women be recruited each month for the Hospital Corps, and the women officers training unit was now dedicated solely to training vitally needed women officers who would serve as physical or occupational ther-apists.[44] Finally, demobilization itself required a substantial amount of manpower.

The WAVES Go Home

On 1 October 1945, the first WAVES began to pass through separation centers. Within thirty days nearly 9,000 WAVES and nurses were separated, and by year's end nearly 21,000 more had been released to civilian life. Most women were released two or three days after arriving at a separation center, having received physical exams, some ori-entation regarding their rights as veterans, a final settling of their pay accounts, and the price of a train ticket to their homes. For Hospital Corpsman Marie Bennett, the process had some moments of *deja vu*:

> It took three days to get through the regu-lar routine of being discharged: lectures and movies on the conversion of our G.I. insurance, the G.I. Bill of Rights, and such. Then the grand finale . . . just like at Boot Camp, X-rays, dental clinic, blood

tests, E.E.N.T., psychologist, and a dozen more . . . .Finally I went to the Admin-istration Building for my mustering out pay of $45 for travel expenses . . . and $165 cash. It was the most I . . . had since the $100 bill . . . the finance officer gave me at Boot Camp and took away immediately for uniform allowance.[45]

The nation's newspapers, which criticized severely both the Army's and the Navy's demobilization of men, praised the WAVES' demobilization. This chapter in Navy women's history thus closed on the same graceful note on which it had opened.

Conclusion

In the midst of wartime turbulence and uncertainty, the WAVES created an invalu-able legacy for all the Navy women who followed them: spirit, hard work, compe-tence, and dignity. As Mildred McAfee Horton later wrote, they

> . . . did not join the military in order to carve out careers for themselves. They knew they were meeting a war need, and they took great satisfaction in doing that. They liked belonging to a great branch of the service . . . .But they . . . .do not like war, with its waste, its worry, its woe.[46]

Yet it was their wartime service that helped secure for women a permanent place in the Navy.

This chapter was adapted by the authors from their book *Crossed Currents: Navy Women From WWI to Tailhook* (Brassey's U.S., 1993)

6

Marine Corps Women's Reserve: Free A Man To Fight

**Colonel
Mary V. Stremlow**
USMCR (Ret.)

Except for 305 Marine Reservists (F), popularly termed "Marinettes," who served a short stint during World War I, the Marine Corps was strictly male until World War II. The unprecedented manpower demands of this two-front war soon threatened the elite image earned by the selective, disciplined Marines and forced the Corps to take several steps which its leaders were extremely reluctant to do. Numbering 143,400 and tasked to add 164,300 to their ranks within a year, the Marines lowered their standards and raised the age ceiling of enlistments to thirty-six. Then, in the fall of 1942, a Presidential Proclamation decreed that the draft would be the sole source of military manpower.

Commandant Thomas Holcomb was then out of options and he did what he had to do. Women were already serving in the Army (WAAC), Navy (WAVES), and Coast Guard (SPARs) in November 1942, when the Marine Commandant asked for estimates of the number of Women Reservists needed to replace office clerks, radiomen, drivers, mechanics, messmen, commissary clerks, etc. He made it clear that, " . . . within the next year the manpower shortage will be such that it will be incumbent on all concerned with the national welfare to replace men by women in all possible positions."

Plans were made to train 500 officers and 6000 enlisted women within four months, with a total of 19,000 women by June 1944. Rank and grades would resemble the men's pattern with minor differences. Officers would include one major and thirty-five captains, with the rest being lieutenants.

The public, anticipating a catchy nickname much like the WAACs, WAVES, and SPARs, bombarded Headquarters with suggestions: MARS, Femarines, Dainty Devil-Dogs, Glamarines, and even Sub-Marines. General Holcomb adamantly ruled out cute names. Answering yet another reporter, he forcefully stated his views in the 27 March 1944 issue of *Life* magazine, "They are Marines. They don't have a nickname and they don't need one. They get their basic training in a Marine atmosphere at a Marine post. They inherit the traditions of Marines. They are Marines."

Marine women of World War II were enormously proud to belong to the only military service that shared its name with them, but, in practice, they were usually called Women Reservists, informally shortened to WRs.

Despite misgivings, Marines went at the task of integrating women with characteristic grittiness to do it right. After three months of planning, on 13 February 1943, General Holcomb announced the formation of the Marine Corps Women's Reserve (MCWR) and the appointment of its first director, Mrs. Ruth Cheney Streeter, with the rank of major.

Major Ruth Cheney Streeter, USMCR, sworn in as Director of the Women's Reserve of the US Marine Corps by Secretary of the Navy Frank Knox.

Biographical Files, Reference Section, USMC Historical Center

By all accounts, Streeter, fiercely patriotic, spirited, high-principled, and blessed with humor and common sense, was an inspired choice. She was a natural leader and ably met the challenge to enlist, train, uniform, house, and put to work 19,000 women within a year. At the same time, her matronly, dignified demeanor allayed the fears of parents who ". . . were not going to let their little darlings go in among all these wolves unless they thought that somebody was keeping a motherly eye on them." As legislation permitted, Streeter became, in turn, lieutenant colonel, then colonel, and served until December 1945.

Major Streeter was not, however, the first woman Marine on active duty. A few weeks earlier, Anne Lentz, a civilian clothing expert who had helped design the uniforms for the embryonic MCWR, was quietly commissioned a captain. She had come to Marine Headquarters on a 30-day assignment from the WAAC and stayed.

Recruiting

Just this once, being last had its merits. The problems of the WAACs, WAVES, and SPARs were noted and avoided by the Marines. More significantly, the other services were generous in sharing advice and resources. From the beginning, the Navy was a partner in getting the MCWR off to a good start. Women were needed immediately for recruiting, so the Navy sounded a call among WAVES officer candidates and nineteen volunteered for transfer and assignment to the Corps. Still dressed in their Navy uniforms, they recruited the first Marine women. Women were asked to "Be a Marine . . . Free a Marine to Fight." Although officially, enlistments were scheduled to begin on

Monday, 15 February, at least one woman, Lucille E. McClarren, signed up on the 13th.

There were strict qualifications regarding age, education, state of health, and marital status. All WRs had to be United States citizens; not married to a Marine; have no children under age 18; be at least 60 inches in height, weigh at least 95 pounds; and possess good vision and teeth.

For enlisted women, age limits were 20 to 35, with at least two years of high school. The age limits for officers were from 20 to 49. Officer candidates needed a college degree or a combination of college and work experience. In time, the wives of enlisted Marines were accepted into the WRs.

Black women were not specifically barred from the segregated Corps, but they were not knowingly enlisted. While it is rumored that several black women "passed" as white and served in the MCWR, there is of course no official record of such.

Early recruiting was so hectic that some women were put to work without military training. American women were determined to do their part even if it meant defying the objections of parents, brothers, and boyfriends.

Marian Bauer's parents were so shaken by her enlistment that they refused to see her off. But there were also lucky ones like Jane Taylor, who remembers the advice from her father, a World War I sailor, "Don't ever complain to me. You're doing this of your own free will. You weren't drafted or forced. Now, go—-learn, travel, and do your job to the best of your ability." Zetta Little, the daughter of Salvation Army officers, joined because " . . . someone waved a flag and said my brother would come home from the war sooner if I did."

Marines were serious about standards, and underweight women devoured bananas and drank water to bring their weight up to 95 pounds. After being rejected, tiny Audrey Bennington gorged herself, and at her second weigh-in the corpsman looked away as she climbed on the scale clutching her fur coat and shoes. Another accommodating medical corpsman leaned on the scale and charted 95 pounds when Danelia Wedge was reweighed. "Wedgie" was afraid her military career was over when a doctor asked how she had lost so much weight since enlistment. He accepted her quick response, "Well, sir, long train rides don't agree with me."

From the start, the directors of the WACs, WAVES, SPARs, and MCWR focused on the war effort. They couldn't help but be distracted, however, by the change in the fickle public whose initial enthusiasm for military women gave way to a nasty, demeaning smear campaign that started as a whisper and grew to a roar. Of all the problems faced by women Marines, ranging from barracks designed for men to the scarcity of uniforms, the most trying were the stares and jeers of the men, which in the words of Colonel Katherine A. Towle, " . . . somehow had to be brazened out."

Nevertheless, the MCWR met its scheduled goal of 18,000 by 1 June 1944. Everyone agreed the MCWR's recruiting success was directly tied to the Corps' reputation. Women like Inga Frederiksen did not hesitate to accept the challenge of joining the most selective. When a SPAR recruiter told her she was smart not to join the Marines because they were a lot rougher, Inga knew she had to be a Marine.

Training

Thanks to the Navy, officer training began when the MCWR was only one month old.

Sharing training facilities saved time and manpower. Moreover, Marines benefitted from the Navy's close relationship with a group of prominent civilian women who gave sound advice based on years of experience with women's programs. Just as important, they offered several prestigious college campuses for WAVE and MCWR training.

Officers were trained at the Navy's schools at Smith College in Northampton, and Mount Holyoke College in South Hadley, both in Massachusetts. Enlisted women were ordered to Hunter College in New York City, and without question, the distinguished reputations of these institutions enhanced the public image of the WAVES and the women Marines.

New WRs received clear instructions before leaving home: bring a raincoat and rain hat (no umbrellas), lightweight dresses or suits, plain bathrobe, soft-soled slippers, easily laundered underwear, playsuit or shorts for physical education (no slacks), and comfortable dark brown, laced oxfords because, " . . . experience has proven that drilling tends to enlarge the feet."

During the first four weeks the MCWR curriculum was identical to that of the WAVES, except for drill, which was taught by reluctant male Marine Drill Instructors (DIs). The women studied Naval Organization, Administration, History, Strategy, Law, Justice, Ships, and Aircraft. The second phase of training was devoted to Marine Corps subjects such as Marine Corps Administration and Courtesies; Map Reading; Interior Guard; Safeguarding Military Information; and Physical Conditioning.

The first group of seventy-one officer candidates arrived at Mount Holyoke on 13 March 1943 and graduated on 4 May. Retired

Colonel Julia E. Hamblet, who twice served as a Director of Women Marines, recalled the comical reactions she and the women of the first officers class received. "That first weekend, we were also mistaken for Western Union girls."

Two weeks after the first officer class began, enlisted women were ordered to Hunter College, where 722 "boots" were billeted in nearby apartment houses. On 26 March twenty-one platoons of women Marines began training with the WAVES and on 25 April they graduated.

Captain Towle, who had been recruited from the University of California at Berkeley and commissioned directly from civilian life, was the senior woman officer on the Marine recruit training staff. Towle, destined to be

Julia Hamblet is sworn into the US Marine Corps by Captain Henry Bransom, Washington, DC, 1943.   Julia Hamblet PC#140, USMC Historical Center

the second director of the MCWR and the first Director of Women Marines after passage of the Women's Armed Forces Integration Act of 1948, described her indoctrination in a 1969 interview:

No one could have been greener or less military than I in those early days. I even came aboard the school in my civilian clothes. My uniforms were still in the process of being tailored for me in New York. I could tie the four-in-hand uniform tie for my uniform khaki shirt, but that was about all. I was soon, however, to learn basic procedures under the kind and watchful tutelage of the Marine Corps detachment's sergeant major, a Marine of some thirty years' service. He really must have had some bad moments.

What you will do when you're a good Marine, is really something. Every day for the first week he would escort me to a quiet room away from curious eyes (which was just as well) and give me instructions in how to salute properly, as well as other helpful lessons on what was expected of a Marine Corps officer. And I shall certainly always be grateful to Sergeant Major Halbert A. McElroy . . . for helping to make a proper officer out of me. He really personified the pride of being a Marine and he soon indoctrinated me with this same feeling. I was determined, no matter what happened, not to let him down after he had spent so much time on me, and I don't believe I really ever did.

A disappointment for early WRs was the scarcity of uniforms. They trained for weeks in civilian clothes and, in fact, the official photo of the first platoon to graduate from boot camp at Hunter College is a bit of deceit because as Audrey L. Bennington tells it,

"Only the girls in the first row—and a few in the second row—had skirts on. We in the other rows had jackets, shirts, ties and caps, but—NO skirts. Lord and Taylor was a bit late in getting skirts to [us]."

Meanwhile, Headquarters Marine Corps decided to consolidate all MCWR training at Camp Lejeune, North Carolina, by 30 June. Marines wanted their own schools not only because the colleges were stretched beyond limits: there was a larger motive—*esprit de corps*. Camp Lejeune, was the largest Marine training base on the East Coast and it offered sobering opportunities for women to see the faces of the young men they would free to fight.

By chance, Mrs. Franklin D. Roosevelt had a hand in the training curricula. On a visit to Mount Holyoke she expressed surprise that American women were not learning as much about weapons as women of other countries. Her remarks lent weight to Major Streeter's request that field exercises be made a regular part of training. As usual, Streeter's instincts were on target, and the envied WRs had regular sessions observing demonstrations in hand-to-hand combat, use of mortars, bazookas, flame-throwers, guns of all sorts, amtracs and landing craft.

Adjustment

Making the change from civilians to Marines began long before arriving at Camp Lejeune. Recruits traveled to Wilmington, North Carolina, on troop trains of about 500 led by a woman lieutenant and two enlisted assistants. At the depot, they were lined up, issued paper arm bands identifying them as boots, ordered to pick up luggage—anybody's luggage—and marched aboard the

Woman Marine private in boot camp, Camp Lejeune, North Carolina.   The Women's Memorial

One thing hadn't changed from the days at Mount Holyoke and Hunter—the male DI's weren't happy. Shaping up a gaggle of women Marines was not what they wanted to do. Feeling the scorn of fellow Marines, the DIs took on a touch more bravado than they had on the college campuses. One boot felt that the DIs resented the women, "... more than a battalion of Japanese troops."

For the first year at least, many male Marines didn't trouble themselves to disguise their resentment. Disregarding the Commandant's wishes about nicknames, more than a few Marines enjoyed using their own derogatory labels. Some women took the insults in stride, but it became tiresome, and many were furious at the putdowns, feeling that they deserved more respect from fellow Marines. The sting of the crude epithets shook the morale of the MCWR to such an extent that the Commandant felt compelled to take steps to end it. In August 1943, he fixed responsibility on unit commanding officers when he wrote:

> Information reaching this Headquarters indicates that some ... officers and men of the Marine Corps treat members of the Women's Reserve with disrespect ... coarse or even obscene remarks are being made without restraint by male Marines in post exchanges, moving picture houses, and other places in the hearing of members of the Women's Reserve ... This conduct ... indicates a laxity in discipline which will not be tolerated. Commanding officers will be held responsible ...

train. At the other end, shouting NCOs herded them into crowded buses and took them to austere barracks with large, open squadbays, group shower rooms, urinals, and toilet stalls without doors.

Patriotism was sorely tested and some women cried, realizing what they had done. Others wondered why they had done it. No time was allowed for adjustment. Processing; medical examinations; uniforming; classification tests and interviews were top priority. Orientation classes and close order drill were scheduled for the first day and training kicked off with 0545 reveille.

By mid-1944, open hostility gave way to a sort of quiet truce and soon the women's competence, sharp appearance, and pride won over a good many detractors. The men's feelings were put in perspective by a young corporal wounded at Guadalcanal, "Well, I'll tell you. I was kinda sore about it [the women Marines] at first. Then it began to make sense—though only if the girls are gonna be tops, understand." In time, Marines could even be counted on to take on soldiers and sailors who dared to harass WRs in their presence.

The Uniform—Worth the Wait

The wardrobe was chosen before the public announcement of the formation of the MCWR. The Commandant was specific; he wanted the women to wear the traditional Marine forest green with red chevrons, and insisted that they look like Marines as much as possible. This was in stark contrast to the Navy, which denied its WAVES officers the privilege of wearing gold braid throughout the war.

Tailored femininity was the goal, and by all accounts, it was achieved. The enthusiastic approval of the attractive uniforms gave everyone's morale a lift, especially since once on active duty, Marines could not wear civilian clothing, even on liberty. Colonel Streeter was especially proud of their appearance and demeanor. In her words, "You know, they had a certain reserve. They always looked good. They held themselves well. They had a certain dignity."

The MCWR uniform mirrored what was worn by all Marines in color and style. For colder seasons, there was a forest green, tailored jacket and skirt worn with a long-sleeved khaki shirt, a four-in-hand necktie, brown shoes and gloves. WRs were easily recognized by their unique, green, visored bell-crowned hat, trimmed with a bright-red cord which set them apart from the WAVES and SPARs, whose hats closely resembled each other. All coats were worn with a red muffler in winter.

The summer uniform was a two-piece green and white seersucker dress, designed for comfort and launderability. When it was realized that officer rank insignia could not be seen on the striped dress, detachable green shoulder boards were added.

The hands-down favorite uniform was the short-sleeved, V-necked white twill uniform worn with gilt buttons, dress emblems, and white pumps. Enlisted women were disheartened when it was discontinued after the war because enlisted men had no equivalent uniform.

For messy work, women Marines wore the olive-drab, utility uniform with the clumsy, high-topped shoes known as boondockers. The trousers with a bib front and crossed straps topped a matching shirt or white tee shirt.

For field nights and exercise, WRs wore the peanut suit, a tan, seersucker, one-piece, bloomer outfit with ties at the bottom of the shorts. In keeping with the times, women covered their legs with a skirt when not actively engaged in sports, exercise or work details.

There were rules for everything. Lipstick and nail polish were encouraged, but the color had to harmonize with the red cord on the winter cap, regardless of the season. The favorite color was Montezuma Red, specifically created to honor the women Marines. Inconspicuous rouge, mascara, and hair coloring were allowed but, realistically, it was nearly impossible for a woman to tint her hair because the color had to match the information on her identification card. Regulations favored feminine hair styles and, by directive hair could touch, but not cover the collar.

Not even underwear escaped regulation. Bras and girdles—whether needed or not—and full length white slips were always worn beneath skirted uniforms. Handkerchiefs could be khaki when the khaki shirt was worn, otherwise, white. Full length, beige, seamed stockings were *de rigueur* with skirted uniforms, but the unpopular cotton hose was worn in ranks. Since nylon, rayon, and silk stockings were rationed, some women in other services were allowed to use leg makeup, but not Marines.

With a clothing allowance of $250 for officers and $200 for enlisted, the women bought winter and summer uniforms, hats, shoes, purse, raincoat, accessories, and undergarments. Unfortunately, the fashionable uniforms belied the never-resolved logistical problems surrounding their procurement, sizing, supply, and distribution.

On the Job

In 1943 the country desperately needed womanpower, but no one knew how far the limits of tradition could be stretched. By custom, working women were mainly in offices, classrooms, hospitals, retail stores, libraries, beauty shops, or in homes as domestics. Although women drove automobiles, few drove trucks or buses, and they certainly didn't fix any vehicles. Women did not work in the trades—plumbing, electricity, carpentry—and they rarely supervised men. Certain jobs were deemed too dirty, too dangerous, too strenuous, or just not suitable for women.

In this social climate, the Corps had to select, train, classify, and assign 18,000 newly recruited women at the rate of over 1,000 a month, and have them at work in the shortest time possible. That it was done so well is a tribute both to the women who made it happen and to the men who allowed it to happen. Colonel Streeter's philosophy was " . . . anything except heavy lifting and combat, they could try."

Captain Cornelia Williams, with a Ph.D. in psychology, was asked to devise a plan balancing the new Marines' skills against the needs of the Corps. After considering the systems used by other services, Williams based the preferred system on the one set up for male Marines.

The same tests were used for officers and enlisted, but for officers, consideration was given to personality and probability of success as leaders and supervisors. While male officers were assigned at the bottom rung of an organization, working under the eyes of senior officers and non-commissioned officers, women officers had neither to guide them. It was sink or swim, teaching and supervising women as green as themselves.

With 500 boots arriving every two weeks, matching women to job openings was challenging and the novelty of using females to fill military titles caused a few miscues. In 1943, Marine recruiting brochures promised women openings in thirty-four job assignments, but final statistics recorded women in over 200.

Men were transferred from boot camp to their first duty station in large troop drafts. In contrast, women were transferred with their names linked to identified jobs because many possessed unique skills. Success depended on the receiving station assigning the women as planned. If, for example, a woman was classified as a telephone operator and was assigned as a clerk the process broke down.

Women Marines translate short wave code messages, Cherry Point, North Carolina, April 1945.

Miscalculations led to bothersome reassignments when high priority jobs were vacant but qualified women were no longer available. For example, the first calls for IBM tabulating machine operators, teletypewriter operators, sewing machine operators, draftsmen, utility repairmen, and telephone operators came only after many women with this civilian training and experience had been assigned to less skilled jobs.

Damaging errors were made because no one knew how many women were needed and Marines underestimated their skills. They requested too many women, especially for office work, because it was assumed that it would take two women to replace one man. Often supervisors requested twice as many women as they thought they needed, expecting to receive only half of what they had requested.

Adding to the confusion was a misunderstanding of job titles. People who could not dictate requested stenographers, and people needing file clerks asked for clerk typists. Large numbers of women felt let down and were bored by assignments that made scant demands on their skills. Colonel Streeter understood their frustration and often visited WRs in the field to give pep talks on the vital importance of every job to the war effort.

One woman who loved her job in Washington was Audrey Bennington, who described it as one of the most important times of her life:

> February 1944, first Woman Marine—oldest Marine Barracks, 8th & Eye Streets, Washington, secretary to the CO and his officers. Every 10 days taken to then Shangri La (Camp David now) to do ration records. That post was where the action was, believe me. I wish I were capable of writing a book—what material I have.

With time, the dilemma of overqualified women resolved itself because as the war progressed there was work for everyone. And after gaining confidence in the women, Marines were more willing to release men.

More than half of all WRs were engaged in clerical work, and others held traditionally female jobs such as cooks and bakers, laundresses, librarians, and clerks in post exchanges. But new ground was broken as women worked as radio operators, parachute riggers, motor transport drivers, aerial gunnery instructors, Link trainer instruc-

tors, control tower operators, motion picture technicians, automotive mechanics, teletype operators, chemists and cryptographers, auditors and statisticians, assembly and repair mechanics, metalsmiths, weather observers, aerial photographers and photograph analysts, and artists, musicians, and writers.

In 1979 Colonel Streeter recalled with amusement that WRs were assigned to Secret and Confidential Files because " . . . they always claim that women can't keep a confidence, you know." One woman working in Secret and Confidential Files presumably had little trouble with the security clearance—Eugenia D. Lejeune, the youngest daughter of Marine Major General John A. Lejeune.

Perhaps because they were pioneers themselves, military aviators were less tradition-bound and requested large numbers of women, willingly assigning them to technical fields. Marines were no exception and right away asked for 9,100. Eventually, nearly one-third of the WRs served at Marine Corps Air Stations.

The Chain of Command

In essence, the MCWR as an organization was always more perception than reality. Generally, the women were regarded as "extra" Marines to be managed as were the men. Furthermore, WRs reported to a commanding officer who was subordinate to the commanding officer of the post, and who, in turn, was responsible to the Commandant. The MCWR Director was a staff officer outside the chain of command, and, in truth, she had nothing to "direct."

There was never any question of the need for an MCWR Director, but her authority

Woman Marine teaching a class at the Radio Radar Section, Marine Corps Air Station, Mojave, California, May 1945.

US Marine Corps

was an illusion. She had influence, but never acted independently. Colonel Streeter was responsible for the tone of the Women's Reserve, and as Marines gained confidence in her judgment, they paid more attention to her suggestions. But, she had no authority of her own; never signed official letters; and was expected not to interfere unless the situation involved blatant disregard of policies. Even then, she merely apprised the Director of Personnel of problems and offered suggestions. Then he took such action as he saw fit.

It was quite a disappointment to Streeter when she learned, quite by chance, the limits of her position. Looking for sympathy, she went to Colonel Littleton W. T. Waller Jr., Director of Reserve, and said, "You know, Colonel, it's a little hard on me. I've got so much responsibility and no authority." She was taken aback by his

answer, "Colonel Streeter, you have no responsibility either." It served her well that no one else—male or female—was ever quite sure just how much authority she did have.

In most cases, men supervised women Marines on the job, but routine discipline was left to women officers. When male officers had serious problems with women at work, they generally turned to the senior woman on board. This unusual idea of shared responsibility was alien to Marines and caused some problems, but in most instances it worked.

There was genuine ambiguity, as well, about the authority invested in women officers and NCOs. Policy said it was limited to the administration of the Women's Reserve and to be exercised solely over WRs. Someone suggested that the relationship of women officers and non-commissioned offi-

Women Marines in fuselage of a Link trainer,
Cherry Point, North Carolina, 1944. US Marine Corps

directions and orders in the proper performance of such duty are the acts of the officer in command, even though such orders are directed to male personnel." This simple statement allowed women to become adjutants, as well as personnel and mess officers.

Lifestyle

In the 1940s, "nice girls" seldom lived away from home or by themselves, and when they did, there was always a chaperone figure in the picture. Even in the midst of such unusual circumstances as women serving in the armed forces, homage was paid to the accepted tradition. To prevent loneli-

cers to enlisted men was akin to that of a civilian teacher in a military school—senior women could give instructions, but matters of discipline and job performance were referred to the man's commanding officer.

In time, the Commandant provided clarification. "It appears that the services of officers and non-commissioned officers of the Marine Corps Women's Reserve are not being realized to the fullest extent due to some doubt as to the scope of their authority . . . " he wrote in March 1944. Explaining that the matter had been considered by the Navy Department, he continued," . . . it is concluded that it is entirely proper for a woman officer to be assigned to duty subordinate to a commanding officer and her

Woman Marine paints airplane parts, Marine
Corps Air Station, El Toro, California.
Courtesy of Eleanor Nocito Tuomi

Women Marines at Henderson Hall, Arlington, Virginia, September 1944. US Marine Corps

ness and avoid unfavorable comments, no fewer than two WRs were assigned to a station; enlisted women were not assigned to a post unless there was a woman officer in the vicinity; and it was customary to assign women officers to units of twenty-five or more WRs.

The relatively few women stationed in large cities were given a monetary allowance to pay for housing and meals. An exception was made in Washington, D.C., where a new, independent post, Henderson Hall, was built to house 2400 WRs. Officially, it was named for the first Commandant, General Archibald Henderson, but understandably, it became "Hen Hall."

When women joined the Corps, they elevated the quality of barracks living. Stark squadbays were often softened with pastel paint and stuffed animals rested on tightly made bunks. Dressers were arranged for privacy, shower curtains were hung, and doors closed off toilet stalls. Day rooms set aside to entertain dates were furnished with

A Native American Woman Marine motor transport driver, Marine Corps Air Station, El Toro, California.   US Marine Corps

board games, pianos, record players and cooking appliances; while hair dryers, and sewing machines were placed in lounges reserved for the women.

Marines weren't happy about the feminine touches, but in time commanding officers were proud to traipse visitors and dignitaries through the immaculate WR barracks and mess halls—clothing hung facing in one direction, sparkling mirrors, no dust kittens under the bunks, and glossy floors buffed to perfection with Kotex.

The Marine Corps, renowned for excellent discipline and morale, had no history to help them bridge the gender gap. These women were not pliant teenagers, but rather adults at least twenty years old; most with work experience; some married; some had children; and a few had grandchildren. Since women were expected to adhere to near-Victorian standards, military leaders assumed a paternalistic attitude and the inevitable occurred—grown, mature women were often treated like school girls. Senior women officers, many with roots in academia, were often more guilty than the men.

One galling rule was that women aboard a base, unlike men of equal rank, could not have an automobile. It added to the allure of the motor pool that the drivers of trucks, jeeps, and buses were more mobile than their sisters.

Hawaii

These same paternalistic thought patterns were responsible for Marine and Navy leaders' initial refusal to send Women Marines and WAVES overseas. Eventually, however, the opinions of military men such as Marine General Holland M. Smith and Navy Secretary James V. Forrestal overcame the original reluctance of Congress. Smith believed that Women Marines stationed in Hawaii would free male Marines stationed there for combat assignments. Forrestal, meanwhile, identified 5,000 positions which women could occupy in Hawaii. Finally, new legislation signed on 27 September 1944 allowed naval servicewomen to be assigned to stations in Hawaii.

Colonel Streeter, anticipating the new policy, asked WAC Director Colonel Hobby for advice on selecting people for overseas. By her own admission, going straight to Colonel Hobby was ". . . not exactly according to Hoyle," but ". . . it was certainly sensible and nobody fussed about it." Colonel Hobby offered simple advice, ". . . a person who's had a good record in this country is likely to have a good record abroad, and a person who's had disciplinary problems in this country, or whose health wasn't good, we wouldn't send abroad."

In October 1944, Colonel Streeter flew to Hawaii to make preparations and inspect the living arrangements. She expected half the women would be stationed at the Marine Corps Air Station, Ewa.

A staging area was established at San Diego where the women underwent intense physical conditioning including strapping on a ten pound pack while ascending and descending cargo nets and jumping into the water from shipboard. They learned about Hawaiians, Allied insignia, shipboard procedures, and safeguarding military information.

On 25 January 1945, five officers and 160 enlisted, with blanket rolls on their backs, marched up the gangplank of the SS Matsonia in San Francisco. Their shipmates were a mixed lot of male Marines, sailors, WAVES, military wives, and ex-POWs, and because of the lopsided ratio of men to women, they were restricted to a few crowded spaces aboard ship.

On 28 January they disembarked as the Pearl Harbor Marine Band played "The Marines Hymn," the "March of the Women Marines," and "Aloha Oe." The WAVES went ashore first—dressed in their best uniform. Then came the WRs—astonished that their no-nonsense appearance in dungarees and boondockers seemed to please the curious Marines who had come to look them over and welcome them to Hawaii.

The majority were quartered in barracks recently vacated by the Seabees. The large, wooden, airy, barracks were comfortable but needed modifications for females, so a few Seabees remained behind to do some reconditioning. Major Wing, the commanding officer, ". . . had a fine way of treating men" according to Colonel Streeter. "No Seabee could pay for a coke. As many cokes a day as he wanted and he couldn't pay for them. We got more work out of those Seabees than you could ever imagine."

In Hawaii, the women worked much the same as in the States, with most assigned to clerical jobs. More than a third of the women at Ewa came from the Marine Corps Air Station, Cherry Point, North Carolina, and lost no time picking up their tools and working on the planes.

At Pearl Harbor, the WRs ran the motor transport section, serving 16,000 persons monthly. Scheduled around the clock and with a perfect safety record, they maneuvered the mountainous roads of Hawaii in liberty buses, jeeps, and trucks carrying mail, people, ammunition, and garbage. Marines became accustomed to the sight of women drivers, but never quite got used to grease-covered female mechanics working under the hood or chassis of a two-ton truck.

The MCWR Band

The most colorful of the WR units was the Marine Corps Women's Reserve Band formed in November 1943 and trained by members of the Marine Band. Prominent music schools and colleges were canvassed and talented enlisted women were auditioned to find forty-three musicians. Its director was Master Sergeant Charlotte Plummer, formerly director of the Portland, Oregon, public school system band.

The Camp Lejeune-based band gave concerts at Marine posts and on national radio programs. It played at guard mounts, inspections, graduations, and dances. It is remembered for performances at the Saturday MCWR recruit depot reviews, marching to the rhythm of its own "March of the Women Marines," written by Musician First Class Louis Saverino of the Marine Band.

Band members were deeply affected by hospital concerts where they entertained Marines on gurneys, in wheelchairs, propped up in bed, and trying to applaud without hands. Playing for wounded Marines added poignancy to graduation parades where they stepped off in front of thousands of men headed for war. And, it was equally hard to be indifferent to the train loads of arriving recruits, greeting them with stirring martial music but thinking of the day when they, too, would go off to war.

Band members rehearsed long hours; toured in crowded, poorly maintained buses; carried heavy instruments in pouring rain, under the broiling sun, and while marching through sucking mud. Because the practice room was unheated, Loudene Grady and Louise Hensinger got up early to build a fire in the coal stove before rehearsals.

Ellen Stone and Bonnie Smallwood recalled the base concerts:

> The weather was changeable . . . One day a cold wind would blow the marching

The Women's Reserve Band performing during a radio broadcast at the Marine Band rehearsal hall, Washington, DC, November 1944.

Courtesy of Audre Fall Wells

women musicians off balance, hitting the instruments against their teeth and bruising their arms. The drums would loosen up and have no tone. Valves on the brass instruments would stick. The clarinets would crack and lips would stick to the brass mouthpieces.

No complaints were heard in August 1945 when the band director announced that Japan was expected to surrender at any moment, ". . . we're to hit the streets in uniform, and we're to parade, parade, and parade!"

They freshened their make-up, rolled up their hair, and waited. When at 7 p.m. on 14 August the news came, the women cheered and fell out for the victory celebration. For three hours they zigzagged throughout the base, playing until their lips were sore, and blisters formed on their fingers and heels.

Thousands of Marines spilled into the streets and danced in and out of their ranks. The women played every march they knew by heart because they couldn't read music in the pandemonium and, when entire sections couldn't play because of tears, the drums just beat out the cadence.

War's End

When the war finally ended with the abrupt surrender of the Japanese, women were in 225 specialties in sixteen of twenty-one functional fields, filling 85 percent of the enlisted jobs at Headquarters Marine Corps and comprising one-half to two-thirds of the permanent personnel at major Marine Corps posts.

Demobilizing the war machine was an administrative process requiring more clerks than warriors. There's an old saw that an army fights on beans and bullets. In 1945, the War Department learned that an army disbands on a mountain of paperwork. Although women were expected to return home quickly, they were needed more, not less. Policies regarding the discharge of women changed daily. While acknowledging their opposition to women in uniform, many men were anxious to keep female clerks to process separation orders, cut paychecks, distribute medals, arrange transportation, assist surviving dependents, and settle the accounts of thousands of Marines.

Announcements called for mandatory release of all WRs by 1 September 1946. Newspapers quoted the Commandant saying that the Marine Corps Women's Reserve would be reduced to 2,638 enlisted and 200 officers by 30 June 1946 and the organization ". . . will completely vanish from the picture by September . . ."

Colonel Streeter resigned on 6 December 1945 and the following day her assistant, Lieutenant Colonel Towle, was promoted to colonel and appointed the second Director of the wartime MCWR. To Colonel Towle fell the dual responsibility of overseeing the demobilization of the women and planning for a postwar women's organization.

A point system was used to control the separations. Women with twenty-five points on 1 September 1945 were eligible for immediate discharge, and the number was progressively reduced. Exceptions were made for married women whose servicemen husbands had been discharged.

The office of the wartime MCWR was closed on 15 June 1946, when Colonel Towle began terminal leave. But in the midst of the drive to demobilize, 300 women were asked to stay and a new unit was opened at Headquarters Marine Corps.

Women Marines celebrate the end of the war in Washington, D.C.   Courtesy of Neva Vredevoogd Austin

An anonymous author summed up the demobilization of the Marine Corps Women's Reserve in an undated, unsigned brief history that begins:

> It is rumored that when it was announced that women were going to be enlisted in the Marine Corps the air was colored with profanity in the language of every nation as the members of the old Corps gathered to discuss this earth-shattering calamity. It is entirely probable that the wailing and moaning which went on that day amongst the old Marines was never equaled—never, that is, until it was announced that the women Marines were going home. Then, with a complete reversal of attitude, many of those same

Marines declared that the women in their offices were essential military personnel and absolutely could not be spared from the office.

Meanwhile, a steady stream of correspondence circulated among the Services exploring various proposals to give women permanent status in the military. Marines had no enthusiasm for the idea and while they did not endorse it, they did not strongly oppose it out of consideration of the wishes of the Army and Navy. The Commandant's plan called for a small women's reserve to be led in peacetime by a director—eventually, Major Julia E. Hamblet—with three officers at Headquarters. About one hundred

WRs remained on active duty at Headquarters, bridging the gap between the end of World War II and the passage of the Women's Armed Services Integration Act of 1948 that authorized women in the Regular as well as the Reserves of the Marine Corps.

Among all the beautifully worded accolades bestowed on women Marines of World War II, is a simple statement made by General Holcomb, the Commandant so opposed in the beginning: "Like most Marines, when the matter first came up I didn't believe women could serve any useful purpose in the Marine Corps ... Since then I've changed my mind."

7

Women In The Coast Guard: SPARs

**Captain
Mary E. McWilliams
USCGR (Ret.)**

Prior to the attack on Pearl Harbor on 7 December 1941, the United States had been in a state of "emergency" declared by President Roosevelt on 8 September 1939. During these two years, the Coast Guard was actively involved in the Battle of the Atlantic—primarily on the Greenland patrol and in escorting convoys. On 1 November 1941, the entire Coast Guard was transferred, by Executive Order, to the Navy from the Treasury Department. This smallest of all the U.S. Armed Forces had increased its personnel, military and civilian, from 17,022 to 29,978 during the "emergency" period.

Rapid expansion of personnel, bases, housing facilities, vessels and equipment became inevitable with the outbreak of World War II. Much of this increase in manpower for the Coast Guard would be taken care of with amendment to the Auxiliary and Reserve Act in June of 1942. Then in July, Congress authorized the establishment of a Women's Reserve in the Navy (WAVES) and one in the Marine Corps—could the Coast Guard be far behind?

Creating the SPARs

Public Law 773, signed by the President on 23 November 1942, established the Women's Reserve of the Coast Guard Reserve, and authorized the replacement of officers and men for duty at sea by women reservists to be assigned to duties ashore at stateside bases. Under terms of an agreement between the Navy and the Coast Guard, the nucleus of the Women's Reserve would come from the Navy—fifteen officers and 153 enlisted women requested discharge from the Navy and were on their way to becoming the original SPARs. Dorothy C. Stratton, on leave from Purdue University, transferred from the Navy and became Director of the Women's Reserve of the Coast Guard. She is

Lieutenant Commander Dorothy C. Stratton, Director, SPARs, with Admiral Waesche.

US Coast Guard

credited with having created the acronym, SPAR, from the first letters of the Coast Guard motto, SEMPER PARATUS—Always Ready.

While early recruiting response was encouraging, problems were bound to develop. There was much uncertainty as to what the manpower needs would be—how many SPARs would be needed and what civilian experience and background would qualify the applicants for those military jobs? Initially, recruiting was done by Navy recruiters, but by 1 July 1943 SPAR recruiters were on the job in all District Coast Guard Offices. When the main chapter of SPAR recruiting came to a close at the end of calendar year 1944, over 11,000 women had signed enlistment contracts.

Women reservists were limited to shore duty within the continental United States and limited as to the commissioned rank they might attain. The highest rank authorized was lieutenant commander and this was to be held by the Director of the program. There could be no more than eighteen in the grade of lieutenant. Military authority of the women officers was to be exercised over women of the Reserve only. In December 1943, Congress, reflecting the increasing awareness and confidence of the American public in the value of the work of military women, removed some of the limitations on rank for women officers of the Coast Guard Reserve. The highest rank was to be captain, but there could be no more than one of them. Captain Dorothy C. Stratton remained Director until September 1945, when she was replaced by Captain Helen Schleman. In September 1944, the assignment of SPARs to "overseas" duty in the territories of Alaska and Hawaii was authorized.

"Don't Be A Spare, Be A SPAR!"

"Don't Be A Spare, Be A SPAR!" read one of the recruiting posters. Early recruiting efforts ran into many difficulties, not the least of which sprang from the societal values of the 1940s. Many families which had willingly sent sons off to the services stopped short of approving a daughter's enlistment. Media coverage ran the gamut from a "wait and see" attitude to downright sleaze. In many cases inexperienced recruiters were

goaded to meet unrealistic quotas. Eager to meet these quotas, some did not have the skills to recognize a fraudulent birth certificate; others may have been under such pressures that they failed to do complete background checks which might have revealed an applicant's inadequate schooling, a prior police record, or time spent in a mental institution. Ultimately, Coast Guard recruiters were given additional training and, very significantly, the assistance of public relations officers in the various Districts. In the

SPARs christen a boxcar bearing the recruiting slogan, "Don't Be A Spare, Be A SPAR."

National Archives

summer of 1944, the music and dance revue, "Tars and Spars," toured East Coast cities in an attempt to heighten the public's awareness of both the Coast Guard and SPAR recruiting program. How much effect the show had on recruiting is debatable, but it did make the public more aware of the Coast Guard.

Who were the women who responded to the recruiting posters? From which walks of life had they come to meet the needs of the Coast Guard to "release a man for duty afloat"? A survey of 1,210 enlisted women in May 1943 reveals some interesting data on their ages, education, and occupational

backgrounds. The median age was 22.73. The youthfulness of the enlisted SPAR group is further emphasized by the fact that 66 percent were under 25 and more than 87 percent were under thirty. More than 66 percent had finished high school. One in four had attended college for at least one year, and 5 percent had graduated. Approximately three out of four had worked in either clerical or sales occupations, another one in ten had professional or managerial experience, and another 10 percent had been employed in industrial occupations. It is interesting to note that the average or mean weekly salary earned by these women in their previous employment was considerably lower than the weekly pay and allowance for a seaman second class.

Previous employment and the personal wishes of the recruit were considered when planning for rate training after boot camp. The needs of the service, however, were given top priority. Eleanor C. L'Ecuyer enlisted in Boston in 1944, completed the nine weeks of boot camp, and vividly recalls the assignment interview.

US Coast Guard SPAR.   The Women's Memorial

Apparently my boot camp grades indicated that there was a school in my future. The interviewer asked all sorts of questions about whether I'd ever volunteered in a hospital or would like to take care of sick people. My responses were firmly negative, but he evidently had a quota to fill, since I was off to Columbia University School of Pharmacy in New York. Rated as Pharmacist Mate 3/c, I reported to CG Air Station, Puget Sound, Washington. I didn't bother to correct my mother's assumption that "Washington" always means the D.C. one. Each Christmas Eve I am reminded of one of my sadder duties while at Puget Sound. It involved four Coastguardsmen in an auto accident just outside the gatehouse. I received a letter of commendation for having administered artificial respiration to the driver, but it was too late. The three passengers survived. Grim holiday. After demobilization, I earned a law degree, was commissioned in the Women's Reserve, served more than twenty years on active duty, and retired as a captain.

Where in the United States did SPAR recruits come from? It seems logical to expect that the appeal of the Coast Guard would be strongest on the salt water coasts of the Atlantic, Pacific, and Gulf of Mexico—the profile of the service itself was high in those areas. A very interesting report on recruiting results for the period July 1943 through June 1944 credits the 9th District in Cleveland with the highest number of enlistments of SPARs! During World War II the Cleveland District had a most irregular shape—running the entire U.S. shoreline of the Great Lakes. Included in the territory were the large urban areas of Buffalo, Cleveland, Detroit, Chicago, and Milwaukee, where the Coast Guard was already a familiar part of the communities. The St. Louis District, covering the vast area drained by the great rivers of the United States—the Ohio, Illinois, Missouri and Mississippi—accounted for the second highest number of women recruits for that same period.

Dorothy Riley Dempsey enlisted in New York. When asked why she had left the comforts of home to venture into the "unknown" of military life, she responded:

Yes, it did take some courage, but it seemed the right thing to do, maybe even the patriotic thing to do—to free a man

for service at sea and be part of the greatest challenge of our time. Boot camp at Palm Beach was a rude introduction to the rigors of community living—eight to a room with four dressers and one bathroom, "white glove" inspections on Saturdays, reporting to morning muster in "quick time," physical exams, and the endless "shots"—occasionally being administered in both arms simultaneously! Feeling very self-conscious in our new uniforms, we all headed for a restaurant on our first liberty, and then to a photo studio. After all, parents and grandparents needed to see what a SPAR really looked like.

Having completed indoctrination and some rate training as boatswains mates, I was assigned to Brandon Hall Barracks in Massachusetts, as Master At Arms. Singing with the 50-voice SPAR chorus eventually led me into some War Bond shows with Chief Boatswains Mate Caesar Romero. These shows toured New England and one time visited the home of then Senator [sic] Margaret Chase Smith to publicize recruiting of women in Maine, Vermont, and New Hampshire. All in all, I feel that we SPARS made a great contribution to the successful and timely end to WWII, and many of us have continued our involvement in community service.

Several months later, a similar survey was conducted among a group consisting of 356 SPAR officers and officer candidates. Both the median and average ages were 29 and 10 percent were over 40. More than nine out of ten were college graduates, one third had done some graduate work, and 20 percent had earned master's degrees. Not surprisingly, half the group had worked in the field of education—the majority as teachers and the others as administrators. Many had worked in government service, industry, retail trades, and social welfare services.

After her March 1943 enlistment in Kansas, and the rigors of boot camp at Hunter College, Bronx, New York, Dorothy Jeanne Gleason reported to the District Office in Cleveland. Less than one year later, she was selected to attend the Pay and Supply Officer School in Palm Beach and, upon commissioning, transferred to the then largest Coast Guard Training Station at Manhattan Beach in Brooklyn. Jeanne recalled:

I was proud to be an officer and enjoyed the prestige and the responsibilities of that single blue stripe. As a junior officer I had my share of tedious little "collateral" duties, but the one I enjoyed most was that of recreational officer for the women—softball and baseball. Our teams challenged the women's teams of the other services. A real distinction that I share with only one other SPAR was that of having been assigned to shore patrol duty in Coney Island on the night of VJ day! Had I been offered the opportunity, I'd have elected to make the service my career, but we were all demobilized. When the Reserve was re-established, I returned and retired as a captain after 35 years.

From her teaching position in Pennsylvania, Vivian Reese Harned reported to Palm Beach for boot camp and remained there to attend Storekeeper School. Her first assignment was to the Third Coast Guard District in New York and she reports:

New York was very exciting—promotions were rapid, and I had the opportunity to see General Eisenhower's Victory Parade

and appear on the Lucky Strike show. But I really wanted a transfer to the West Coast. Although the regular OCS classes had been terminated in November 1944, Coast Guard Headquarters had scheduled a Pay and Supply Officer class in August 1944 for which I was accepted. VJ Day created a dilemma, but we were commissioned and I was assigned to Coast Guard Headquarters in Washington in the travel section of Disbursing.

The cost and other difficulties of living "on the economy" in Washington shocked us. Not only were rooms expensive and almost unavailable, but also landlords did not want to rent to women—too messy and left stockings hanging in the bathroom! After demobilization in 1946, I returned to the Reserve Program, and retired as a captain with 37 active and Reserve years. A happy note—in 1979 I married a Coast Guard captain to whom I'd paid travel vouchers in 1946!

While most women enlisted in the SPARs in the traditional fashion—a visit to a nearby recruiting office, interviews and tests, and swearing-in—Florence Ebersole Smith had to travel half way 'round the world! The daughter of a former U.S. soldier and a Filipino mother, Mrs. Smith was working for the U.S. Army when the Japanese occupied Manila. Claiming Filipino citizenship, she was able to avoid immediate internment. She joined the underground and smuggled food, medicine, and other supplies to the American captives. Eventually, however, she was arrested by the Japanese, tortured, and sentenced to three years imprisonment. After having served five months of her sentence, she was liberated by American forces.

Returning to the United States aboard a Coast Guard transport, she headed for

Buffalo, New York, her father's home town. She enlisted in the Coast Guard to help avenge the death of her husband, Charles Smith, a Navy PT boat crewman killed at Corregidor. Smith was the first SPAR to receive the Pacific Campaign ribbon in recognition of her service in the Philippines. At the end of the war she was awarded the U.S. Medal of Freedom.

In 1995 the Coast Guard paid tribute to Florence Ebersole Smith Finch of Ithaca, New York, by naming Base Honolulu's new administration and operations building the Smith building. At the time, she said, "I couldn't believe it! I wouldn't have imagined this in my wildest dreams. It's a combination of sorrow and joy."

Uniforms and Training

The selection of appropriate uniforms for the SPARs apparently did not present too much of a problem. Since the uniforms of the men in both the Navy and the Coast Guard were similar except for the small identifying insignia, why not have the SPAR uniforms similar to those worn by WAVES! One innovation in this area for the Coast Guard, however, was the addition of the gold Coast Guard seals on jacket lapels and shields on sleeves—white on enlisted and gold above the blue braid for officers. Early uniforms had been acquired from the Navy, but by June of 1943 the Coast Guard had assumed complete responsibility for uniforming SPARs.

By prior agreement with the Navy, Coast Guard women would be trained at Navy training schools—a tremendous help to the smaller service! Enlisted recruits reported to the Naval Training School, Bronx, New York (Hunter College) for five weeks of

SPAR uniforms. National Archives

indoctrination training. At the conclusion of "boot school" those with prior training in needed skills were sent directly to duty assignments while others were selected to attend specialized WAVE training schools—yeoman training at Cedar Falls, Iowa, and Stillwater, Oklahoma; storekeeper training at Bloomington, Indiana; Boston, Massachusetts and Milledgeville, Georgia. Radioman schools were at Madison, Wisconsin and Oxford, Ohio.

In March 1943, it became evident that the Coast Guard needed a separate training facility and the Palm Beach Biltmore Hotel was leased for the duration of the war. More than 7,000 women went through "boot" training at the Florida station in the

SPAR Regimental Review, US Coast Guard Training Station, Palm Beach, Florida.   US Coast Guard

following year and a half. In addition, there were four enlisted specialist schools located at Palm Beach for yeoman, storekeepers, cooks and bakers, and pharmacist's mates; as well as a school for pay and supply officers. Specialist (rate) training expanded and was diversified to the point where, by the end of the war, enlisted women were serving in a wide variety of jobs in the Coast Guard—many of them highly "nontraditional for women." A partial listing would include: parachute rigger, radioman, Link trainer, radio technician, coxswain, air control tower operator, gunner's mate, musician, photographer, motion picture technician, radarman, quartermaster, and chaplain's assistant.

Despite the requirement of having to wait two months for release from her defense job at General Electric, Bostonian Alice Jefferson enlisted in January 1944 and remembered:

The thought of boot camp at Palm Beach was particularly intriguing in January! I also felt that there might be greater opportunity for advancement in the smaller service, thus ending my plan to enlist in the Navy. After a short first assignment at the Brooklyn Supply Depot, transfer orders sent me back home to the Finance Department in the Boston District. Having advanced to Chief Storekeeper, I applied for transfer to Hawaii and almost made it but the war ended, dashing that dream.

SPARs study an automobile engine.

I returned to active duty after the re-establishment of the Women's Reserve and retired after almost 25 years of service. Following the 1973 legislation, I became the first woman officer sworn into the Regular Coast Guard.

The recruiting and training of SPAR officer candidates evolved in much the same way as the programs for enlisted women. Initially, officer training was in two phases: the first with the WAVES at Northampton, Massachusetts; then candidates were transferred to the Coast Guard Academy at New London, Connecticut, for three weeks. By July 1943, the Coast Guard decided to give the entire officer indoctrination at the Coast Guard Academy. This did not affect the arrangement whereby women communications officers would continue to receive their training at the WAVES Communications School at Northampton. SPAR officers from later classes attended Coast Guard Communications School at Atlantic City, New Jersey.

Early recruiting efforts were targeted toward filling two types of billets open to SPAR officers—those in which the requirements were general in nature, and those requiring specialized training and experience. For the "general duty" officers, recruiters sought women with broad backgrounds who appeared to be adaptable and able to learn quickly. Women with experience and training in technical areas were targeted for assignments in legal, engineering, intelligence, and some other fields. The Coast Guard encouraged enlisted SPARs to apply for officer training. Eventually about 31 percent of those commissioned had been drawn from the enlisted community. Most of the Pay and Supply officers received both their specialist training and their officer indoctrination at the Palm Beach Station. During the waning days of the war, an additional group of women was trained in pay and supply and commissioned at the Manhattan Beach Training Station.

After training, most general duty SPAR officers were assigned to duties in Coast Guard District Offices or large stateside bases from Port Angeles, Washington, to the Florida Keys. Others performed duties in Coast Guard Headquarters in Washington, D.C. Many served in the administration of SPAR barracks located in areas where there were large concentrations of enlisted women to be housed. Some remained at the training stations to continue training new recruits.

It had been somewhat of a surprise to many Coast Guard leaders to learn that women could, indeed, learn new skills, live in barracks, and adapt to military discipline. While their enthusiasm for adding women to their work force during the early days of the program was, at best, lukewarm, it became difficult to fill their personnel requests once they learned that SPARs were a valuable asset and that the buildings would not crumble upon the arrival of women! While a few SPARs may have encountered some difficulties in becoming part of a military organization, the vast majority have expressed very positive recollections of their service. Lorraine Jacyno Dieterle from Michigan recalled that:

When I enlisted in the Coast Guard in 1944, I never expected that I would be the first female photographer in the Third Naval District. Every morning I rode the New York City subway to the Photo Lab located in the Barge Office in lower

SPARs on parade, Washington, D.C.   US Coast Guard

Manhattan right next to the Staten Island Ferry. Because of prior experience as a photographer, I was put right to work training young Coast Guardsmen in aerial, motion picture, still photography, and darkroom procedures. My duties in the District Public Affairs Office also included the cataloguing of incoming photographs from all theaters of Coast Guard activities and distribution to newspapers, newsreels, magazines and the National Archives. My most memorable experiences, however, were during the homecoming of our troops through the Port of New York. I had the opportunity of photographing many of the parades which included General Wainwright, President Truman, and Admiral Halsey. When I approached his car to get a better closeup shot of him, Admiral Halsey ordered the car stopped and gently warned me 'Be careful, young lady, we don't want you to get hurt. You want to go home too.' I had great rapport with the young Coast Guardsmen with whom I worked. I suspect that they viewed me as their mother or sister, or perhaps their girlfriend back home.

LORAN

A small group of SPARs was assigned to one of the most important, highly classified, and little publicized activities of the war effort: LORAN. When the Coast Guard took over the Lighthouse Service in 1939, it took on the responsibilities for "aids to navigation"— lighthouses, lightships, fog signals, buoys, day beacons, and radio beacons. As the Battle of the North Atlantic raged, dimouts and even blackouts of these aids were initiated in cooperation with the Army and the Navy. This forced amazingly rapid acceleration in research by scientists in both the United States and Canada on an alternative system

for navigational aid, resulting in the birth of LORAN (Long Range Aid to Navigation), a classified system which enabled navigators of air and surface craft to fix positions under all weather conditions. LORAN is an electronic system whereby two stations, situated 200-600 miles apart in LORAN-A and 600-1,000 miles apart in LORAN-C, transmit synchronized signals. These signal pulses are received aboard ship by a LORAN receiver which electronically measures the interval between the times of their reception in millionths of a second. The time difference obtained from the receiver is known as the "LORAN reading." While LORAN stations were eventually constructed in the Pacific, the original stations were on the Atlantic coasts of the United States, Canada, Greenland and Great Britain.

During the summer of 1943, Coast Guard Headquarters made the decision that LORAN Monitoring Stations would be manned by SPARs. The women selected for this highly classified duty were sent for special training at the Naval Training School (Navigation) at the Massachusetts Institute of Technology. The monitoring required 24-hour watch standing and taking and recording measurements every two minutes.

The first Commanding Officer of the all female station at Chatham, Massachusetts, Lieutenant (junior grade) Vera Hamerschlag, made some interesting observations about the duty:

> Little had I realized when I was told I would be commanding officer of a LORAN monitor station how many angles it involved. I was operating and engineering officer, medical officer, barracks officer, personnel officer, training officer—and even Captain of the Head! I had to learn the intricacies of plumbing, of a coal fur-

nace, of a Kohler engine that supplied emergency power when the main line was out—and being on the Cape, where nor'easters are frequent, the times were many! I remember the feeling I had when I looked at the 125' mast for the station's antenna and wondered which SPAR would climb the riggin' if something went wrong. Inasmuch as LORAN is considered one of the outstanding scientific developments of this war, it is a satisfaction to know that SPARS were given the opportunity to participate in its operation.

The unit at Chatham on Cape Cod is believed to have been, at the time, the only one of its kind staffed completely by women. The Commandant's letter of commendation stated: ". . . the operation of Unit 21 under the SPARs has been carried out in a most efficient manner and the efforts of the SPAR

personnel have contributed greatly to the overall efficiency of the LORAN system during World War II." When the SPARs celebrated their 50th anniversary in 1992, then Secretary of Transportation Andrew Card sent special greetings to members of the all-SPAR Unit 21, Chatham, Massachusetts: ". . . where they filled a tremendous void for our nation in time of dire strife."

Epilogue

As the war came to a close, the SPARs, along with the women in their sister services—WACs, WAVES, and Marine Corps Women Reservists—were scheduled to be disbanded since the laws under which they operated provided only for their service during the war. With the cessation of hostilities, recruiting and training of women came to a halt.

Crew of Unit 21, LORAN Station, Chatham, Massachusetts

Courtesy of Betty Bean

By the middle of 1946, most of the women in the Coast Guard Reserve had been released from active duty and, in July 1947, when Congress terminated the emergency Coast Guard legislation, all SPARs were discharged in the general demobilization.

Following World War II, with the Coast Guard returned to Treasury Department jurisdiction, there were significant developments concerning the women of the other services. In 1948 Congress passed the Women's Armed Services Integration Act, providing both Regular and reserve status for women throughout the Army, Navy, Marine Corps and the newly established Air Force. The Coast Guard was not covered by this DOD legislation. However, in 1949 the Women's Reserve of the Coast Guard Reserve was re-established and many World War II veterans re-affiliated and began careers on active duty and in reserve units. During the Korean conflict, some thirty to forty women returned to active duty and approximately sixteen of them served long enough to retire. The tenacity of a small group of women reservists finally paid off, but not until twenty-five years later. In December 1973 legislation was enacted giving women in the Coast Guard the same opportunities as women in the other services.

The Saga of the CGC *SPAR*

A unique tribute to the Coast Guard Women Reserves of World War II was given by the Coast Guard on 21 November 1943 when the cutter *SPAR* was launched at the Marine Iron and Shipbuilding Company in Duluth, Minnesota. Commissioned on 12 June 1944, CGC *SPAR* was quickly put to work in convoy duty in support of antisubmarine warfare off the coast of Brazil. At the close of

World War II, *SPAR* was home ported in Woods Hole, Massachusetts. Later home ports included Bristol, Rhode Island; Boston, Massachusetts; and South Portland, Maine. In 1957 *SPAR* conducted oceanographic operations through the Northwest Passage. The culmination of that assignment occurred when the cutters *SPAR, Storis,* and *Bramble* became the first vessels to circumnavigate the North American continent. President Dwight D. Eisenhower sent his personal congratulations to all hands for this significant accomplishment.

CGC *SPAR* added to its illustrious history by logging over 17,000 miles visiting Iceland, Norway, Denmark, Germany and Ireland while conducting an oceanographic charting expedition in the North Atlantic in 1966. Later duties included the servic-

The first SPAR to report for duty in Alaska, September 1944. National Archives

ing of aids to navigation over an area from Portsmouth, New Hampshire, to Quoddy Head on the northeastern tip of Maine; search and rescue; ice breaking in the Cape Cod Canal and Buzzards Bay; and enforcement of laws and treaties.

On 28 February 1997 CGC *SPAR* was decommissioned at the U.S. Coast Guard Base in South Portland, Maine, completing fifty-three years of distinguished service to the nation. Among the guests attending the ceremony and braving the icy blasts coming off Casco Bay were about a dozen World War II SPARs who had come from all across the country. The words of Ella Wheeler Wilcox in her poem, "Winds of Fate," express the moment:

> One ship drives east and another drives
>   west
> With the selfsame winds that blow.

'Tis the set of their sails and not the gales Which tells us the way to go.

Looking Back

An extraordinary number of the women who trained as SPARs retained a strong sense of identification with and loyalty to the Coast Guard. Evidence of this "sense of belonging" has been the great numbers of women who have attended the reunions held periodically to celebrate the November anniversary. For many, their service during World War II opened windows on a new world—newly acquired skills, a wider circle of acquaintances, and views of parts of the country they had never known before. Not surprisingly, some of them married men they had met during their service time, and yes, the children and perhaps grandchildren of some are in today's Coast Guard. **SEMPER PARATUS!**

Women Airforce Service Pilots: WASP

Lieutenant Colonel
Yvonne C. Pateman
USAF (Ret.)

Frankly, I didn't know in 1941 whether a slip of a girl could fight the controls of a B-17 in the heavy weather they would naturally encounter in operational flying.

General "Hap" Arnold
Commander U.S. Army Air Forces

Thirteen women pilots did qualify to fly B-17 bombers and flew them on various missions within the United States during World War II. In fact, before the end of the war, Women Airforce Service Pilots (the WASP) had flown seventy-eight different military aircraft, almost every type of plane in the Army Air Forces inventory at the time. Not only did they fly trainers (PT-19, BT-13, AT-6) and utility aircraft (UC-78, C-46, C-47) but combat pursuits (P-38, P-39, P-40, P-47, P-51, P-63) and bombers (A-20A, B-24 thru the B-29 Super Fortress). Thus, in the graduation address to the last WASP class at Avenger Field, General Arnold, the Commander of the U.S. Army Air Forces, with high praise acknowledged:

> You have shown you can fly wing tip to wing tip with your brother. If ever there was a doubt in anyone's mind that women can become skilled pilots, the WASP have dispelled that doubt . . . We haven't been able to build an airplane you can't handle.[1]

Origins

Of course, it was known in aviation circles prior to World War II that there were highly skilled women pilots around, and by 1941 there were plenty of examples. The problem was to convince the military to use them when and if they were needed in the war effort. Two highly competent female aviators, Jacqueline

Cochran and Nancy Harkness Love, championed this effort. Even before Pearl Harbor, each woman, independent of the other, had submitted a formal proposal delineating how to use women pilots in case of war and had expressed her willingness to direct such a program. Both plans were turned down, however, not because of lack of merit, but because they were considered premature; it was believed that there were plenty of male pilots to do what needed to be done.[2]

The British, on the other hand, were already sorely in need of pilots and were actively recruiting them from other countries. They were also using women in the British Air Transport Auxiliary (ATA), under the direction of Pauline Gower, to ferry combat aircraft. Aware that the ATA would consider using American women pilots, General Arnold suggested to Jacqueline Cochran in August 1941 that she formally apply to the ATA and recruit other women to join her.[3] Twenty-five women

were selected by Cochran and sent in groups of four or five to Montreal, Canada, for screening and final acceptance by the ATA. The women signed an 18-month contract with an option to extend and were sent to England by ship, the first group arriving there in January 1942. The last of the Cochran contingent arrived in London on 2 September 1942. These women became known as the "ATA-gals," and piloted British pursuits, bombers and miscellaneous aircraft from base to base within England under the most hazardous war time conditions.

The success of the British ATA and an apparent shortage of male pilots finally convinced the U.S. Army Air Forces to organize a women's pilot program. Jacqueline Cochran returned from England to become the director of women's flight training.[4] In September 1942, both Cochran and Love were given the go-ahead to start recruiting women pilots and to implement their respective plans.

Major General Harold L. George congratulates Nancy Harkness Love on her appointment as Director, WAFS.

National Archives

The Air Transport Command (ATC) was particularly keen on putting women immediately into the jobs of ferrying aircraft from the factories to bases or ports of embarkation thus freeing male pilots for overseas combat. Nancy Love's plan suited this purpose nicely as she proposed to recruit a few highly skilled women pilots who could, after a minimum of transition time, commence these ferrying duties. The women were required to have a commercial license, at least 500 hours flying time (fifty of which had to be in the last six months), and a log book entry certifying to having qualified in aircraft in the 200 horsepower category. They had to be within 21-35 years of age, and a high school graduate. Women who accepted the challenge were required to report at once and at their own expense to New Castle Army Air Base, Delaware.[5]

As the women reported in, they were personally interviewed by Nancy Love, then given physical exams and flight checks. Out of approximately eighty women contacted by Mrs. Love, twenty-eight were finally selected. After a thirty-day transition period, the women commenced ferrying aircraft on 21 October. All were assigned to the Women's Auxiliary Ferrying Squadron (ATC) and became known as WAFS. Mrs. Love selected a distinctive uniform for them to wear for all flying duties, to be purchased at the women's own expense.

On 28 December 1942, selected WAFS were transferred from New Castle's 2nd Ferrying Group to the following ferrying groups: the 3rd at Romulus, Michigan; the 5th at Dallas, Texas; and the 6th at Long Beach, California. They were to continue their ferrying duties and to prepare for the arrival of future women pilots from Cochran's Flight Training Program.

WASP in Training

The plan developed by Jacqueline Cochran was greater in scope in that it was designed to recruit licensed women pilots (the initial goal was 500) for specialized group training that would qualify them to accomplish a variety of flight assignments in addition to ferrying duties.

In Cochran's plan, the women were required to have a minimum of 200 hours of flying time and a commercial license. They had to have completed high school and be between 18 and 24 years of age. The first batch of applications were sent to 150 women, 130 of whom responded. Each of the respondents was personally interviewed by Cochran, and thirty were selected to make up the first class. The women were notified by telegram of their selection for Army Air Forces training, and ordered to report to the Rice Hotel in Houston, Texas, at their own expense.

> . . . bring such street clothing as you deem desirable together with funds for living expenses for thirty days. Provisions have been made for your employment on civil service status at the rate of one hundred and fifty dollars per month during your satisfactory pursuance of flying instruction under Army control. Upon satisfactory completion of Army instruction course and if physically qualified, you will be eligible for employment as utility pilot at a rate of two hundred and fifty dollars a month.
> *Telegram from General Barton Yount, Commander, Air Training Command.*[6]

The women arrived at the Rice Hotel in a variety of outfits from tailored suits to cowboy boots. Cochran was there to meet them and explained that their training was classified, that there would be no publicity and no glory, just hard work, and that the future of women in military aviation depended on them.[7]

The commanding officer of the Women's Flying Training Detachment was a male captain, not too pleased with his assignment. He addressed the group and told them:

> If you think you're hot shots, I'd advise you to forget it. You are here to learn the way the army flies. The best way to get along here is to be where you're supposed to be and do what you're supposed to do. There are three things for which you can be washed out of the course. The first is you can't fly. The second is that you can't do ground school work. The third is that your attitude isn't good.[8]

Thus was the first class of WASP introduced to the "Army Way."

There was no central housing arrangement; each woman was given a list of places near the airport, and it was up to her to find a place to live and eat and still get to the airport in time for the start of classes. Some of the women elected to live in boarding houses for working girls, while others teamed up and rented hotel or motel units.

The first class (43-1) commenced training at Hughes Airport, Houston, Texas on 16 November 1942, and were assigned to the 319th Women's Flying Training Detachment (WFTD). Up before dawn, the trainees spent nearly 12 hours a day at the airfield: half the day flying in very crowded air space (hundreds of male pilots were training at the same time) doing stalls, spins, turns, take offs and landings; the other half spent in ground school studying navigation, weather, communications, Morse code, and aircraft mechanics. Five months later, on 24 April 1943, twenty-three out of thirty trainees graduated and earned their wings. They were qualified to fly PT-19s (a military training aircraft) and other aircraft in the utility series.

WASP ready to get into the cockpit of a Stearman PT-17, Avenger Field, Texas.   USAF Neg. # B-36486AC, Courtesy of NASM, Smithsonian Institution

Because no official uniform had been designed for them, the women purchased khaki caps, slacks and white shirts with open collars as a uniform for duties at the air-field. The Army Air Forces issued, at no expense to the women, a fatigue coverall in olive drab color as well as an A-2 leather flight jacket.

While the first class was training at Houston, Jacqueline Cochran searched for a better place to conduct the program. She looked for a training facility with central-ized housing on base, classrooms, repair hangars, a dining hall, more air space, a fenced perimeter and the availability of BT-13s and AT-6s for advanced training. Eventually Cochran located such a facility at Avenger Field, Sweetwater, Texas. The ear-lier use of Avenger Field by the women was not possible as it was occupied by Canadian airmen being trained under contract with Aviation Enterprises. There were simply not enough aircraft, facilities or instructors to accommodate both groups.

By February 1943, the 318th Women's Flying Training Detachment (WFTD) was activated at Avenger Field. There were eigh-teen WASP training classes in all, the first two completing all their training at Houston. Class 43-3 was programmed to move up to Avenger Field in May to complete advanced training on AT-6s and the UC-78, a twin-engine trainer. Half of the new class of 43-4 reported for training at Avenger in February, with the remainder of 43-4 report-ing to Houston. Class 43-5 arrived on 24 March 1943 and was the first class to com-plete all primary, basic and advanced train-ing at Avenger Field, graduating on 11 September 1943. All subsequent training (Class 43-6 through 44-10) was completed at Avenger.

As the women graduated, they were reas-signed to one of the four ferrying groups where a cadre of WAFS initiated them into the operation of ferrying aircraft. Once assigned to a Ferry Command Group, the women (except WAFS who already had a uni-

Jacqueline Cochran visits pilot trainees of Class 43-W-4 at Avenger Field, Texas, May 1943.

National Archives

WASP preparing to get into AT-6 aircraft, 1944.
The Women's Memorial

form) were required by the squadron commander to purchase male officer's "pinks and greens" to wear as the official uniform (no hat was prescribed).

The two programs, initiated and directed by Cochran and Love respectively, were meshing well, and the women pilots were recognized as a much needed asset to the war effort. On 5 August 1943, the training program and the women pilots were merged to form the Women Airforce Service Pilots (WASP). Jacqueline Cochran was appointed Director of Women Pilots, Army Air Forces,

and Nancy Love was appointed WASP Executive, Ferrying Division, Air Transport Command.[9]

Duties as Assigned

On 7 August 1943 the fourth WASP class graduated 112 women, the largest group of all the training classes. Eighty-seven of the graduates were sent to one of the four Ferrying Groups while twenty-five others were sent to Camp Davis, North Carolina, on a classified assignment. When they arrived on station, they learned that their assignment was to tow target sleeves behind A-24s and A-25s, war-weary Navy attack planes. Antiaircraft gunner trainees would practice their firing skills by shooting at the target sleeves. The aircraft were to be flown on both high and low level tracking missions along the shoreline.[10]

In October 1943, seventeen women were selected out of classes 43-5 and 43-6 to attend the B-17 school at Lockbourne, Ohio. Thirteen of the B-17 "gals" graduated in January 1944, nine of whom were sent to Buckingham AAB, Fort Meyers, Florida. There they towed targets at high altitudes for flexible gunnery practice by pilots in pursuit aircraft. Three of these women were later sent to Roswell AAB, New Mexico, to tow targets and conduct engineering test flights. One B-17 WASP pilot was sent to Las Vegas, Nevada for similar operational duties.[11]

Other graduates from 43-5 and 43-6 were assigned to B-26 transition training at Dodge City, Kansas. The WASP who completed the class in the B-26, known as the Martin Marauder, were qualified as first pilots immediately. Later, other WASP were given a shorter class at Dodge City and other bases

WASP, trained to ferry the B-17 Fortress, leave their aircraft at the four engine school at Lockborne AAB, Ohio. USAF Neg. # 160449AC, Courtesy of NASM, Smithsonian Institution

to become qualified copilots, thus relieving male copilots for overseas assignments. In November 1943, nineteen WASP graduates of the class of 43-7 went directly to B-25 school at Mather Air Base, California, after which they were reassigned to training bases in California and Texas to tow targets.[12]

Also by November 1943, a program was started to train women pilots to fly pursuit (fighter) aircraft. Two WASPs were sent to Palm Springs, California, for pre-pursuit transition and then retained as instructors for incoming students. The first class of both male and female students convened in December 1943, and subsequent classes followed each month thereafter until April 1944, when the school moved to Browns-ville, Texas. There the students learned to fly four different fighter aircraft: the P-40, P-47, P-51 and the P-39. Classes continued at Brownsville until the pursuit school closed to women on 15 October 1944. Not all women who flew pursuits attended the

school for check-outs. Some women transitioned at their home base or learned to fly the fighters at the aircraft factory prior to taking them on a ferry mission.[13] Such was the case for thirty-one women who qualified to fly the Lockheed Lightning P-38.

There was a variety of flying jobs to which WASP were assigned other than ferrying aircraft. They flew tracking and searchlight missions; towed gliders and targets; and delivered weapons, cargo, and personnel. Some became instructor pilots, and many others were involved in the engineer testing of aircraft. One highly classified project at that time was flying radio-controlled target planes. In this operation, a WASP sat in a tiny PQ-8 aircraft which was controlled by a second WASP in a "mother ship," using radio controls. The pilot in the PQ-8 was exposed to all sorts of flight maneuvers and it was a unique experience, to say the least, for a pilot accustomed to controlling her own aircraft.

Production line maintenance test pilots, Shaw Air Base, November 1944.   USAF Neg. # 85-15657,
Courtesy of NASM, Smithsonian Institution

Fifteen months into the program, a distinctive official uniform became available for trainees and WASP to wear for all nonflying official duties. WASP class 44-1 was the first class to wear the uniform for its graduation ceremony on 11 February 1944. The smart-looking uniform was in Santiago Blue and consisted of winter and summer skirts with jackets as well as winter and summer slacks and a winter beret. These items were issued by the Army Air Force, while shirts and accessories, e.g. purse, tie, and insignia, were purchased by each woman from clothing stores. Functional pilot clothing was issued (at no cost to the WASP) and included an "Ike" jacket, new flight coveralls with a hidden drop seat, a flight cap and a trench-type overcoat.[14]

There was one job in the Training Command that men pilots often simply refused to do, one that was critical on every training base across the country . . . that of test pilot. These future combat pilots thought that if they were going to risk their lives, it should be in combat . . . not in the maintenance testing of aircraft in student training squadrons. This was another essential task where the WASP were used to relieve the men from "dishwashing jobs." In March 1944, Cochran began sending WASP to bases where their primary duty was to test-hop patched-up aircraft, and aircraft that had been "written up" by an instructor or student following a flight operation. Some write-ups, for example, stated that an aircraft "smelled funny" or "wouldn't complete a right turn." Approximately 130 WASP served

WASP reviewing chart before a flight, Romulus Army Air Field, Michigan.
USAF Neg. # A-29684AC,
Courtesy of NASM,
Smithsonian Institution

in this risk-filled, hazardous duty at forty-eight bases, including repair depots.[15]

In March 1944, Congress considered legislation to militarize the WASP. This had been a long-time objective of Jacqueline Cochran and was supported by General "Hap" Arnold. There was much ado on how this would be done. General Arnold thought the WASP should be brought into the Army Air Forces by direct commission and fought for that during Congressional hearings. As civilians, the WASP had no insurance, no burial benefits, no military rank and no veterans benefits. By contrast, women serving as WACs, WAVES, SPARs and Women Marines had all these benefits. The WASP had been led to believe that they too would be given military status.

In late March 1944, a memo from Major General H. A. Craig, AAF Headquarters, was sent to the Commanding General, AAF Tactical Center, Orlando, Florida. The memo stated that in anticipation of the commissioning of the WASP, it was desirable that they receive basic military courses, including training in organization and staff procedures and the exercise of command. Thus a WASP Military Course of about four weeks' duration was established, and in April some women were placed on orders to attend officer training. The first group to complete the training returned to home base on 12 May 1944. Three other groups attended the school, but the training was terminated when it became apparent that the WASP would not be commissioned.[16]

WASP discuss flying.
The Women's Memorial

On 21 June 1944, a bill for the militarization of the WASP was defeated in Congress by only nineteen votes. As a consequence, the WASP flying training program was terminated and Class 44-10, already in training at Avenger Field, was the last class. Graduation ceremonies were held on 7 December 1944. The more devastating decision to deactivate the entire WASP program was not made until later.

On 3 October 1944, a letter from Jacqueline Cochran "TO ALL WASP" dashed their hopes of being commissioned into the AAF. It read: "General Arnold has directed that the WASP program be deactivated on 20 December 1944. Attached is a letter from him to each of you, and it explains the circumstances leading up to his decision."[17]

The War Department announced to the press, "the decision to disband the WASP was based on indications that by mid-December there would be sufficient male pilots available to fill all flying assignments in the U.S. and overseas, thus canceling the need for women to fly the routine jobs in this country . . . " The same release quoted General Arnold, AAF's Commanding General, "I am proud of the WASP and their record of skill, versatility and loyalty. They have done outstanding work, even exceeding expectations. What they have proven, including flying B-29s, would be of inestimable value should another national emergency arise."[18]

Even though all would be going home very soon, well over 900 WASP continued their service to the last minute of the final hour.

The WASP flew. They were proud to fly for their country. They expected to continue doing so until the war was over. They were unaware of the debate and political ramifications over the status of their militarization and continued service. It was therefore a shock to learn they would be so abruptly disbanded before the war was to end.

Epilogue

In Jacqueline Cochran's final report to General Arnold on the WASP, she stated that:

> More than 25,000 women applied for training. 1830 were accepted. 1074 made it through a very very tough program to graduation. These women flew approximately 60 million miles for the Army Air Forces with fatalities of 38, or one to about 16,000 hours of flying. The statistics compared favorably for male pilots in similar work: women had as much endurance, were no more subject to fatigue, flew as regularly and as many hours as the men.[19]

On 4 January 1949, four years after the deactivation of the WASP program, the United States Air Force and Army offered reserve commissions to former members of the WASP in the grades of 2nd lieutenant through major. Grades were awarded according to WASP length of service (excluding trainee time) in World War II. One hundred of 300 women who accepted commissions in the reserves were recalled to active duty during the Korean War, although in a non-flying status. Nine of these women served on extended active duty until retirement, five of whom served in Southeast Asia during the Vietnam War. Fifteen others left active duty but continued to serve

Jacqueline Cochran and General Henry H. Arnold at Avenger Field, Texas, for final graduation of the last WASP class, December 1944.

USAF Photo, Dora Dougherty Strother Collection,
Texas Woman's University

in reserve assignments until eligible for full retirement.

Those who volunteered for active duty were entitled to veterans benefits. The majority of the WASP, however, did not receive recognition of their World War II service until November 1977, when veterans status was approved under Public Law 95-292, Section 401.

9

Army Dietitians, Physical Therapists and Occupational Therapists

Colonel Ann M.
Ritchie Hartwick
USA (Ret.)

During World War II, a seldom-heralded group of medical care-takers, women numbering in the thousands, served their country with courage, dedication, ingenuity, and stamina. They established standards of professional practice under combat conditions which still influence Army medical staffs in today's changing world. Their moments on the world's stage invite us to glimpse, if ever so briefly, the commitment of dietitians, physical therapists and occupational therapists to the combat soldier in World War II and the historical settings in which they served.

Dietitians and physical therapists had served in the Army Medical Department as civil service employees even before the United States entered World War I. They had established nationally accredited training programs, and many had served overseas, where some received decorations from foreign governments and others found their final resting places. Male and female occupational therapists, numbering several thousand during World War I, were by 1940 employed for individual Army hospital projects only.

When President Franklin Delano Roosevelt declared a state of national emergency in September 1939 in response to the German occupation of Austria and Czechoslovakia, the anticipated U.S. Army wartime requirements for dietitians, physical therapists, and occupational therapists far exceeded the staffing ceilings of the Army Medical Department. In fact, these new requirements exceeded the total number of these professionals nationwide as recorded by their professional organizations. The recruitment of trained medical professionals by the Army was sluggish due to Civil Service Commission testing procedures, low salaries compared to similar civilian positions, and the recognized lack of wartime protection provided civilians employed by the United States Army. To meet personnel needs, the Army established training programs for qualified medical personnel in civilian institutions as well as in Army hospitals. National training programs for dietitians alone increased from thirty-eight in 1939 to sixty in 1941.

On 7 December 1941, without a formal declaration of war, Japan attacked the United States at Pearl Harbor, Hawaii, destroying the majority of aircraft and naval vessels assigned there and effectively crippling the United States Pacific Fleet. The United States declared war against Japan on 8 December as Japanese attacks on American bases in the Philippines and other Pacific Islands continued. On 11 December, Congress declared war on the other two Axis Powers, Germany and Italy.

Located in Manila to support the armed services and American Embassy personnel was Sternberg General Hospital (Army) with its outlying support hospitals and clinics. Three American staff dietitians and one physical therapist were captured by the Japanese and held as prisoners of war. Mrs. Anna Bonner Pardew, a dietitian and daughter of an Army chaplain, was captured at the Fort McKinley Station Hospital near Manila when the Japanese occupied the city. During the battle of Manila, Miss Brunetta A. Kuehlthau, a physical therapist from North Bend, Oregon, and dietitians Miss Ruby F. Motley, from Columbia, Missouri, and Mrs. Vivian R. Weissblatt, who was married to a United Press correspondent in Manila, were transported from Sternberg Hospital to the Army hospital "topside" on Corregidor and to General Hospital No. 2, an open-air hospital of 6000 beds on the Bataan Peninsula.

On the night of 8 April 1942, merely hours before the Bataan jungle hospital was over-

run by the Japanese, the women serving on Bataan were transferred by boat to the Malinta Tunnel Hospital (1,500 beds) in the island rock of Corregidor. Following the fall of Corregidor (May 1942), the dietitians and physical therapist were interned by the Japanese on 3 July 1942 in the 4,000-person Santo Tomas prisoner of war camp for Allied civilians in Manila. The four women remained at Santo Tomas, caring for the internees as needed, and utilizing the meager provisions (some of which were purchased with their own money) to best maintain the nutritional status of all POW personnel—men, women and children. In the final months of their internment, the prisoners subsisted on starvation rations, until they were liberated by American armed forces in February 1945. They later said that they knew their rescue was close at hand when they smelled the fuel exhaust from the American armored vehicles. When rescued, none of the women weighed over 90 pounds, and Mrs. Wiessblatt had been wounded by shrapnel. After returning home, 1st Lieutenant Ruby Motley spoke before the House of Delegates of the American Dietetics Association on 17 October 1945, relating her experiences at Santo Tomas. Following is an excerpt of her presentation.

We had to dig pits in which to build a fire . . . we used a 50 gallon oil can with the top cut off . . . this was placed over the fire pit, and in it we cooked the rice, which was our main food . . . In our camp we had a small garden, so we had to do most of the planting on a mass production basis. It takes a lot of vegetables to feed 4,000 people! We found a plant called talinum which grew very rapidly, a green vegetable similar to spinach except that it is rather slick when cooked. We found that we fared much better if we had this green vegetable along with the rice. Many didn't like it, but they ate it and were glad to get it . . . We formed lines for everything. People fainted in the lines because they were so weak but they would get up and keep going . . . At the end there were three to four deaths every day, mostly due to malnutrition . . . people trying to work with such small caloric intake naturally would lose their strength . . . I have seen many horrible things, but I have also seen many acts of bravery,

courage and sacrifice that make me proud to think I am an American.

The official oral military histories recorded by Misses (later Majors) Motley and Keuhlthau mention their disappointment and concern at not being selected to be part of the group, which included General MacArthur and his family, that evacuated Corregidor by ship. During the several days when such options remained open, Motley and Keuhlthau reportedly were never told

A wounded war veteran runs a printing press to exercise an injured leg while an occupational therapist and a visitor watch, October 1944.

National Archives

exactly what criteria were used, or who made the final decision in choosing the women to be saved. They surely did know, as the Japanese shells fell hourly on their small rocky fortress, that they had been left behind to uncertain fates at the hands of the enemy. They said that the sounds of the last transport leaving were especially painful.

Following the U.S. declaration of war in December 1941, the Army Surgeon General organized hospitals to support the British armed forces. In May, 1942, the same month that Corregidor fell in the Philippines, the first of these general hospitals to be assigned overseas duty, the 5th General Hospital, embarked for Ireland with two dietitians assigned.

Major Helen Burns, Director of Dietitians, Surgeon General's Office, U.S. Army, and dietitian, Lieutenant Margaret Anderson watch meat preparation for patients of the 16th Evacuation Hospital, Fifth Army, Italy.   US Army

During the invasion of North Africa in the fall of 1942, code-named Operation TORCH, dietitians and physical therapists were assigned to the hospital ships of the invasion fleet and to the 7th Station Hospital established in Oran, Algeria, two weeks after British and American troops landed. These women were the first of hundreds of dietitians and physical therapists to serve overseas and on hospital ships in World War II. Prior to December 1942, they went as civil service volunteers since, by law, civilians could not be ordered to work abroad.

Dietitians and physical therapists served in every theater of war: the European, Pacific, Mediterranean, and China-Burma-India Theaters, as well as "the Zone of the Interior," or the continental United States. Occupational therapists served only in the United States.

In 1943, dietitians and physical therapists were given relative military rank as officers for the duration of the war plus six months. Occupational therapists retained civilian status throughout the war. On 22 June 1944, landmark legislation passed by Congress provided commissioned officer status for dietitians, physical therapists and nurses in the Army, granting them the same allowances, rights, benefits, and privileges as other commissioned officers.

The bill was sponsored by Republican Congresswoman Frances P. Bolton of Ohio's 22nd District. This legislation (P.L. 78-350) established physical therapists and dietitians, as commissioned officers, with military pay and allowances, and benefits including financial support for dependents and long-term medical care. More importantly, however, the legislation protected these officers when they served in combat theaters abroad,

Ward food service for ambulatory patients, 171st Station Hospital, New Guinea, 1943.
US Army Center of Military History

giving them increased protections under Articles of the Geneva Convention. They were allowed to purchase war-risk insurance and were provided with military death benefits. Prior to passage of the Bolton Bill, dietitians and physical therapists had served as civilian volunteers in combat zones without the above benefits, which had been legislated for WAC personnel months earlier.

Dietitians and physical therapists served in England in the Office of the British Quartermaster and cared for patients in London during the blitz. In France, dieti-tians operated large hospital messes serving 6,000 to 7,000 meals daily. Subsistence (food) deliveries were unreliable, equipment novel and varied, and patient census fluctuated rapidly as convoys of battle casualties arrived and were dispersed. Physical therapists and dietitians also supported combat troops in Algeria, Sicily, Italy, Belgium, Germany, Iran, Australia, New Guinea, the Philippines, New Caledonia, Guam, Wake Island, Guadalcanal, and in the China-India-Burma Theater. The enemy was often tropical disease, torrential rains, and the bore-

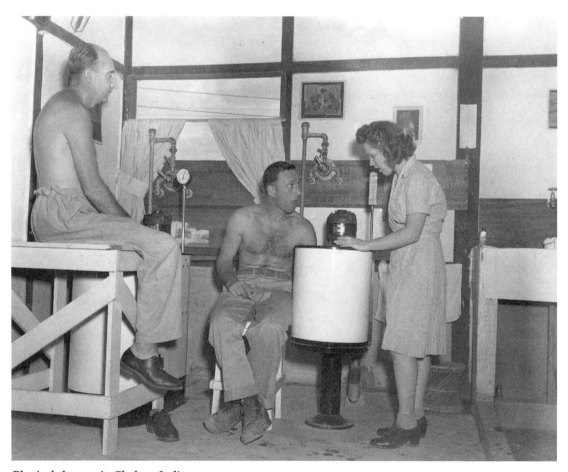

Physical therapy in Chabus, India.

dom of subtropical heat. They extended hands of compassion to the casualties of war . . . Allied and enemy wounded, injured civilians, prisoners of war . . . and with determination helped heal the soldier and feed the hungry of many nations.

1st Lieutenant Helena D. Quinn, stationed at the 49th General Hospital at Milne Bay, New Guinea, told a 1944 Christmas story related to subsistence delivery. As it happened, personnel from the 49th had unloaded long awaited patient subsistence on Christmas Eve from quartermaster transports in the bay, and had taken it to the hospital. Lieutenant Quinn's Christmas Day logbook entry touches the heart.

> There were fresh apples, oranges, frozen asparagus, and many other things . . . eggs in particular. We were so happy to receive them . . . but the Q.M. called and said it was a mistake . . . that they were supposed to be shipped forward. It was like parting with diamonds, but after much persuasion and excuses, we were finally told to keep them, as we had been the only hospital that had sent the detail down the night before. We really feasted for the next weeks.

Forty-two dietitians and two physical therapists served aboard the twenty-four Army World War II hospital ships transporting patients across the Atlantic, Mediterranean and Pacific oceans. These floating hospitals were generally self-sufficient luxury ships, refitted for patient care, and used during combat in support of amphibious landings as offshore hospitals, and as patient transport vehicles from war zones to general hospitals. The staffing complement was one dietitian per 1,000 patients on the manifest, and two for sailings with over 1,000 patients.

Because of the difficulty in performing proper physical therapy due to the ship's roll, confined ward space, and other factors, physical therapists were dropped from hospital ships' complements after the second voyage of USAHS *Acadia.*

In April 1945, the hospital ship *Comfort* was bombed by the Japanese during the battle for Okinawa, causing sixty-nine casualties. In her operations report for 28 April 1945, the hospital ship's dietitian, 1st Lieutenant Edna Rayburn wrote: "At a time like that you can do things you never thought you'd be able to do, put broken arms in place, administer first aid to open wounds, and even assist in giving plasma."

Equipment for physical therapy use had been evaluated and standardized in the late 1930s through the efforts of the American Medical Association's Council on Physical Therapy, and since 1939 Army equipment purchase requests were processed in anticipation of wartime requirements. Physical therapists operating in the early months of the war, or in remote locations, however, often rehabilitated the wounded with improvised equipment utilizing ingenuity and a "can do" work ethic. Mess tables were used as plinths (exercise/treatment tables); water for whirlpools was heated on field ranges; weights for resistance exercises were made from cans filled with dirt, rocks and sand. Large basins and bathtubs became whirlpools. Paraffin came from melted candles (or in Khorramshahr, Iran, from an oil refinery). Bamboo, scrap lumber, and salvage parts from vehicles or aircraft were utilized to construct innovative apparatus for physical therapy programs. Water was often in short supply and electrical current variable. Given these unusual challenges, the physical therapists in World War II demonstrated con-

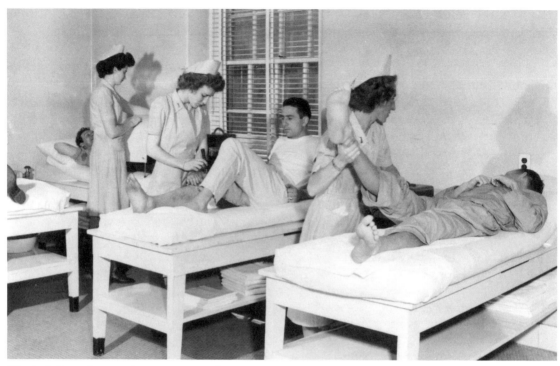

Physical therapists treating patients, Walter Reed General Army Hospital, 1945.

US Army Center of Military History

clusively that wounded soldiers experienced less trauma and healed more quickly and effectively when physical therapy was employed as soon as possible after injury.

Lieutenant Geraldine D. Lindberg, a physical therapist assigned to the 31st Station Hospital (tentage) in New Caledonia, wrote in her official report to Headquarters in 1945:

> Technique in treatment was changed a bit because of local conditions. We had been taught never to remove our hands from a patient during massage, but the author of that idea must never have worked in a mosquito-ridden swamp land. We learned to massage with one hand and swat with the other any mosquito threatening to lunch on either patient or operator.

On 8 May 1945, Germany capitulated. After V-E Day, Army resources, including medical assets, were redirected to the Pacific. Policy provided that married women who were also commissioned officers could relinquish their commission on the same date that their servicemen husbands were discharged from the service, wherever they were located, and both returned to civilian life. They were not required to remain in service for the duration of the war plus six months. By August 1945, of the thousands of women who had served in these professions during the war, Army dietitians on active duty numbered 1,580; Army physical therapists 1,129 300; and occupational therapists (Civil Service employees) 899. On 2 September 1945, Japan formally surrendered.

The standards of professional excellence these women demonstrated during the war and their "can-do" mind set and work ethic were best stated, eloquently but simply, by Colonel Emma E. Vogel in a speech to personnel. "Return the patient to duty or to his rightful place in society in the shortest time by the best means." Colonel Vogel was Director of Physical Therapists, Office of the Army Surgeon General, throughout World War II, and, in 1947, was selected as the first Chief, Women's Medical Specialist Corps.

Some dietitians and physical therapists remained on active duty the "six months" after the end of the war which was the condition of their commissions. Others accepted civil service appointments such as those held by occupational therapists. Most returned to civilian life.

The historical imprint they collectively have left for us to study and admire is truly a multifaceted legacy. They served selflessly—healing the injured in locations more global, more varied, and more distant from their homeland, than had any American women in their professions before them. They were awarded military decorations for heroism in North Africa, Sicily, and the Pacific. They were all volunteers, either as civil service personnel at the war's beginning or volunteering to serve as commissioned officers after legislation was passed. They were well educated. Some were married,

WAC enlisted physical therapy aides at a stateside Army Hospital, 1945.   The Women's Memorial

some single, and, yes, some met their husbands in the military. They loved their country and enriched its traditions by their bravery. They were the girls next door.

The World War II post graduate educational programs which were begun to train women in these specialties accredited by their national professional organizations continued to train thousands of military women and men for the following fifty years. Military personnel changes of the 1990s reduced the number of these programs. The training locations in Army Medical Centers rekindles memories for many generations . . . Walter Reed, Letterman, Brooke, Valley Forge.

The dedicated record of service by dietitians, physical therapists, and occupational therapists in meeting the medical needs of the combat soldier was instrumental in establishing the Women's Medical Specialist Corps. Public Law 80-36 was sponsored by Congresswoman Margaret Chase Smith of Maine and signed by President Harry Truman on 16 April 1947. The Corps welcomed male officers in 1955, and was redesignated as the Army Medical Specialist Corps. In 1992, President George Bush signed legislation incorporating the Army physician assistants as the fourth section of the Army Medical Specialist Corps.

This chapter is dedicated by the author to those who served.

10 *We Also Served*

Judith Lawrence
Bellafaire, Ph.D.

Civilian women served their country during World War II by volunteering as members of service organizations which provided support to Armed Forces personnel. In the course of their service, some women volunteered to go overseas, where they shared the hardships endured by American troops stationed around the world. Other women volunteered on the homefront; they organized civil defense efforts, conducted blood drives, collected scrap materials, wrapped bandages, and manned canteens for service personnel around the country. Patriotism was so high during World War II and the list of volunteer service organizations so long that it is not possible to describe them all here; only selected groups are discussed below.

The American Red Cross

Women volunteering with the American Red Cross (ARC) served on every major military base and in every theater of war. Red Cross nurses were among the first American women to experience the war firsthand. In July 1941, months before the United States officially entered the war, a ship carrying Red Cross nurses to Great Britain to work in hospitals there was torpedoed 400 miles off the coast of Greenland. Four nurses spent twelve days in an open boat on the Atlantic before they were rescued; the ordeal of two others lasted nineteen days. A final group of four were lost at sea. Red Cross nurses helped tend wounded sailors at Pearl Harbor, and several were on the Philippine Islands when the Japanese attacked American installations there. Red Cross nurses were aboard the vessel S. S. *Mactan,* which sailed from Manila to Darwin, Australia in January 1942 with some 200 seriously wounded U.S. soldiers. The Japanese, who controlled the waters around the Philippines, monitored the ship's progress but allowed it safe passage. One Red Cross nurse was among U.S. personnel captured in the Philippines and held by the Japanese as POWs for over two-and-one-half years.[1]

American Red Cross workers from the 298th General Hospital unit, after their arrival at Utah Beach, France, July 1944.

The Women's Memorial

When American forces reached North Africa, Sicily, Italy, Europe, China, India, Burma and the Southwest Pacific, the Red Cross sent recreation workers to Army hospitals in every theater of war. Other ARC women were assigned to Red Cross Clubs located close to wherever U.S. troops were stationed. An innovation called the Clubmobile (a converted Army two-and-one-half-ton truck) allowed some ARC women to reach the troops in the field near the front lines. Surprised soldiers in North Africa, Italy, Normandy and Germany flocked to these mobile kitchens for freshly brewed coffee and the immensely popular fresh doughnuts.

Red Cross women made over 1.6 million doughnuts over the course of the war, and served these confections at a rate of 400 a minute during 1944 and 1945.[2] The doughnut, and the smiling Red Cross girls serving them at stationary clubs and in traveling clubmobiles, seemed to represent home to the American soldier. Only a letter from home was more precious to the average GI, and the Red Cross was often able to help with this as well. Mary Ferebee Howard, assigned to a Red Cross club on the island of New Caledonia, remembers:

Often men were unable to write and wanted us to write a letter home for them. One boy from North Carolina said that he had been away from home for eighteen months and had never received a letter. He told me what to write and I wrote it just as he spoke the words. About a month later he came into the club waving a letter. Someone in his family could read and write and had let him know what was happening at home.[3]

Red Cross Clubs Overseas

The Red Cross established more than 1,800 recreational facilities for the soldiers overseas. The "Rainbow Corner," run by the Red Cross in London, was one of the most popular overseas clubs. The Rainbow was open twenty-four hours a day, and was manned by 400 paid staff in addition to 400 volunteers. Soldiers visited the club for a hot meal, a shave and a haircut, friendly conversation, pinball machines, American music, and the chance to relax in a homey environment.[4]

Many Red Cross clubs were located in isolated areas where volunteers coped with primitive conditions. Mary Thomas Schiek (later Sargent) was assigned to a B-29 Air Base in India's Bengal Desert near the town of Salua, where she and three other ARC workers ran a club for a population of about 5,000 servicemen. Temperatures on the desert often hit 115 degrees, and sometimes reached as high as 125 degrees. When the air base was bombed by the Japanese, Mary spent the night in a trench. She wrote:

> We were all scrunched down on the bottom of the trench and it was so dark, you couldn't tell up from down . . . the night

American Red Cross worker attached to the 5th Air Force sits in an ARC Mobile Canteen, Nadzab, New Guinea.
The Women's Memorial

was full of big blasts from our large bore guns and the black sky was stitched with red tracer bullets. The ground shook as the Japanese bombers dropped their loads in their pass across the center of the air strip.[5]

While alerts in the Bengal Desert were infrequent, Americans stationed in New Guinea were not so lucky. Helen Hall, Director of Red Cross Clubs in the South Pacific, remembered sitting in a dark, wet trench in Port Moresby with other Red Cross workers and Army Nurses:

We sat in our coveralls and fought the mosquitoes together. After two hours the all clear sounded and I was free to climb under my mosquito netting and into bed . . . an hour later came another alert . . . and I staggered to the trench again . . .[6]

Clubmobile Service

The Red Cross Clubmobile Service was orga-nized into ten groups designated "A" through "L" (the letters "I" and "J" were not used). Each group consisted of eight Clubmobiles, manned by two to three volunteers.[7] ARC women drove the Clubmobiles and dis-pensed coffee, doughnuts, candy bars and general good cheer to the troops in the field. The women traveled to as many units as possible, and given the highly mobile nature of the European campaign, frequently found themselves very close to the front lines.

The women from Clubmobile Group D experienced some strafing while in Normandy during the fall of 1944. Gail Wild, Kay Marshall and Janet Whittaker

all piled under the truck. Jan got herself so firmly ensconced that when the planes passed, she found she was stuck between

the wheels. Two GIs extricated her, and the three jumped into the truck to move on, whereas Kay [driving], ran over a pile of hand grenades. The crowd of GIs dis-persed in all directions. Happily they were all duds. What a terrible day. The fat spilled all over the floor too.[8]

Helen Potter of the same group recounted another strafing at the expense of colleague Dottie Stout:

Dottie, running like mad, dodged into the Clubmobile. There was a cluster of coffee urns in the corner and, ostrich-like, Dottie leaned over and put her head into one of them with the rest of her vulnera-ble to shock and shell. When the danger was over Dottie came out of the coffee urn, slightly red in the face, and serving went on as usual.[9]

Mary Coleman of the Clubmobile AUGUSTA, Group A, found herself too close to the front lines during the early stages of the Battle of the Bulge in December 1944:

The infantry retreated back to the high ground where we were serving. We were then right in the front lines. Shells started whistling, and when Ruth Gray heard someone shout, we all ducked. I was cut-ting candy but when I heard a rat-tat-tat like a machine gun, I didn't stop till I was under the truck, way down under my helmet—real small.[10]

Clubmobile Group F was camped at Bastogne when the Battle of the Bulge started. The women manning the five Clubmobiles that comprised Group F re-treated quickly with the troops and got out of the danger zone. One member of the group, Peggy Henry, had been on temporary assignment running a Red Cross club at a rest center for combat troops at Clervaux in Luxembourg. When the Germans suddenly attacked the town, the American soldiers who had been sent to Clervaux for rest and recuperation took up rifles and carbines and prepared to defend the town. The commanding officer gave Peggy instructions on what she should do if she were captured. That night, Peggy was placed on an Army convoy, which broke out of town under severe shelling. She eventually made it back to her colleagues and returned to her job, a bit jumpy but otherwise fine.[11]

Four ARC workers of Clubmobile Group K were recruited as drivers for the Red Ball Express for six weeks, taking truckloads of supplies from Cherbourg to Paris and from Paris to an Army supply depot on the Belgian-German border.[12]

ARC recreation workers frequently visited hospitals set aside for trench foot patients. Although the condition of these GIs necessitated enforced bed rest, the majority of them felt well enough to be bored and many were vulnerable to guilt and depression. The unknown author of a report written on the activities of Clubmobile Group E remembered:

> We'd come bouncing in with a great deal of chatter and foolishness and stay as long as we could . . . these GIs were like children, and they loved having an American girl talk with them. They all wanted to go back to the front . . .[13]

The author also described her Clubmobile's sojourn with the 634th Tank Destroyers:

> In the evenings the Clubmobile was left in a camouflaged position; then we'd go down to the basement of our billet and listen to the men giving orders to the 3" guns in our backyard. A 15 minute lull in firing would be the signal for us to dash out with coffee and doughnuts for the gun crew.[14]

Red Cross Clubmobiles operated in the North African, Mediterranean and European Theaters. They were not used in the China-Burma-India or Southwest Pacific Theaters due to geographic conditions. Those volunteers who worked in Red Cross Clubmobiles and in overseas clubs provided an incalculable morale lift to GIs in every theater of war; however the proximity of Red Cross volunteers to the fighting front exacted a price—twenty-nine ARC women died in service overseas.[15]

Homefront Activities

Over 6 million Red Cross volunteers on the homefront worked in military hospitals and staffed recreational canteens at hundreds of isolated military posts across the country. The Red Cross also shipped weekly food packages to 115,000 American POWs and more than 1.3 million Allied POWs in Europe and the Far East. Volunteers working on assembly lines processed 1.4 million of these packages monthly. Additionally, Red Cross volunteers produced 2.5 billion surgical dressings and nearly 16 million "ditty bags" which contained comfort items for troops and refugees.[16]

The Red Cross also ran a blood donor service, collecting and transporting blood and plasma to U.S. fighting forces around the world. By the end of the war, the ARC had collected 13 million pints of blood for the American military services. Getting the blood and plasma to the front was also the responsibility of the Red Cross.[17]

The military services acknowledged the critical importance of the Red Cross blood and plasma service to the war effort. One Navy surgeon credited the Red Cross blood program with saving the lives of 4,000 Marines at Tarawa. The Surgeon General of the Navy said, "Only one percent of the Navy personnel wounded in the Pacific died, thanks in a large part to plasma." The Army named one hard-contested hill in New Guinea "Plasma Ridge," because of the number of wounded saved by plasma during the operation. When the invasion of Normandy occurred, plasma was dropped by parachute to the evacuation hospitals which had been established as early as D-Day. General Dwight D. Eisenhower, the Commanding General of Allied Forces in Europe, said, "If I could reach all America—there is one thing I would like to do—thank them for blood plasma and for whole blood. It has been a tremendous thing."[18]

Servicemen and women probably remember the Red Cross most for the essential communication services they provided for soldiers overseas and their families back home. Soldiers received messages via the Red Cross relating to the birth of a child, messages requesting their presence home for a funeral, and messages pertaining to other significant personal events. On their side of the world, families would receive messages telling them that loved ones were in an Army hospital; subsequent messages written by Red Cross hospital workers told them of the patient's progress. During the war, the Red Cross sent a total of 42 million such communications.[19]

United Service Organizations

Six civilian volunteer aid organizations: the Young Women's Christian Association (YWCA); the Young Men's Christian Association (YMCA); the National Catholic Community Service; the National Jewish Welfare Board; the Traveler's Aid Association; and the Salvation Army decided to band together under one umbrella organization in 1941, enabling them to pool their resources. They formed the United Service Organizations for National Defense—later shortened to United Service Organizations. The overall mission of the USO was decided by President Roosevelt. He wanted the USO to handle the on-leave recreation of the men and women in the Armed Forces stationed everywhere in the United States and in foreign lands. Many of them were away from home for the first time and yearned for a non-military environment where they could relax—a "home away from home." USO clubs operated at over three thousand locations, providing a "time out" from the war for over 12 million men and women in uniform.[20]

On the homefront, young women from local communities volunteered as hostesses and dancing partners, and participated in other social activities such as cards and ping pong. Other volunteers helped soldiers write letters, sewed on buttons, and manned photographic studios, craft shops, and lending libraries. The USO also distributed 13 million books and 3 million magazines to service personnel stationed around the world.[21]

Well-known movie stars volunteered for traveling road shows that entertained the troops in the United States and around the world. Gary Cooper, James Cagney, Clark Gable, Carole Lombard, Gertrude Lawrence, Fred Astaire, Bob Hope, Marlene Dietrich, Bing Crosby, and Martha Raye were among those who performed. Wherever there were

USO volunteer Marlene Dietrich with WACs in France, 1944.   USO

troops, the stars entertained: Alaska, the Aleutian Islands, Belgium, Bermuda, Brazil, Burma, Canada, the Caribbean, China, Egypt, England, France, Germany, Greenland, Guam, Hawaii, Iceland, Iran, Iraq, Italy, Labrador, Luxembourg, the Netherlands, New Caledonia, the Philippines and the Soviet Union. The performers faced many of the same dangers as the soldiers. Thirty-seven USO entertainers died in plane crashes during the course of the war, and one husband/wife comedy duo was captured by the Germans and released after twelve days. By the end of the war, USO Camp Shows had given more than 428,000 performances to military audiences totaling 213 million.[22]

Lassie Moores Smith, a USO entertainer in the George Abbot play "What A Life," remembers a special performance in the Philippines on 15 August 1945:

We were playing a hospital. There must have been a thousand men there that night, all in their pajamas, all looking exhausted and drawn . . . some without arms, without legs. Some with heads bandaged, some with eyes bandaged . . . At the end of the play, the Commandant announced that the Japanese had surrendered. Every man there was a skyrocket of joy. Such exultation! Every man was yelling, screaming, hugging, crying. We knew, no more death due to mines. No more death due to bayonets. No more death due to grenades. Our servicemen were at last free from the horrors of war.[23]

Salvation Army

The Salvation Army was a member of the USO during World War II. Women Salvation

PHS Officer Josephine Clapp
Courtesy of Josephine Clapp Osbun

The Public Health Service and the Cadet Nurse Corps

The Public Health Service (PHS) worked closely with the American military throughout the war. Forty-nine PHS nurses served with the Coast Guard, and twenty-three were assigned to hospitals which served civilians working on the Alaskan Military Highway project. Other PHS nurses worked at the "relocation" camps where thousands of Japanese-Americans were transferred after the attack on Pearl Harbor. Some nurses of Japanese descent living in other areas of the country volunteered to work at these west coast camps. The shortage of nurses of Japanese ancestry led to the use of student nurses and nurses aides at some of these camps.[25]

Ida Albertina Bengtson, Ph.D., a Public Health Service scientist, helped to develop a vaccine which protected American troops against typhus, a major wartime disease.[26]

In 1943, Congress acted to alleviate a shortage of professionally trained nurses which had been exacerbated by the demands of World War II by passing the Bolton Act, which established the Cadet Nurse Corps. The Public Health Service, under the Surgeon General, was responsible for the administration of the Corps, and promptly established the Division of Nurse Education (DNE) to allocate aid to participating nurse schools. Lucile Petry Leone headed the Cadet Nurse Corps. Later she became the Chief Nurse Officer of the PHS and in 1949 the first woman to achieve the rank of Assistant Surgeon General.[27]

To qualify for the Cadet Nurse Corps, nursing students had to be between 17 and 35 years of age; had to have received good

Army volunteers worked in USO Clubs and Red Shield Clubs located outside Army posts and Navy and Marine bases in the United States. Troops visiting these clubs found activities such as ping pong, shuffleboard, and dancing. Each facility also had a small library, handicraft and language classes, writing desks, and plenty of stationery.

Women in the Salvation Army also organized and participated in large sewing projects making thousands of garments for distribution to service members and their families in temporary difficulties.[24]

US Cadet Nurse Corps mass induction, New York City, May 1944.   National Archives

grades and a degree from an accredited high school; and had to be in good health. To participate in the Cadet Nurse Corps program, three-year nursing schools had to be accredited. These requirements allowed 85 percent of the nursing students and nursing schools in the country to participate in the Cadet Nurse Corps program. The Federal government provided nursing students who qualified and who were enrolled in participating schools with scholarships which paid tuition, fees, the cost of uniforms, and a monthly stipend. The stipend was fifteen dollars a month for the first nine

months of training, and twenty dollars a month for the next fifteen to twenty-one months. The Corps also paid up to forty-five dollars a month for room and board during the first nine months of training. Participating schools received funds to upgrade their programs. October 1945 was the final date for admission, and the last students graduated in 1948. Upon graduation, Cadet nurses were expected to work at military hospitals, veterans hospitals, Indian reservations, or perform other "essential" nursing services for the duration of the war.

Between 1943 and 1948, more than 124,000 nurses, 3,000 of whom were black, graduated from the Cadet Nurse Corps. Twenty-one nursing schools for black women participated in the program, as had thirty-eight schools with racially integrated classes.[28] The Office of War Information considered the Cadet Nurse Corps Program to be the most successful of all the wartime recruitment programs. From 1944-1946, 46 percent of the Public Health Service's budget was devoted to the Cadet Nurse Corps program.

Cadet nurses also helped the cause of medical research. During the war, Dr. Carroll E. Palmer, head of the research unit of the division of tuberculosis control of the Public Health Service, conducted a study of the disease using as his subjects all student nurses living in Baltimore, Philadelphia, Detroit, Minneapolis, Kansas City, Denver, San Francisco, Los Angeles, New Orleans and Columbus, Ohio. The results of this test helped to distinguish between tuberculosis itself and a related fungal disease.[29]

Conclusion

The members, workers, volunteers and personnel of service organizations performed numerous essential duties during the war effort, many of which the military could not hope to do for itself, yet which it could not do without. It is easy to see the importance of blood and plasma; more difficult to acknowledge the importance of the morale boost provided by a hot cup of coffee and a cheerful smile. Let us not forget the contributions made by those men and women who helped the American soldier win the war.

11 *The Legacy*

**Major General
Jeanne M. Holm**
USAF (Ret.)

*Let the generations know that women in uniform also guaranteed
their freedom. That our resolve was just as great as the men who
stood among us. With victory our hearts were just as full and
beat just as fast—that the tears fell just as hard for those we left
behind.*

Army Nurse, World War II

World War II changed the world profoundly; it altered both
America's position in the world, and the lives of all who served.
The war also left an indelible legacy of American women in
military service for their country. The record of their accomplishments, devotion to duty, and courage under difficult and
often dangerous circumstances proved their worth to a reluctant military and challenged the historical premise that the
armed forces were not a proper place for women. By war's end,
it was becoming evident that the unexpected success of this
new endeavor could well become a major turning point in the relationship of American women to national defense.

For the United States, the war was a rare period when self-
interest and parochialism were replaced by a national unity of purpose in pursuit of a common goal in the United States during World
War II. Americans seldom questioned why they were fighting
or who the enemies were. To those who complained about the
hardships and inconveniences, there was a stock reply, "Don't you
know there is a war on?"

For those who served in the Armed Forces, World War II was
an intensely personal experience. Even today, after more than fifty
years, the memories remain vivid and emotions lie close to the surface. World War II veterans still experience a great sense of
pride knowing that they had been part of one of the transform-
ing events of history. They still marvel at what they accomplished during those few hectic years. And they still grieve for their
buddies and loved ones who didn't make it home.

WACs march down the Champs Elysees, Paris, May 1945.   National Archives

War's End

The war ended in Europe in May 1945 with the unconditional surrender of Germany. Then on 2 September, aboard the battleship USS *Missouri*, the official instrument of surrender was signed by representatives of the Japanese government. Years later Agnes Rothman Hersey, who served as a WAVE, recalled her feelings:

> The overwhelming joy of knowing the war was over, that thousands of American servicemen would be coming home soon, is still beyond description. The city exploded into a singing, dancing party . . . A glorious celebration that remains a vivid memory all these years."[1]

By war's end, nearly 400,000 women had served their country in the Armed Forces performing a wide range of noncombat duties once reserved for men. They had served at military installations in the United States releasing men for duty at sea and in combat theaters. WACs deployed to every theater of operation, as did Army and Navy Nurses and medical specialists who also served aboard hospital ships at sea.

In addition, many thousands of women gae direct support to the military troops both at home and overseas as members of civilian organizations.

Taking Stock

Perhaps the ultimate recognition of the contribution of America's women to the war was paid by Albert Speer, Adolph Hitler's weapons production chief:

How wise you were to bring your women into your military and into your labor force. Had we done that initially, as you did, it could well have affected the whole course of the war. We would have found out as you did, that women are equally effective, and for some skills, superior to males."[2]

For most men, military service held few mysteries. They had grown up playing soldiers and listening to their fathers, older brothers and male friends tell of military experiences. But for women, entering the military was a giant leap into the unknown. Regimented service life and military trappings were alien to most women's life experiences. "We hadn't a clue what we were getting into but the Army didn't know what to make of us either," a WAC veteran recalled fifty years later. "We learned a lot together. The experience shaped the rest of my life. And our being there changed the Army too . . . for the better."

Thousands of well-educated women gave up good jobs and prospects of high-paying defense employment for low-paying military jobs and the uncertainties of military life. Many had husbands who were in uniform and some had already become widows. Some had children whose custody they had relinquished in order to join. A few were even grandmothers whose sons and husbands were in the service. Some were already Gold Star Mothers.

During the three years of war, the American military and American women adapted to one another to such a degree that surprised them both. From the outset, to the astonishment of many military traditionalists, the women not only adapted quickly but proved to be excellent, hardworking and dedicated soldiers, sailors, Marines and Coast Guardsmen in whatever jobs they were assigned. Before long, requests from the field for service women were pouring into military headquarters. Commanders who had once stated that they would accept women "over my dead body" were soon welcoming them and asking for more. Testifying before Congress after the war, General Eisenhower acknowledged that when the formation of a women's corps was first proposed at the beginning of the war, "like most soldiers, I was violently against it." He admitted that he had predicted "tremendous" difficulties. He then added: "Every phase of the record they compiled during the war convinced me of the error of my first reaction."[3]

As the war progressed, requests for women in all the services soon outstripped the services' abilities to recruit and train them. Programs that had started out as half-hearted schemes in response to outside pressures quickly escalated into serious, occasionally desperate, efforts by the military to recruit women for a wide variety of jobs. As the national pool of qualified male draftees dwindled, it became clear that for every woman recruited, one less man had to be drafted. Women volunteers came to be viewed not just as a source of women's skills, but as a valuable source of high-quality personnel to meet the overall manpower requirements for the massive military buildup. On more than one occasion, the Army became so desperate for women that its leaders seriously considered requesting Congressional approval to draft them.

Initially, the services had assumed that enlisted women would be assigned to fill traditional "women's" jobs so that men stationed at desk jobs in headquarters could be reassigned to combat or duties at sea. The principal role of female officers would be to organize, recruit, train and supervise the enlisted women. However, almost from the start, officers and enlisted women began moving into an ever-widening range of jobs. In the end, there were few noncombatant jobs in which women did not serve.

It was originally assumed that the only women who would serve outside the continental United States would be nurses. But within months, WAAC officers and enlisted women were deploying to combat theaters. By war's end, like the nurses, WACs were serving in every combat theater. Army women followed closely behind the combat forces into Normandy, New Guinea, and the Philippines. They were exposed to the same hardships and dangers as the men with whom they worked. And, like all good soldiers, the women griped about the field rations, the mud, the mosquitoes, and the lack of mail. Both Generals Eisenhower and MacArthur later observed that not only were the women eager to serve as close to the fighting as they could get, but the closer they got to the front and the greater the hardships, the higher was their morale.

The chief complaint of the WAVES, SPARs and the Women Marines was that they were excluded from overseas assignments for most of the war. Only in the last months of the war was the ban lifted, at least partially, when they were allowed to go to the territories of Hawaii and Alaska.

Of all the women who served in the war, the Army nurses were those most exposed to combat and danger and thus suffered the heaviest casualties.

Black Women: The Double-bind

For black women veterans, memories of their wartime experiences elicit deeply con-

flicted emotions: pride at having served their country during a time of crisis and anger at some of the treatment they had to endure. Those who joined the military hoping that they might escape the corrosive racism running through American society were in for a rude awakening. Although the racial policies of the services began to break down in response to political pressure and manpower needs, segregation and discrimination remained institutionalized in the military culture for most of the war. In the last year, the sea services began to integrate in response to an order from the Navy Secretary, but even then, implementation was grudging at best. The toll these service policies and attitudes exacted in terms of wasted talents, fractured dreams and injustices to say nothing of the costs and inefficiencies they generated, were incalculable.

The only service to actively recruit black women throughout the war years was the Army. The Navy and Coast Guard opened their doors to black women in the closing days of the war but only to small numbers. The segregated Marine Corps continued to ban them from its ranks. Ironically, of the four services, the Army had the best record of utilizing black women, yet it came under the heaviest scrutiny of civil rights activists during the war.

Black women joined the military with high hopes of making a contribution to their country's defense in a time of national crisis while at the same time improving their own status and gaining valuable experience. But to their dismay, they soon found themselves in the double-bind of racism and sexism. Despite the frustrations and disappointments they encountered, many were able to fulfill their aspirations. And they took justifiable pride in the knowledge that their record of commitment and dedication contributed to the Allied victory and to the abolition of segregation in the military. Recounting her feelings about her service in the WAC during the war, and expressing the feelings of many of her colleagues, Dr. Martha Putney stated in a 1994 interview: "It was rough, unfair, but worth enduring."[4]

In July 1948, President Harry Truman issued an Executive Order directing equality of treatment and opportunity for service personnel. Although Truman's order did not immediately end segregation and prejudice in the Armed Forces, it signaled the end of officially sanctioned racism and ultimately resulted in racially integrating the military.

Demobilization

"V-J Day came. The war was over but there was still work to be done," recalled WAC veteran Doris Ede. "That evening as I sat alone outside my barracks and sewed my new staff sergeant stripes on my uniform, I told myself that I had accomplished what I had set out to do in the service. I helped win the peace."[5]

Annie Lea Sirmon expressed the sentiments of many when she recalled her arrival back in the United States from New Guinea on the evening of 18 November 1945:

> . . . the rail of our ship was crowded with WACs, looking at the lights of San Francisco on the horizon. That was the USA! We were home. We were leaving our [Army] friends, probably never to see them again. But the war was over! Peace at last! Were the last three years of my life worth it? Yes! We did our part. It's great to be an American.[6]

The suddenness of the Japanese surrender had caught nearly everyone by surprise. Some called it a "sneak surrender." The services were unprepared for peace. They had no acceptable plans for the instant demobilization demanded by the American public, the Congress and their war-weary troops.

With the end of hostilities, millions of servicemen and women were eager to go home . . . to return to loved ones and start new families, to find jobs and use new-found skills, or to advance their education under the G.I. Bill of Rights. For most, it was not a question of *if* they would leave, but of *when*. Yet the process of returning was not a simple matter. It would require thousands of people, reams of paper, and two long years.

For the majority of women, getting out was hardly a choice. With the exception of the two nurse corps, there were no provisions for servicewomen in the postwar military. The laws authorizing the wartime WAC, WAVES, SPARs and Women Marine Reserve were due to expire six months after the President declared the war at an end. Circumstances dictated that if the services wanted it otherwise, action would have to be taken and none too soon.

A New Beginning

Even before the last shots were fired, a new and unexpected manpower crisis was taking shape which would ultimately regenerate interest in military women.

By the time the war ended, the United States had evolved into a world power with global military commitments. Clearly, the American armed forces would have to carry the major burden of keeping the peace as well as the military occupation of Germany, Austria and Japan. At the same time, the services had to set up and staff new processing centers all over the country for the speedy discharge of returning troops. The Army and Navy also needed to staff extensive systems of medical facilities to care for thousands of sick and wounded service personnel. These requirements imposed enormous unforeseen demands on the service's dwindling manpower resources.

The precipitous demobilization soon decimated U.S. military forces stationed around the world, to the extent that it threatened the services' ability to meet their postwar commitments. Many of the jobs in growing demand were those in which women excelled and for which they were preferred, e.g. clerical, administrative, personnel and medical fields. Unfortunately, the recruitment and training of women had been shut down because the WACs, WAVES, Women Marines and SPARs were all scheduled to disband in June 1948.

The manpower problems were further compounded by the fact that the flow of male conscripts had dried up because the wartime draft law had been allowed to run out. The services were in the impossible position of having to rely solely on male volunteers to meet all their military personnel replacement requirements. That was totally impractical, for young men were not remotely interested in volunteering.

Meanwhile, new military tensions were mounting in Europe with the Soviets raising the specter of yet another general war. Military leaders, who were in the middle of a massive demobilization, now found themselves having to examine their manpower options in the event of new hostilities. At that point, serious consideration was given to reinstating the draft—not a politically popular idea right at the end of a major war.

Another option which could hardly be ignored, considering the country's recent wartime experience, was to call on womanpower again. Although there was great reluctance in many circles to embrace the idea, it had growing support among top wartime military leaders. Gradually, all of the services but the Coast Guard got behind legislation to provide a permanent place for women in the armed forces.[7] Some members of Congress, who normally would not have supported the idea, found it attractive as a means of reducing pressures for a new draft.

There was never any doubt about the future of the two nursing corps. The need for professional military nursing skills was a foregone conclusion. They would be required in whatever force structure evolved after the war. There was only the unresolved issue of their military status. Although at the peak of the war the Army and Navy nurses were finally granted reserve officer status, they were still not authorized to hold commissions in the Regular Army or Navy.

Their problems were resolved in 1947 when Congress passed the Army-Navy Nurse Act, making the Nurse Corps permanent staff corps in the Regular Army and Navy. The new law also established the Women's Medical Specialist Corps.[8] Two years later the newly created Air Force followed suit by establishing its own Nurse Corps and Medical Specialist Corps. Typical of the sex bias at the time, membership in these corps of health professionals continued to be limited to women. It would be several years before men would be admitted.

By contrast to that of the nurses, the future of the WACs, WAVES, Women Marines and SPARs were anything but assured. There was strong opposition within and outside the Armed Forces to continuing these women's components. There were even opposing views on the subject among the women themselves. Like most men in the service, the vast majority of women had no interest in staying on after the war. They had joined to help in the war and were eager to leave when it was over. Most felt that the programs had fulfilled their wartime missions and it was time to go home.

However, a small and growing segment of military women did not agree. They saw a continuing need for the women's services in the immediate postwar period and even perceived the possibility of careers in the peacetime military. Notable among these were Mary A. Hallaren of the Women's Army Corps and Joy Bright Hancock of the Women's Naval Reserve, both of whom took up the fight for legislation to authorize permanent status. They would become the first directors of the WAC and WAVES in the postwar era.

During the Congressional hearings on the legislation, the senior leaders of the Army, Navy, Marine Corps and Air Force (established as a separate service in 1947) personally testified to the need for the legislation. The support of General Eisenhower, then Army Chief of Staff, was especially persuasive:

> In the event of another war, which would be even more truly global than the last in its effects upon the entire population, it is my conviction that everybody in this country would serve under some form of call to duty . . . I assure you that I look upon this measure as a "must."[9]

On 2 June 1948, after two years of rancorous, sometimes ludicrous, and often acrimonious debate, Congress passed the Women's Armed Services Integration Act. (P.L. 625-80th Congress). It was signed by President Truman on 12 June. Another milestone had been crossed. Women could now serve as commissioned officers and enlisted women in the permanent Regular and reserve of the Army, Navy, Marine Corps and Air Force.

Congresswoman Margaret Chase Smith (R-Maine), an influential member of the powerful House Armed Services Committee, had put her full weight behind the legislation. Years later, as a Senator, Smith recalled the proud day on 12 June 1948 when she joined President Truman in the White House for the bill signing ceremony. In reflecting on the legislative battle, she said:

> It was a tough fight. But I say now with the greatest pride that the performance of women in the Armed Services since that time has fully justified and vindicated the faith that I had in them and the fight that I made for them in the face of overwhelming odds.[10]

Over the ensuing months, women who had served in the wartime WAC, WAVES, and Women's Marine Reserve were offered the opportunity to be sworn into the peacetime Army, Navy, Marine Corps and Air Force in either Regular or reserve status. Although the Coast Guard deactivated the SPARs, the women could apply for commissioning or enlistment in the other services. Nor were the women who had served as pilots in the WASP forgotten. They were offered commissions in the Army and Air Force reserves, but not as pilots.

By the time the Integration Act was passed, most women, like the men, had already returned to civilian life in the general demobilization. But those who stayed on and those who returned to duty became the nucleus for the peacetime women's military components and for the next wartime mobilization of womanpower, which would not be long in coming.

Women of all races and creeds who served our country in World War II never claimed to be heroines. They just did their duty—what they felt they had to do to help their country in time of need in whatever capacity they were allowed to serve and whatever the dangers. Fifty years later they constitute the largest segment of the female veteran population of the United States. It is altogether fitting that these gallant women who served America in the largest war in history are among those honored by the Military Women's Memorial at the entrance to Arlington National Cemetery near our Nation's Capital.

The Women's Memorial salutes them all, as do the authors of this volume.

About the Authors

Brigadier General Wilma L. Vaught, USAF (Ret.)

Wilma Vaught is a native of Illinois, and earned a Bachelor of Science Degree at the University of Illinois and a Master of Business Administration at the University of Alabama before joining the Air Force. During her military career, she held various positions in the comptroller field at Barksdale Air Force Base, Louisiana; Zaragoza AFB, Spain; McCoy AFB, Orlando, Florida; Headquarters, Military Assistance Command, Saigon, Vietnam; Air Force Logistics Command, Wright Patterson AFB, Dayton, Ohio; the Air Staff, the Pentagon, Washington, D.C.; and Deputy Chief of Staff, Comptroller, Air Force Systems Command, Andrews AFB, Maryland. Her last military assignment was as Commander of the U.S. Military Entrance Processing Command, North Chicago, Illinois, where she served from 1982 until her retirement in 1985. General Vaught served as Chairperson of the NATO Women in the Allied Forces Committee from 1983 to 1985, and was the senior woman military representative to the Defense Advisory Committee on Women in the Services from 1982 to 1985. General Vaught is the President of the Board of Directors of the Women in Military Service For America Memorial Foundation, Inc.

Major General Jeanne M. Holm, USAF (Ret.)

Jeanne Holm enlisted in the Women's Army Auxiliary Corps (WAAC) in July, 1942. After a short stint as an Army truck driver, Holm attended Officer Candidate School and was assigned to the WAAC Training Center at Ft. Ogelthorpe, Georgia. Holm rose to the rank of captain, and after leaving active duty at the end of the war attended college on the G.I. Bill. In 1948, Captain Holm was called back to active duty and was assigned to the WAC training center at Ft. Lee, Virginia. She then received an appointment as a captain in the Air Force, and took up duties at Erding Air Force Base, Germany as war plans officer during the Berlin Airlift. In the ensuing years she held a variety of staff positions in the U.S. and overseas. From 1965 to 1972 she served as Director of Women in the Air Force. In 1971 she was the first Air Force woman promoted to brigadier general. Two years later, while director of the Air Force Personnel Council, she was promoted to major general; the first woman in the Armed Forces to hold two-star rank. After retiring from the military in 1975, General Holm was appointed Special Assistant to President Gerald Ford. She was then appointed to a three-year-term on the Defense Advisory Committee on Women in the Services (DACOWITS). During the Reagan Administration General Holm was appointed to the Veterans Administration Committee on Women Veterans and served as its chair. General Holm wrote the definitive history of women in the military, *Women in the Military: An Unfinished Revolution* in 1992.

Colonel Mary T. Sarnecky, USA (Ret.), RN, DNSc

Mary Sarnecky received a B.S. in nursing from St. Louis University, a Masters of Nursing from the University of South Carolina, and a doctorate in nursing from the University of San Diego. She served in the United States Army Nurse Corps from 1962 to 1965 and 1977 to 1996, fulfilling roles in community health nursing, critical care nursing, nursing administration, nursing education, infection control and nursing research. While an Army officer, she held every grade from second lieutenant to

colonel. During her break in service, she was employed as a general duty nurse in a civilian institution and subsequently as a school health nurse in the Department of Defense school system in Nuremberg, Germany. In her last Army assignment as a nurse researcher at Walter Reed Army Medical Center and Assistant Professor at the Uniformed Services University of the Health Sciences, Colonel Sarnecky researched and wrote the bulk of a manuscript that focuses on the history of the Army Nurse Corps. The manuscript will be published in 1998 by the University of Pennsylvania Press.

Susan H. Godson, Ph.D.

Dr. Godson received a B.A. from George Mason University and an M.A. and Ph.D. in history from The American University. She is the author of *Viking of Assault: Admiral John Lesslie Hall, Jr., and Amphibious Warfare* (1982) and a co-author of *The College of William and Mary: A History* (1993). She is currently writing a history of women in the U.S. Navy. She has published numerous articles on naval history, women's history, and educational history.

Colonel Bettie J. Morden, USA (Ret.)

Bettie J. Morden entered the WAAC in October 1942 and served as an enlisted woman throughout World War II, primarily at the WAC Training Center in Fort Oglethorpe, Georgia. After discharge in 1945, she entered Columbia University and received a B.A. in 1949 and an M.A. in 1950. She rejoined the Army as a 1st Lieutenant in 1952 and served on active duty for a total of 33 years, retiring as a colonel in 1982. Her career included assignments at the Army Security Agency; the Defense Language Institute; Fort Riley, Kansas; Heidelberg, Germany; and Fort McClellan, Alabama. She served as Executive Officer and Deputy Director, WAC, in the Office of the Director Women's Army Corps, at the Pentagon for six years. She is a graduate of the Army Command and Staff College and the Army Management School. She was assigned to the U.S. Army Center of Military History in 1974 where she wrote *The Women's Army Corps, 1945-1978*, which received "Best Book Award" in 1990 from the Society of Military Historians. She has been president of the Women's Army Corps Foundation, Fort McClellan, Alabama since 1973.

Jean Ebbert and Marie-Beth Hall

Jean Ebbert holds a B.A. and M.A. from the State University of New York at Albany. In 1952 she was commissioned an ensign in the U.S. Naval Reserve. Following two years active duty and augmentation to Regular Navy, she resigned as a lieutenant (jg). She has been a Naval Academy Information Officer (1977-1990), a featured columnist in *Navy Times* (1978-1992), and a regular contributor to One Woman's Voice, a nationally syndicated newspaper column (1989-1991). Her first two books were published by the Naval Institute Press in 1974 and 1977. Jean began working with Marie-Beth Hall, a writer and analytic editor with the Energy Information Administration, in 1978. Marie-Beth holds a B.A. in History from Radcliffe. She is the daughter of a Naval Academy graduate and the wife of a retired Navy captain, with two sons and a daughter-in-law in the Navy. Since 1990 she has been an editor, researcher and writer in the Office of Economic Policy at the Federal Energy Regulatory Commission. Ebbert and Hall's first book, *Crossed Currents: Navy Women From WWI to Tailhook*, was published by Brassey's in 1993.

Colonel Mary V. Stremlow, USMCR (Ret.)

Mary Stremlow has a B.S. from New York State University College at Buffalo. Her Marine Corps service includes experience as a company commander; staff operations officer; executive officer, Woman Recruit Training Battalion, Paris Island; inspector-instructor, Woman's Reserve Platoon, 3d Infantry Battalion, Boston; instructor at the Woman Officer School, Quantico; woman officer selection officer for the 1st Marine Corps District; and officer-in-charge, mobilization station, Buffalo, New York. She is the author of an official history, *A History of the Women Marines, 1946-1977*, and of *Coping With Sexism in the Military*. Colonel Stremlow retired from the Reserve in 1985. In 1986 she was appointed Deputy Director, New York State Division of Veteran's Affairs. She served on the U.S. Department of Veterans Affairs Advisory Committee on Women Veterans for three years.

Captain Mary E. McWilliams, USCGR (Ret.)

Mary McWilliams served on active duty with the Coast Guard during World War II, assigned to the Intelligence Division of Headquarters and the 9th Coast Guard District in Cleveland, Ohio. Upon release from active duty, she returned to school and received a B.A. from Brooklyn College and an M.A. from Columbia University. She taught at elementary and secondary schools in New York City and Great Neck, New York, retiring in 1975. Paralleling her teaching career, Captain McWilliams was continuously assigned to Coast Guard Reserve units in the New York area from 1951 until her retirement in 1979. In 1971 she was appointed Officer in Charge of a Reserve unit—a first for women in the Coast Guard. She became the first Officer in Charge of the Coast Guard school for women petty officers at Yorktown, Virginia in 1972. In 1980, Captain McWilliams was appointed to a three-year term as a member of DACOW-ITS. She has also remained active in teacher unionism—serving as a delegate to American Federation of Teachers.

Colonel Ann M. Ritchie Hartwick, USA (Ret.)

Colonel Ann Hartwick, RD., Ph.D., is a registered dietitian who has served in the Army Medical Specialist Corps under two direct commissions, one in 1959 and the second in 1974. She finished her dietetic internship at Walter Reed Army Medical Center in 1960, served at Ft. Knox, Kentucky and then left the service to accept a teaching fellowship at Cornell University, followed by executive positions in civilian industry. Among other military assignments she has been the Director of Nutrition Care at three Army Medical Centers in the United States and overseas. Her last assignment was as Historian, Army Medical Specialist Corps, United States Army Center of Military History in Washington D.C., where she wrote *The Army Medical Specialist Corps, 45th Anniversary*, published by CMH in 1993.

She has also served as a contributing author for two other publications: *Celebration of Patriotism and Courage* and *Rehabilitation of the Injured Soldier*.

Lieutenant Colonel Yvonne C. Pateman, USAF (Ret.)

Yvonne "Pat" Pateman served as a member of the Women's Airforce Service Pilots (WASP) during World War II. She was assigned to the 3d Ferrying Group at Romulus Army Air Base, Michigan, and later to Shaw AFB in South Carolina, where she served as an engineering test pilot. In 1948 she accepted a commission in the Air Force Reserve. Recalled to active duty in the Air Force in 1951, Colonel Pateman served in intelligence assignments stateside with 15th Air Force at March Air Force Base and overseas with the 13th Air Force in the Philippines; the 5th Air Force in Japan; the Alaskan Command; and the 7th Air Force at Ton Son Nhut, Vietnam 1969-1970. Upon return from SEA she was assigned to the Defense Intelligence Agency in Washington D.C. until her retirement in 1971. Colonel Pateman has published articles in *Aviation Quarterly* and *Minerva, Quarterly Report on Women in the Military*. Her book on female test pilots, test engineers and astronauts, *Women Who Dared*, was published by Norstahr Publishing in 1997.

Judith Lawrence Bellafaire, Ph.D.

Judith Bellafaire received her Ph.D. in American History from the University of Delaware in 1984. She taught American History and Museum Studies at Armstrong State College, Savannah, Georgia from 1984 to 1985. In 1986 she became the Curator of Collections and Education at the Barrington Area Historical Society in Barrington, Illinois. She taught American History at Austin Community College in Austin, Texas for two years and then accepted the position of Historian at the U.S. Army Center of Military History in Washington, D.C., which she held from 1989-1996, when she left to become the Curator at the Women In Military Service For America Memorial Foundation, Inc. Dr. Bellafaire is the author of two 50th Anniversary of World War II Commemorative Studies, "The Women's Army Corps," and "The Army Nurse Corps." She is a contributing author of the Army's official history of Operation DESERT STORM, *The Whirlwind War*, published in 1995.

Chronology

The introduction of large numbers of women into the United States Armed Forces during World War II was historically unprecedented. It can only be fully appreciated in the context of the military circumstances of the period. A chronology of major events of the war as they correlate with each phase of women's assimilation into the military services is provided below. The purpose of this chronology is to provide the reader with a historical framework leading up to decisions and events described in the various chapters of this volume.

The column headed "Major Military Events," rather than including all military actions of the war, lists only those which had an impact, direct or indirect, on decisions related to the service's employment of women in military roles. The column headed "Highlights: Military Women," identifies some of the most significant actions, dates, names and places associated with the introduction of women into what, up to that point, had been an essentially male institution.

1939

Major Military Events	Highlights: Military Women
June: Active duty strength of U.S. military forces totals 334,500	Military nurses begin to mobilize:
	Army Nurse Corps (ANC) (established in 1901), Superintendent Maj. Julia O. Flikke
1 September: Germany invades Poland; Britain and France declare war on Germany	
	Navy Nurse Corps (NNC) (established in 1908), Superintendent Capt. Sue S. Dauser
U.S. proclaims neutrality; President Roosevelt declares limited national emergency, authorizes modest increases in military forces; Gen. George C. Marshall appointed Army Chief of Staff	Marshall predicts critical manpower shortages; orders study of a women's corps for other than nurses

1940

Major Military Events	Highlights: Military Women
June: France capitulates	June: ANC strength—942 Regular and 15,770 nurses enrolled in first reserve of the American Red Cross Nursing Service
British troops evacuate Dunkirk	
August: Battle of Britain begins	July: NNC strength—458 Regulars
27 August: Congress authorizes mobilization of National Guard and reserves	November: First reserve nurses called up
16 September: Congress enacts Selective Service law to conscript men.	

1941

Major Military Events	Highlights: Military Women
Battle for the North Atlantic; German U-boats attack Allied shipping	May: Rep. Edith Nourse Rogers introduces bill to establish women's corps in Army
June: Germany invades USSR	Nurses, dietitians, physical therapists in Hawaii, Philippines and Guam come under fire
7 December: Japan attacks Pearl Harbor and strikes Western Pacific (Philippines and Guam 8 December)	
8 December: U.S. declares war on Japan	
11 December: Germany and Italy declare war on U.S.	
Mobilization of U.S. military and civilian economy goes into high gear	

1942

Major Military Events	Highlights: Military Women
January-May: U.S. forces battle Japanese on Philippines (Bataan and Corregidor)	Nurses, dietitians and therapists taken POW
March: Gen. Douglas MacArthur leaves Philippines for Australia to take command of forces there	Nurses continue to deploy overseas with combat forces
April: Philippines fall; Americans taken prisoner	May: Women's Army Auxiliary Corps (WAAC) established; Oveta Culp Hobby appointed Director; WAAC training begins at Ft. Des Moines, Iowa
June: Dwight Eisenhower appointed Commander of U.S. forces in Europe	30 July: Navy Women's Reserve established with acronym WAVES; Mildred McAfee appointed its head
November: U.S. forces deploy for campaign in North Africa; Eisenhower takes command of Allied forces	August: WAVE officer training begins at Smith College, Northampton, Massachusetts
Manhattan Project to develop atomic bomb established	September: Army begins recruiting women pilots; Nancy Love organizes Women Auxiliary Ferrying Squadron (WAFS); Jacqueline Cochran organizes Women's Flying Training Detachment (WFTD)
	October: First enlisted WAVES begin specialized training in Oklahoma, Wisconsin and Indiana
	23 November: Women's Coast Guard Reserve established with acronym SPAR; Dorothy C. Stratton appointed Director
	December: First WAVE boot camp established at Cedar Falls, Iowa
	First WAACs deploy to North Africa

1943

Major Military Events	Highlights: Military Women
May: War in North Africa ends	January: Maj. Emma E. Vogel named Director of Physical Therapists, U.S. Army
July-August: Invasion of Sicily	February: WAVES boot training opens at Hunter College, Bronx, New York
December: Eisenhower named Supreme Commander of Allied Forces Europe	13 February: Marine Corps Women's Reserve established; Ruth Cheney Streeter named Director
	Training of enlisted SPARs separated from WAVES training and set at Palm Beach, Florida.
	SPARs assigned to secret LORAN station
	WAACs assigned to top secret Manhattan Project.
	July: 1st WAAC Separate Battalion arrives in England
	Law enacted to establish Cadet Nurse Corps
	All MCWR training consolidated at Camp Lejeune, North Carolina
	August: WAFS and WFTD merge to become WASP (Women Airforce Service Pilots); Cochran designated Director, Women Pilots in AAF
	September: WAAC converts to WAC (Women's Army Corps)
	October: WACs arrive in New Delhi, India (CBI Theater)
	November: USCGC *SPAR* launched
	Plane crashes in Albania with 13 Army nurses aboard

1944

Major Military Events	Highlights: Military Women
January: Allies land at Anzio, Italy	February: Six Army nurses killed at Anzio
May-August: Burma Campaign	Black Army nurses in CBI
June: D-Day landings at Normandy	June: Temporary commissions authorized for nurses, dietitians and physical therapists
December: Battle of the Bulge	Bill to militarize WASP defeated in Congress
	September: Law passed authorizing WAVES, SPARs, and Women Marines to serve in Hawaii and Alaska
	December: WASP deactivated

1945

Major Military Events	Highlights: Military Women
U.S. forces under MacArthur land in the Philippines	January: WAVES and Women Marines arrive in Hawaii
7 May: Germany surrenders, ending war in Europe	February: 6888th Postal Directory Battalion arrives in England
U.S. military active forces peak at over 12 million	April: Hospital Ship *Comfort* attacked by Japanese suicide bomber; six Army nurses killed, four wounded
Allied Occupation Forces set up in Germany and Austria; some U.S. troops re-deploy to Pacific	May: Number of military women peaks at 266,300
August: Atomic bombs dropped on Hiroshima and Nagasaki	Nurses and WACs assigned to occupation Forces in Europe
2 September: Japan signs instrument of surrender on battleship USS *Missouri*, ending war in Pacific	June: women naval officers designated as Naval Air Navigators
	July: Col. Hobby resigns and Westray Battle Boyce named Director, WAC
U.S. Military Occupation forces set up in Japan	August: Recruiting of WACs, WAVES, SPARs, and MCWRs discontinued
Demobilization begins	September: Nurses and WACs assigned to occupation forces in Japan
Wartime draft expires	December: Col. Streeter resigns, Katherine Towle named Director, MCWR
	Capt. Stratton resigns, Helen Schleman named Director, SPAR

1946

Major Military Events	Highlights: Military Women
June: Demobilization reduces U.S. military strength to 3 million	Capt. McAfee resigns; Jean Palmer named WAVES Director
Tensions build between western Allies and Soviet Block	Most women leave services during general demobilization; services try to retain some women for vital jobs
	Pressures build to authorize peacetime status for WACs and WAVES

1947

Major Military Events	Highlights: Military Women
July: National Security Act unifies the armed services	April: Army-Navy Nurses Act makes nurse corps permanent staff corps of Regular Army and Navy and establishes Army Women's Medical Specialist Corps (WMSC)
September: United States Air Force established as a separate service under the Department of Defense	Heading Regular Corps: Col. Florence A. Blanchfield, Chief, ANC; Capt. Nellie Jane DeWitt, Superintendent, NNC; Col. Emma Vogel, Director, WMSC
	July: SPAR program deactivated

1948

Major Military Events	Highlights: Military Women
May: Strength of U.S. military forces falls to postwar low of less than 1.4 million	12 June: Women's Armed Forces Integration Act signed, providing for women to serve in the Regular and reserves of the Army, Navy, Marine Corps and Air Force. Appointed as directors were: Col. Mary A. Hallaren, WAC; Capt. Joy Bright Hancock, WAVES; Col. Katherine Towle, Women Marines; Col. Geraldine May, Women in the Air Force (WAF)
April: USSR blockades Berlin. U.S. and British planes provide Berlin Airlift to sustain West Berlin	
24 June: New military buildup begins. Selective Service Act signed providing for registration of men	
30 July: President Truman orders equality (racial) in armed services	Recruiting and training programs set up and women sworn into the Regular Army, Navy, Marine Corps and Air Force

1949

Major Military Events	Highlights: Military Women
May: Berlin Blockade lifted	July: Air Force establishes Nurse Corps (AFNC) and Women's Medical Specialist Corps (AFWMSC)—Chiefs: Col. Verina Zeller (AFNC); Col. Miriam E. Perry (AFWMSC)
June: U.S. troops withdrawn from Korea, leaving only a small contingent of military advisors	

1950

Major Military Events	Highlights: Military Women
Mobilization for war in Korea. Draft escalates; reserves called up for new military buildup	Women in reserves called up. Nurses deploy to Korea. DoD embarks on ambitious joint recruiting campaign for women in all components
	Failure to reach recruiting goals leads to establishment of DACOWITS in 1951

Cover Key

1. Physical therapy in Chabus, India.
National Archives

2. New WAAC recruits in men's overcoats, Fort Des Moines, Iowa, March 1943.
The Women's Memorial

3. Women Marines in fuselage of a Link trainer, Cherry Point, North Carolina, 1944.
US Marine Corps

4. Women Marines translate short wave code messages, Cherry Point, North Carolina, April 1945.
National Archives

5. SPAR uniforms.
National Archives

6. WACs arrive for duty in North Africa, 1944.
National Archives

7. Women Marines study to be celestial navigation operators, Marine Corps Air Station, Edenton, North Carolina.
US Marine Corps

8. Army flight nurses arrive in China to serve with the 14th US Army Air Force, 1944.
National Archives

9. Woman Marine private in boot camp, Camp Lejeune, North Carolina.
The Women's Memorial

10. A wounded war veteran runs a printing press to exercise an injured leg while an occupational therapist and a visitor watch, October 1944.
National Archives

11. American Red Cross workers from the 298th General Hospital unit, after their arrival at Utah Beach, France, July 1944.
The Women's Memorial

12. Company 3, Platoon 2, Sections 217-219 in typing class at the Oklahoma A&M Yeoman School, July 1943.
The Women's Memorial

13. Army nurses, Tagap, Burma, April 1945.
National Archives

14. First Navy flight nurse to reach Iwo Jima, Ensign Jane Kendeigh, March 1945.
Naval Historical Center

15. Army nurses assigned to the 153d Station Hospital, New Guinea, November 1942.
ANC Collection, US Army Center of Military History

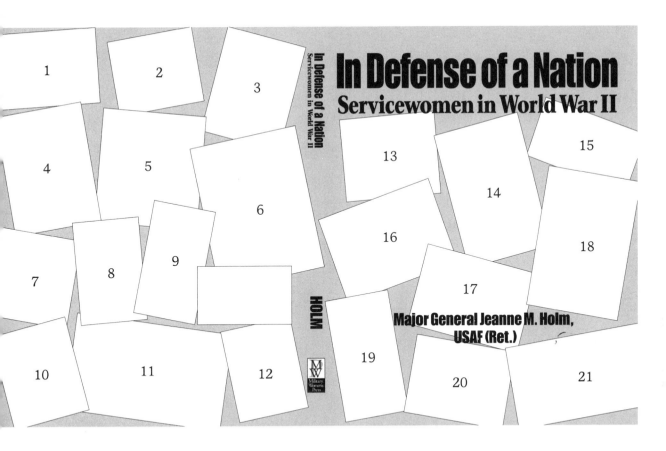

In Defense of a Nation
Servicewomen in World War II

HOLM

Major General Jeanne M. Holm,
USAF (Ret.)

16. Japanese-American Nisei WACs,
General Headquarters, Toyko, 1945.
National Archives

17. Colonel Ruth Streeter, Director,
Women Marines, watching Women
Marines at work, Atlanta, Georgia, 1943.
*Personal Papers Archives PC-137-1A11,
Folder 4, USMC Historical Center*

18. Air WACs repair airplane.
US Army Air Forces

19. Lieutenant (j.g.) Harriet Ida Pickens
and Ensign Frances Wills were the first
black WAVES commissioned, November
1944.
National Archives

20. WAFs stationed at Love Field, Dallas,
Texas.
Courtesy NASM, Smithsonian Institution

21. WAVES training to become aviation
machinist's mates, US Naval Training
Station, Norman, Oklahoma, April 1943.
National Archives

Abbreviations

AAB	Army Air Base
AAF	Army Air Forces
AFNC	Air Force Nurse Corps
AFWMSC	Air Force Women's Medical Specialist Corps
AGF	Army Ground Forces
ANC	Army Nurse Corps
ARC	American Red Cross
ASF	Army Service Forces
AWOL	Absent without leave
CBI	China-Burma-India Theater of Operations
CONUS	Continental United States
CNO	Chief of Naval Operations
DI	Drill Instructor
ETO	European Theater of Operations
GI	Government Issue (any Army soldier)
HR	House Resolution
LORAN	Long Range Aid to Navigation
M.A.E.T.S.	Medical Air Evacuation Transport Squadron
MCWR	Marine Corps Women's Reserve
NAACP	National Association for the Advancement of Colored People
NCO	Noncommissioned Officer
NNC	Navy Nurse Corps
OCS	Officer Candidate School
OD	Olive Drab
P.L.	Public Law
POW	Prisoner of War
SOS	Services of Supply (Army)
SPAR	Acronym denoting the Coast Guard Women's Reserve from Coast Guard motto: "**S**emper **Par**atus—**A**lways **R**eady"
SWPA	Southwest Pacific Area
USCGC	United States Coast Guard Cutter
USO	United Services Organization
USPHS	United States Public Health Service
V-E Day	Victory in Europe Day—8 May 1945
V-J Day	Victory in Japan Day—2 September 1945

WAAC	Women's Army Auxiliary Corps
WAC	Women's Army Corps
WAF	Women in the Air Force
WAFS	Women's Auxiliary Ferrying Squadron
WASP	Women Airforce Service Pilots
WAVES	Acronym denoting the Navy Women's Reserve—derived from Women Accepted for Volunteer Emergency Service
WMSC	Women's Medical Specialist Corps

Notes and Sources

Chapter 1

[1]According to Charity Adams Earley, author of One Woman's Army: A Black Officer Remembers the WAC (Texas A & M University Press), "Negro" was the accepted racial designation during World War II, although the term "colored" was also used. Earley explains that before the 1960s the term "black" was considered derogatory and inflammatory. In this book, the authors have chosen to use the current terminology.

[2]Mary Daily, address to a group of Navy women in Seattle, 17 November 1983.

Sources

Fisher, Ernst F. "World War II." *Encyclopedia of American History*. (1994). pp. 939-984.

Holm, Jeanne M. *Women in the Military: An Unfinished Revolution*. (1992).

MacGregor, Morris J. "Minorities in the Armed Forces." *Encyclopedia of the American Military*. (1994). pp. 2056-2057.

Chapter 2

[1]Ruth Evelyn Parks, "Inside Looking Out," *American Journal of Nursing* 41 (June 1941): 641.

[2]Monica Conter, "My Army Career," January 1943, Conter Collection, AMEDD Museum, Fort Sam Houston, Texas.

[3]R.N., Hawaii, "The Honor Column," *American Journal of Nursing* 42 (April 42): 425-426.

[4]Lucy Wilson Jopling, *Warrior In White* (San Antonio: The Watercress Press, 1990), p. 42.

[5]Myrtle E. Arndt, "The Women's Angle," in *54th Review: A Resume of the Activities of the 54th General Hospital, 1943-1945*, n.p., ANC Archives, U.S. Army Center of Military History, Washington, D.C.

[6]Edna C. Mahar, "Northern Australia, 1942," *American Journal of Nursing* 43 (December 1943): 1063-1064.

[7] Margaret K. Grace, "Informal Report, Subject: Seeing It Through With The ANC in Calcutta," n.d., 3-4, ANC Archives, U.S. Army Center of Military History, Washington, D.C.

[8] C.M. Buchanan, "Army Nurse Along the Stilwell Road, Roundup, India-Burma Theater, 14 June 1945," 3, ANC Archives, U.S. Army Center of Military History, Washington, D.C.

[9] Daryle E. Foister, "Historical Report, Army Nurse Corps, 383d Station Hospital," 30 July 1945, 6, ANC Archives, U.S. Army Center of Military History, Washington, D.C.

[10] Mabel Keaton Staupers, *No Time For Prejudice* (New York: The MacMillan Company, 1961), p.114.

[11] Viola M. Boosalis, "The ANC In Eskimo Land," *The Army Nurse* 1 (November 1944): 5.

[12] Edna D. Umbach to Louise S. Heyen, type-written letter, 9 October 1941, ANC Archives, United States Center of Military History, Washington, D.C.

[13] Office of Public Relations, Bowman Field Army Base, "History of Air Evacuation at Bowman Field, Kentucky, News Release: 22 January 1944," Leora Stroup Collection, AMEDD Museum, Fort Sam Houston, Texas.

[14] Mae M. Link and Hubert A. Coleman, *Medical Support of the Army Air Force in World War II* (Washington, D.C.: Department of the Air Force, 1955), pp. 490-493; Amy Porter, "Balkan Escape," *Colliers* (1 April 1944): 14, 64, 66.

[15] Wilma Weatherford Ford, "Air Evacuation," December, 1993. Typewritten manuscript from the files of Colonel Patricia Chamings, USAFR, Greensboro, North Carolina.

[16] Maxine Davis, *Through the Stratosphere, The Human Factor in Aviation* (New York: The MacMillan Company, 1946), p. 227.

[17] Marjorie Peto, *Women Were Not Expected* (West Englewood, New Jersey: Published by the Author), p. 9.

[18] Ibid., pp. 47-48.

[19] Theresa Archard, *G.I. Nightingale, The Story of An American Army Nurse* (New York: W.W. Norton & Company, 1945), p. 45.

[20] Ruth G. Haskell, *Helmets and Lipstick* (New York: G.P. Putnam's Sons, 1944), pp. 111-112.

[21] Raymond Scott, "Eleventh Evacuation Hospital in Sicily," *American Journal of Nursing* 43 (October 1943): 925-926.

[22] Bill Mauldin, *Up Front* (Cleveland: The World Publishing Company, 1945), pp. 164-167.

[23] "Annual Report, 220th Hospital Ship Complement, USAHS *Blanche F. Sigman*, 1944," pp.5-6, Record Group 112, Entry 54A, National Archives, Washington, D.C.

[24] Anna Lisa Moline, *Reminiscences, My Life and Nursing Career* (Denver: Cherry Creek Graphics, 1987), pp. 30-31.

[25] Anna Lisa Moline, "U.S. Army Nurses in Russia," *American Journal of Nursing* 45 (November 1945): 904-906.

[26] Letter from Lt. Mary Louise Carpenter to family, 7 June 1944, quoted in Alma Lutz, *With Love, Jane, Letters From American Women on the War Fronts* (New York: John Day Company, 1945), pp. 23-25.

[27] Mary Jose, "Hi, Angels!" *American Journal of Nursing* 45 (April 1945): 267-270.

Chapter 3

[1] Barbara B. Tomblin, "Beyond Paradise: The U.S. Navy Nurse Corps in the Pacific in World War II," pt. 1, *Minerva* 11 (Spring 1993): 36-38; Doris M. Sterner, *In and Out of Harm's Way: A History of the Navy Nurse Corps* (Seattle: Peanut Butter Publishing, 1996), pp. 107-08.

[2] Sterner, p. 109; Grace B. Lally, "On Being a Chief Nurse," *R. N.* (September 1943): 22.

[3] Bureau of Medicine and Surgery, *The History of the Medical Department of the United States Navy in World War II* (Washington: GPO, 1953), 2: pp. 154-55.

[4] Philip A. Kalisch and Beatrice J. Kalisch, "Nurses under Fire: The World War II Experience of Nurses on Bataan and Corregidor," reprinted in *Pages from Nursing History: A Collection of Original Articles from the Pages of "Nursing Outlook," the "American Journal of*

Nursing" and *"Nursing Research"* (New York: American Journal of Nursing Co., 1984), pp. 106-07, 111, 113, 115, 119-20; J.M.G., "Nurses Stood By to the End," *Trained Nurse and Hospital Review* (March 1945): 182-83.

[5] Capt. Sue S. Dauser, official bio, Officers' Bio Files, Operational Archives, Navy Historical Center, Washington, D.C.; Sue S. Dauser folder, box 1, entry 48D, record group 52, National Archives and Records Administration, Washington, D.C.

[6] Nurse Corps Monthly Census, folder 42 (6), box 35, series 6, Navy Nurse Corps Records, OA, NHC.

[7] American Red Cross . . . procedure, 24 January 1944, folder 55 (1), box 15; National Nursing Council for War Service, Army and Navy Needs, 1 March 1945, folder 37, box 13; Digest of Information on Nurse Procurement, and Survey of Cadet Nurses, 31 July 1945, both in folder 55 (6), box 16, all in series 3, NNC Records, OA, NHC.

[8] Bureau of Medicine and Surgery, *Manual of the Medical Department of the United States Navy: 1945* (Washington, D.C.: GPO, 1945), pp. 76-77; Qualifications for Appointment, enclosure 5, Bureau of Naval Personnel, Procurement Directive 4-45, folder 55 (2), box 15, series 3, NNC Records, OA, NHC.

[9] Personnel . . . by State of Residence, folder 42 (8), box 35, series 6; NNC, Nursing Information Bureau, 15 June 1945, folder 68 (1), box 19, series 3, both in NNC Records, OA, NHC.

[10] Author interview with R. Adm. Alene B. Duerk, 11 October 1996.

[11] "Indoctrination Course," *American Journal of Nursing* 43 (December 1943): 1144.

[12] Thelma F. Laird, "R.H.I.P. and the Navy Nurse," folder 1 (2), box 20, series 4, NNC Records, OA, NHC. [R.H.I.P. = Rank Has Its Privileges.]

[13] *Uniform Regulations: United States Navy, 1941* (Washington, D.C.: GPO, 1941), pp. 50-51; *Nurse Corps Chronology*, pp. 23, 28.

[14] *Nurse Corps Chronology*, p. 35; *Secretary of the Navy Report: 1945*, p. A-93.

[15] Bureau of Naval Personnel, *Naval Administration: The United States Navy Medical Department at War, 1941-1945*, 2 vols. (Navy Department Library), 2: pp. 404-09.

[16] Page Cooper, *Navy Nurse* (New York: Whittlesey House, 1946), p. 137.

[17] Jessie F. Evans, no title but re Ens. Margaret Allen, folder 49, box 14, series 3; Nellie Mae Quinn, "Navy Nurses in Alaska," folder 1 (1), box 20, series 4, both in NNC Records, OA, NHC.

[18] *Nurse Corps Chronology*, pp. 23-25, 27; BuMed, *Medical Department . . . WW II*, 1: pp. 13, 22, 38.

[19] *Nurse Corps Chronology*, pp. 26-27; quote in "Lt. Dymphna Van Gorp, NC, USNR," folder 1 (3), box 20, series 4, NNC Records, OA, NHC.

[20] Ens. Elizabeth Torrance's account in Sterner, *Harm's Way*, p. 169.

[21] Quote from Ens. Mary V. Demarais, "Navy Nursing on D-Day Plus 4," *American Journal of Nursing*, 45 (January 1945): 12.

[22] BuMed, *Medical Department . . . WW II*, 1 p. 30; Tomblin, "Beyond Paradise," pt. 1, pp. 44- 45.

[23] Lt. Sarah O'Toole, "They Pioneered on Tinian"; Lt. (j.g.) Mary H. Staats, "Navy Nurses in the Solomons," both in folder 49, box 14, series 3, NNC Records, OA, NHC.

[24] Lt. Martha E. Page, "With the Navy Nurses at a Base Hospital in the South Pacific"; Ens. Helen H. Johnson, "The Training of Operating Room Technicians by Navy Nurses in Australia," both in folder 49, box 14, series 3, NNC Records, OA, NHC.

[25] Quotes from *Goodnow's History of Nursing*, 10th ed., p. 258; Kathi Jackson, "50 Years Ago--World War II and the Navy Nurse," *Navy Medicine* (July-August 1995): 22.

[26] Dauser, memo, 21 February 1946, folder 40, box 14, series 3, NNC Records, OA, NHC.

Chapter 4

[1] Treadwell, Mattie E., *The Women's Army Corps, The United States Army in World War II*, Special Studies, CMH Pub. 11-8 (Washington, D.C.:

U.S. Army, 1954) pp. 18-25. In addition to citations to specific information from this source, the general information in this chapter, unless noted otherwise, is also from this volume.

[2] Ibid., p. 66.

[3] Act of 14 May 1942, Public Law 554, 77th Cong. Sec I, War Dept. Bulletin #25.

[4] PL 544, 77th Cong, Establishment of the WAAC, Sec 1: "The total number of women enrolled or appointed in the WAAC shall in no event exceed 150,000." Also, Treadwell, p. 62.

[5] Olga Gruhzit-Hoyt, *They Also Served: American Women in World War II* (New York: Burch Lane Press, 1993).

[6] Georgia B. Watson, *World War II in a Khaki Skirt* (Moore Haven, Florida: Rainbow Books, 1985), pp. 20-21.

[7] Roy Terry, *Women in Khaki, The Story of the British Woman Soldier* (London: Columbus Books, 1988), pp. 152-156.

[8] Watson, pp. 38-39.

[9] Treadwell, p. 326.

[10] Eleanor Stone Roensch, *Life Within Limits* (Los Alamos, New Mexico: Los Alamos Historical Society), p. 5.

[11] Transcript of the historical video tape "Remembering Los Alamos, World War II," Los Alamos Historical Society, Los Alamos, New Mexico, 1993, p. 7.

[12] Roensch, p. 43

[13] Ibid., p. 39

[14] Ibid.

[15] Treadwell, p. 360

[16] Sara Ann Allen, ed. *Daughters of Pallas Athene: Cameo Recollections of Women's Army Corps Veterans* (Kansas City, Missouri: Aero Graphics Inc. 1983), pp. 66-67.

[17] Larson, C. Kay, *'Til I Come Marching Home': A Brief History of American Women in World War II* (Pasadena, Maryland: The Minerva Center), pp. 72-3.

[18] Hallaren, Mary A., "The Civilians Are Coming," ltr. to ETO WACs, June 1946, from Hallaren folder "Early Service" in WAC Museum Historical Collection, Fort McClellan, Alabama.

[19] Treadwell, p. 408.

[20] Strength of the Army Report (STM-30) for 31 Dec 1943.

[21] It was a goal that was never to be achieved during the course of the war despite the WAC's best recruiting efforts.

[22] Brenda Moore, *To Serve My Country, To Serve My Race* (New York and London: New York University Press, 1996), p. 194.

[23] Mary B. Johnson, "The WAC as Cryptographers," Poulos, Paula N., Editor, *A Woman's War Too: U.S. Women in the Military in World War II* (Washington, D.C.: National Archives and Records Administration, 1996).

[24] Treadwell, p. 460.

Chapter 5

[1] Navy Department, Bureau of Naval Personnel, *U.S. Naval Administration in World War II, Women's Reserve*, p. 7; *Eleventh Naval District*, p. 575; letter from L.E. Denfeld, Assistant Chief of the Bureau of Navigation, 20 April 1942, and replies, entry 90, Folder QR8, Box 2328, Record Group 24, National Archives, Washington, D.C.

[2] Virginia Gildersleeve, *Many a Good Crusade* (New York: MacMillan Co., 1954), p. 272.

[3] Mildred McAfee Horton interview by John T. Mason, 25-26 August 1969, Randolph, New Hampshire, (typed manuscript, Naval Institute, Annapolis, Maryland), p. 50.

[4] Mary Daily, address to a group of Navy women at Seattle, Washington, 17 November 1983, copy sent to authors, quoted with permission.

[5] Jean Palmer interview by John T. Mason, Jr., 19 May 1969, New York, New York, (typed transcript, Naval Institute), pp. 3, 11-12.

[6] Mary Daily interview by Jean Ebbert, 30 July 1982, Seattle, Washington; Etta Belle Kitchen, interview by John T. Mason Jr., 30 November 1983, Annapolis Maryland (typed transcript, Naval Institute), p. 7.

7 Bureau of Naval Personnel, *Women's Reserve*, pp. 230-233, 240-242, 313; letter to alumnae, 1942, "The Navy Comes to Smith," WAVES general folder, World War 1939-1945, War Service Collection, Smith College Archives; Joy Bright Hancock, *Lady in the Navy*, (Annapolis, Maryland: Naval Institute Press, 1972), pp. 76-78; Bureau of Naval Personnel, *Women's Reserve*, p. 242.

8 Bureau of Naval Personnel, *Women's Reserve*, p. 242.

9 Elizabeth Crandall, interview by Etta Belle Kitchen, 18 July 1970, Palo Alto, California (typed transcript, Naval Institute), p. 5.

10 Bureau of Naval Personnel, *Women's Reserve*, pp. 260-264.

11 Bureau of Naval Personnel, *U.S. Naval Administration in World War II: Office of Naval Operations, School of Oriental Languages*, pp.1-15, 22, Appendixes 23-25; Mary Josephine Shelly, interview by John T. Mason Jr., 9 February 1970, New York, New York, (typed transcript, Naval Institute), p. 25.

12 Hancock, pp. 88-90; *Annual Report of the Secretary of the Navy, 1945*, p. A-11; *The New York Times,* 27 July 1945, p. 12.

13 Hancock, pp. 80-81; O'Dea conversations with Marie-Beth Hall, 30 October 1988, Annapolis, Maryland and 18 February 1989, Bowie, Maryland.

14 Department of the Navy, *Statistics Yearbook*, p. 80.

15 Bureau of Naval Personnel, *U.S. Naval Administration in World War II: Enlisted Personnel*, p. 44; Mildred McAfee Horton, interview, p. 74.

16 Mary Josephine Shelley, interview, pp. 19-20.

17 Copy of talk given by Ensign Quait before the Cedar Falls High School Girls Reserve, 9 February 1943, Gladys Hearst Collection, University of Northern Iowa Archives.

18 Bureau of Naval Personnel, *Women's Reserve*, p. 58; memo to the Secretary of the Navy from the Chief of Naval Personnel, 30 December 1942, Folder 30, Box 4, Series I, ACNP(W), Navy Operational Archives.

19 Bureau of Naval Personnel, *Women's Reserve*, Vol. II, pp. 46, 53; Eleanor Rigby, interview by Etta Belle Kitchen, 19 July 1970, Palo Alto, California (typed transcript, Naval Institute) pp. 13-14; Marie Bennett Alsmeyer, *The Way of the WAVES* (Conway, Arkansas: Hamba Books, 1981), p. 17.

20 Patricia G. Morgan, unpublished memoir, copy sent to Jean Ebbert on 14 May 1983, quoted with permission.

21 Alsmeyer, pp. 15-16.

22 Bureau of Naval Personnel, *Women's Reserve*, Vol. II, p. 56.

23 "Training Program for Members of the Women's Reserve," Folder 29, Box 4, Series I, ACNP (W), Navy Operational Archives; Bureau of Naval Personnel memorandum, 24 June 1943, Folder QR8/NC, Box 2330, Record Group 24, National Archives.

24 Seven-page history of the Women's Reserve, Folder 29, Box 4, Series I, ACNP(W), Navy Operational Archives; Hancock, pp. 145-146; Alsmeyer, pp. 29-30.

25 Hancock, pp. 127-142; La Verne Bradley, "Women in Uniform," *National Geographic*, October 1943: 454.

26 Hancock, pp. 138-142; Judy Barrett Litoff and David C. Smith, "The Wartime History of the WAVES, SPARS, Women Marines, Army and Navy Nurses, and Wasps," in *A Woman's War Too*, p. 53.

27 Department of the Navy, *Annual Report of the Secretary of the Navy, 1945* (Washington, D.C.), p. A-15.

28 Veronica Mackey Hulick interview by Jean Ebbert, 19 May 1983, Alexandria, Virginia.

29 Joy Bright Hancock, interview, pp. 87-88.

30 Louise Wilde, interview by John T. Mason Jr., 2 December 1969, Washington, D.C., (typed transcript, Naval Institute), p. 14.

31 Mildred McAfee Horton interview by Jean Ebbert.

[32] Navy Department press release, March 6, 1943, Marriage Policies (1942-1954), Folder 37, Box 5, Series I, ACNP(W), Navy Operational Archives.

[33] Bureau of Naval Personnel, *Women's Reserve*, pp. 116-118, 155-156; Jean Palmer interview, p. 39; Bureau of Naval Personnel letter 45-612, dated 15 June 1945, Maternity Care (1945-1949), Folder 38, Box 5, Series I, ACNP(W), Circular Letter 122-45, 1 May 1945. Discharge Policies: 1943-1949, Folder 12, Box 2, Series I, Navy Operational Archives; Hancock, p. 117, states that only one WAVE was convicted of a felony and "sentenced by a general court martial to a federal prison for the crime of forgery."

[34] Bureau of Naval Personnel, *Women's Reserve*, p. 102; Hancock, p. 210.

[35] Hancock, pp. 175-179.

[36] Mary Daily, address to a group of Navy women, Seattle, Washington, 17 November 1983, copy sent to authors.

[37] Mary Josephine Shelly interview, p. 32; document P14-2, subject file QRB, record group 24, National Archives; "Sounding Off," 31 September 1944, publications folder "WAVES," War Service collection, World War 1939-1945, Smith College archives; Bureau of Naval Personnel, *The Negro in the Navy,* p. 98; "World War II Account of Lois Logan Horn," pp. 31-32, WIMSA Register; Mildred McAfee Horton oral history, p. 48.

[38] Morris J. MacGregor, *Integration of the Armed Forces, 1940-1964* (Washington, D.C.: Defense Studies Series, U.S. Army Center of Military History, 1981), p. 88; Navy press release dated 19 October 1944, Folder 29, Historical Data Concerning Women's Reserve (1942-1962), Box 4, Series I, ACNP(W), Navy Operational Archives.

[39] Letter to Port Director of Twelfth Naval District from Assistant to Operations Officer of Twelfth Naval District, 16 January 1945, Fourteenth Naval District (1943-1953), Folder 50, Box 7, Series I, Navy Operational Archives; Hancock, p. 199.

[40] Navy Department press release, 21 July 1945, Press Releases on WAVES (July 1942-December 1947), Folder 3, Box 18, Series II, ACNP(W), Navy Operational Archives.

[41] Three-page typescript of an article by McAfee intended for the *Army-Navy Journal,* Speeches, Statements and Articles of Captain M.M. Horton (1943-1945), Folder 2 of Folder 101, Box 16, Series I, ACNP(W), Navy Operational Archives.

[42] Letter from Chief of Naval Information to Assistant Secretary of Defense, 13 March 1963, Historical Matters (1944-1968), Folder 33, Box 5, Series I, ACNP(W), Navy Operational Archives; magazine distributed at the Navy Women's 50th Anniversary Convention, Norfolk, VA, 1992, ed. by Senior Chief Journalist Cindy Adams, U.S. Navy, p. 14.

[43] *Annual Report of the Secretary of the Navy, 1945,* p. A-15, 22.

[44] Bureau of Naval Personnel, *U.S. Naval Administration in World War II: History of Field Administration,* p. 374; *Women's Reserve,* p. 135.

[45] Alsmeyer, pp. 181-182.

[46] Mildred McAfee Horton, *American Journal of Sociology,* March 1946: 450.

Chapter 6—Sources

The primary sources for this chapter are the author's previously published, *Free A Marine To Fight: Women Marines In World War II* (Washington, D.C.: History and Museums Division. Headquarters, U.S. Marine Corps, 1994); *History of the Marine Corps Women's Reserve: A Critical Analysis of Its Development and Operation, 1943-1945,* by Colonel Ruth Cheney Streeter and Colonel Katherine Towle (Washington D.C.: 1945); *Marine Corps Women's Reserve in World War II* by Lt. Colonel Pat Meid (Washington D.C.: Historical Branch, G-# Division, Headquarters, U.S. Marine Corps, 1968); *Women Marines: The World War II Era* by Peter Soderbergh, (Westport

Connecticut: Praeger Publishers: 1992) and *Musical Women Marines: The Marine Corps Women's Reserve Band in World War II* by Ellen Stone Doukoullos & Bonnie Smallwood Medin, published privately in 1981.

Transcripts of oral history interviews with Colonel Streeter, *Ruth Cheney Streeter, A Lively Life* (Morristown, N.J.: 1979), and Colonel Katherine A. Towle, *Katherine A. Towle, Administration and Leadership* (Berkeley, University of California: 1970), give behind the scenes insights into the era.

Chapter 7—Sources

Commandant's Bulletin, May 1995. *Paying Tribute to Dedication, Dignity and Distinction— Asian Pacific Islanders.*

Gurney, Gene. *The United States Coast Guard: A Pictorial History.* New York: Crown Publishers, Inc., 1973.

Holm, Jeanne M. *Women in the Military: An Unfinished Revolution.* Novato, California: Presidio Press, 1992.

Kaplan, H.R. and James F. Hunt. *This Is The Coast Guard.* Cambridge, Maryland: Maritime Press, Inc., 1972.

Larson, C. Kay. *'Til I Come Marching Home.'* Pasadena, Maryland: The Minerva Center, 1995.

Lyne, Mary C. And Kay Arthur. *Three Years Behind the Mast: The Story of the United States Coast Guard SPARs.* Washington, DC: U.S. Coast Guard, 1946.

New York Times, Saturday, July 25th, 1945, p. 13, "Only SPAR to Wear Pacific Ribbon Tells of Japanese Cruelties."

Thompson, Robin J. *The Coast Guard and the Women's Reserve in World War II.* Washington, D.C.: Coast Guard Historian's Office, 1992.

U.S. Coast Guard, Public Information Division, *Women's Reserve, Volume 22, The Coast Guard At War.* Washington, D.C.: 1946.

Willoughby, Malcolm F. *The U.S. Coast Guard in World War II.* Annapolis, Maryland: Naval Institute Press, 1989.

Chapter 8

[1] Kay Gott, *Women In Pursuit* (McKinleyville, California: 1993), pp. 52-54.

[2] Sally Van Wagenen Keil, *Those Wonderful Women In Their Flying Machines: The Unknown Heroines of World War II*, (New York: Four Directions Press, 1990), pp. 98-99.

[3] Ibid.

[4] Jacqueline Cochran and Maryann Bucknum Brinley, *Jackie Cochran: An Autobiography* (New York: Bantam, 1987), p. 196.

[5] Byrd Granger, *On Final Approach: The Women Airforce Service Pilots of World War II* (Scottsdale Arizona: Falconer Publishing, 1991), pp. 53, Appendix D A-71.

[6] Marianne Verges, *On Silver Wings, 1942-1944: The Women Airforce Service Pilots of World War II* (New York: Four Directions Press, 1990), p. 69.

[7] Ibid., p. 70.

[8] Ibid., p. 71.

[9] Cochran and Brinley, p. 207.

[10] Keil, pp. 194-199.

[11] Yvonne C. Pateman, *Aviation Quarterly*, Vol 8, No. 2, pp. 194-199.

[12] Granger, p. A-47/B.

[13] Gott, pp. 58-61.

[14] Granger, p. A-90 Appendix E.

[15] Yvonne C. Pateman, *Women Who Dared: American Female Test Pilots, Flight Test Engineers, and Astronauts, 1912-1996* (Norstahr, 1997), pp. 123-130 Appendix A.

[16] Granger, pp. 329-342.

[17] Keil, p. 290.

[18] Ibid, p. 291.

[19] Jacqueline Cochran, *Stars At Noon* (Boston: Little, Brown & Co., 1954) pp. 128-9.

Chapter 9—Sources

Excellent sources of material relating to dietitians, physical therapists and occupational therapists who served in World War II are located in the Historical Archives, AFIP; the National

Library of Medicine, the National Archives, Suitland, MD, and the Archives of the American Physical Therapy Association and American Occupational Therapy Association, all in the Washington D.C. area. Oral histories are held in the U.S. Army Center of Military History (Washington D.C.) and in the U.S. Army Military History Institute. Carlisle Barracks, PA. Source material is also collected in the AMEDD Historical Holding, AMEDD Museum, Fort Sam Houston, Texas.

Two official military histories are available. *The Army Medical Specialist Corps*, edited by Colonels Anderson, Lee, and McDaniel which was published in 1968 by the Office of the Army Surgeon General and reprinted in 1986 by the Government Printing Office, and *The Army Medical Specialist Corps: 45th Commemorative* written by Colonel Hartwick and published in 1993 by the U.S. Army Center of Military History and the Government Printing Office. The first text addresses history of the Corps through 1960. The second text addresses Corps history from World War I through 1992, and includes a chronology and Corps insignia in color.

Chapter 10

[1] George Korson, *At His Side: The American Red Cross Overseas In World War II* (New York: Coward-McCann, Inc., 1945), pp. 16-20; Patrick F. Gilbo, *The American Red Cross: The First Century* (New York: Harper & Row, 1981), p. 145.

[2] Gilbo, p. 158.

[3] Mary Ferebee Howard, *No Drums, No Trumpets: Red Cross Adventure,* (North Carolina: Wesleyan College Press, 1992), p. 9.

[4] Gilbo, p. 152.

[5] Mary Thomas Sargent, *Runway Towards Orion,* (Grand Rapids, Michigan: Triumph Press, Inc, 1984), pp. 70, 87-88.

[6] Korson, p. 66.

[7] Marjorie Lee Morgan, Ed., *The Clubmobile—The ARC In The Storm*, (St. Petersburg, Florida: Hazlett Printing and Publishing Inc., 1982), p. 45.

[8] Ibid., p. 134.

[9] Ibid.

[10] Korson, p. 281.

[11] Morgan pp. 150-151.

[12] Ibid., p. 87.

[13] Morgan, p. 118.

[14] Ibid.

[15] Korson, p. 59.

[16] Gilbo, pp. 148, 165.

[17] Charles Hurd, *The Compact History of the American Red Cross,* (New York: Hawthorne Books Inc., 1959), pp. 234-235; Stan Cohen, *V For Victory: America's Homefront During World War II* (Missoula, Montana: Pictorial Histories Publishing Co. Inc., 1991), p. 363.

[18] Hurd, pp. 235-236.

[19] Gilbo, p. 154.

[20] Frank Coffey, *Always Home: Fifty Years of the USO* (Brassey's Inc. 1991), p. 3.

[21] Cohen, p. 354.

[22] Coffey, pp. 26-27.

[23] Lassie Moores Smith, WIMSA Register # 342474.

[24] "The Salvation Army During World War II," Information Sheet in the Curator's Office at WIMSA.

[25] Fitzhugh Mullen, M.D., *Plagues and Politics: The Story of the United States Public Health Service* (New York: Basic Books, Inc., 1989), p. 115; Bess Furman and Ralph C. Williams, M.D., *A Profile of the United States Public Health Service 1798-1948,* (Washington, D.C.: U.S. Department of Health, Education and Welfare, 1973), pp. 422-423; Ralph Chester William, M.D., *The United States Public Health Service 1798-1950,* (Washington, D.C.: Commissioned Officers Association of the U.S. Public Health Service, 1951), pp. 641, 736.

[26] Jeannette Barry, *Notable Contributions To Medical Research by Public Health Service*

Scientists, (Washington, D.C.: U.S. Department of Health, Education and Welfare, 1960), p. 434.

27 Mullen, p. 120.

28 Ibid.

29 Furman, p. 432.

Chapter 11

1 WIMSA Register, Agnes Rothman Hersey, # 041352.

2 As reported by Ira Eaker, Lt. Gen. USAF (Ret.) *Air Force Times,* 6 December 1976 (see Holm, p. 100).

3 Mattie E. Treadwell, *The Women's Army Corps: The United States Army In World War II,*

(Washington, D.C.: U.S. Army Center of Military History, 1954), p. 748.

4 Interview with Dr. Martha Putney conducted by Rudi Williams, Armed Forces Information Service, *Pentagram,* 25 February 1994.

5 WIMSA Register, Doris Ede, # 027383.

6 WIMSA Register, Annie Lea Sirmon, # 015552.

7 By this time the Coast Guard was no longer in the Department of the Navy; in 1946 it reverted to the Treasury Department.

8 The Medical Specialist Corps incorporated dietitians, physical therapists and occupational therapists.

9 Treadwell, p. 748.

10 Ware Graduation Exercises, Newport, Rhode Island, 25 April 1952.

Sources

Fisher, Ernst F. "World War II," *Encyclopedia of American Military.* (1994), pp. 939-984.

Holm, Jeanne M. *Women In The Military: An Unfinished Revolution.* (California: Presidio Press, 1992).

MacGregor, Morris J. "Minorities in the Armed Forces," *Encyclopedia of the American Military* (1994), pp. 2056-2057.

Selected Bibliography

Archard, Theresa. *G.I. Nightingale: The Story of An American Army Nurse.* New York: W.W. Norton, 1945.

Aynes, Edith A. *From Nightingale to Eagle: An Army Nurse's History.* Englewood Cliffs, New Jersey: Prentice-Hall, 1973.

Bell, Iris Y. *Los Alamos WAACS/WACS: World War II 1943-1946.* Sarasota, Florida: Coastal Printing, 1993.

Bellafaire, Judith. *The Army Nurse Corps: A Commemoration of World War II Service.* Washington, D.C.: U.S. Army Center of Military History, 1993.

Bellafaire, Judith. *The Women's Army Corps: A Commemoration of World War II Service.* Washington, D.C.: U.S. Army Center of Military History, 1993.

Camp, LaVonne Telshaw. *Lingering Fever: A World War II Nurses Memoir.* Jefferson, North Carolina: McFarland, 1997.

Cochran, Jacqueline, with Floyd Odum. *The Stars At Noon.* (Reprint), New York: Arno, 1980.

Cochran, Jacqueline, and Maryann Bucknum Brinley, ed. *Jackie Cochran: An Autobiography.* New York: Bantam, 1987.

Coffey, Frank. *Always Home: 50 Years of the USO: The Official Photographic History.* Washington, D.C.: Brassey's, 1991.

Collins, Winifred Quick. *More Than A Uniform: A Navy Woman in a Navy Man's World.* Denton, Texas: University of North Texas Press, 1997.

Cooper, Page. *White Task Force.* New York: Whittlesey House, McGraw-Hill, 1945.

Danner, Dorothy Still. *What A Way To Spend A War: Navy Nurse POWs in the Philippines.* Annapolis, Maryland: Naval Institute Press, 1995.

DeWitt, Gill. *The First Navy Flight Nurse on a Pacific Battlefield: A Picture Story of a Flight To Iwo Jima.* Fredericksburg, Texas: Admiral Nimitz Foundation, 1983.

Dulles, Foster Rhea. *The American Red Cross: A History.* Westport, Connecticut: Greenwood Press, 1971.

Earley, Charity Adams. *One Woman's Army: A Black Officer Remembers the WAC.* College Station, Texas: Texas A & M University Press, 1989.

Ebbert, Jean, and Marie Beth Hall. *Crossed Currents: Navy Women From WWI to Tailhook.* Washington, D.C.: Brassey's, 1993.

Feller, Carolyn M. And Constance Moore. *Highlights in the History of the Army Nurse Corps.* Washington, D.C.: U.S. Army Center of Military History, 1995.

Friedel, Vicki L., comp. *Women In The United States Military, 1901-1995: A Research Guide and Annotated Bibliography.* Westport, Connecticut: Greenwood Press, 1996.

Gott, Kay. *Women In Pursuit: Flying Fighters For the Air Transport Command Ferrying Division During World War II: A Collection and Recollection.* McKinleyville, California: K. Gott, 1993.

Granger, Byrd Howell. *On Final Approach: The Women Airforce Service Pilots of World War II.* Scottsdale, Arizona: Falconer, 1991.

Gruhzit-Hoyt, Olga. *They Also Served: American Women in World War II.* Secaucus, New Jersey: Carol Publishing, 1995.

Hancock, Joy Bright. *Lady in the Navy: A Personal Reminiscence.* Annapolis, Maryland: Naval Institute Press, 1972.

Hartwick, Ann M. Ritchie. *The Army Medical Specialist Corps: The 45th Anniversary.* Washington, D.C.: U.S. Army Center of Military History, 1993.

Holm, Jeanne. *Women in the Military: An Unfinished Revolution.* (Revised Edition), Novato, California: Presidio Press, 1992.

Johnson, Jesse. *Black Women in the Armed Forces 1942-1974: Missing Pages in U.S. History.* Hampton, Virginia: Hampton Institute, 1974.

Keil, Sally Van Wagenen. *Those Wonderful Women in Their Flying Machines: The Unknown Heroines of World War II* (revised and expanded edition), New York: Four Directions, 1990.

Litoff, Judy Barrett and David C. Smith, eds. *We're In This War Too: World War II Letters From American Women in Uniform.* New York: Oxford University Press, 1994.

Lyne, Mary C. And Kay Arthur. *Three Years Behind the Mast: The Story of the United States Coast Guard SPARs.* Washington, D.C.: U.S. Coast Guard, 1946.

Meid, Pat. *Marine Corps Women's Reserve in World War II.* Washington, D.C.: Historical Branch, G-3 Division, Headquarters, USMC, 1968.

Moore, Brenda Lei. *To Serve My Country, to Serve My Race: The Story of the Only African-American WACs Stationed Overseas During World War II.* New York: New York University Press, 1996.

Morden, Bettie J. *The Women's Army Corps, 1945-1978.* Washington, D.C.: U.S. Army Center of Military History, 1990.

Morgan, Marjorie Lee, ed. *The Clubmobile: The ARC in the Storm.* St. Petersburg, Florida: Hazlett, 1982.

Pateman, Yvonne C. *Women Who Dared: American Female Test Pilots, Flight-Test Engineers, and Astronauts, 1912-1996.* Norstahr, 1997.

Putney, Martha. *When the Nation Was in Need: Blacks in the Women's Army Corps During World War II.* Metuchen., New Jersey: Scarecrow Press, 1992.

Redmond, Juanita. *I Served On Bataan.* (Reprinted Edition), New York: Garland, 1984.

Rosenthal, Rose. *Not All Soldiers Wore Pants: A Witty World War II WAC Tells All.* Rochell Park, New Jersey: Ryzell, 1993.

Seeley, Charlotte Palmer, compiler, revised by Virginia Cardwell Purdy and Robert Gruber. *American Women and the U.S. Armed Forces: A Guide to the Records of Military Agencies in the National Archives Relating to American Women.* Washington D.C.: National Archives and Records Administration, 1992.

Soderbergh, Peter A. *Women Marines: The World War II Era.* Westport, Connecticut: Praeger, 1992.

Sterner, Doris. *In and Out of Harm's Way: A History of the Navy Nurse Corps.* Seattle: Peanut Butter Press, 1996.

Stremlow, Mary V. *Free A Marine To Fight: Women Marines In World War II.* Washington, D.C.: U.S. Marine Corps, History and Museums Division, 1994.

Thomson, Robin J. *The Coast Guard and the Women's Reserve in World War II.* Washington D.C.: Coast Guard Historian's Office, 1992.

Tomblin, Barbara Brooks. *G.I. Nightingales: The Army Nurse Corps in World War II.* Lexington: University Press of Kentucky, 1996.

Treadwell, Mattie E. *The Women's Army Corps: The U.S. Army In World War II.* Washington, D.C.: Office of the Chief of Military History, 1954.

Verges, Marianne. *On Silver Wings: The Women Airforce Service Pilots of World War II 1942-1944.* New York: Ballantine, 1991.

Williams, Denny. *To The Angels.* San Francisco, California: Denson Press, 1985.

Yianilos, Theresa Karas. *Woman Marine: A Memoir of a Woman Who Joined the U.S. Marine Corps in World War II to "Free a Marine to Fight."* La Jolla, California: La Jolla Book Publishing, 1994.

Index

Acadia, USAHS, 129
Adams, Major *Charity,* 5, 50, 171
Aircraft Warning Service, 45, 49
Air evacuation. *See* Flight nursing
Air Force Nurse Corps (AFNC), 19, 148
Air Force Women's Medical Specialist Corps (AFWMSC), 148
Air WACs, 51, 53-54
Air Training Command, 113, 118
Air Transport Command (ATC), 113, 116
Alaska, 16, 19, 33, 98, 109, 139, 140, 146
Algeria, 20, 34, 45-46, 127-28
Allen, Margaret, 33
Anderson, Lieutenant Margaret, 126
American Red Cross, 7, 12, 18, 31, 65, 133-38
  Clubmobile 134, 136-37
  Clubs 134-36
  Home front 137-38
Antiaircraft Artillery (AAA), 43-44, 116
Anzio, Italy, 22
Archard, Lieutenant Theresa, 20
Army Air Forces (AAF), 7, 19, 45, 47, 51, 53-54, 111-13, 115-16, 118-20
Army Air Force Tactical Center, 119
Army Ground Forces (AGF), 45, 53, 54
Army Medical Department, 123

Army-Navy Nurses Act of 1947. *See* Legislation
Army Nurse Corps (ANC), 1-4, 6, 9-28, 41, 127, 136, 143-44, 147-48
  demobilization, 147
  status, 147
Army Service Forces (ASF), 45, 53
Arndt, Major Myrtle E., 11
Arnest, Gertrude B., 29
Arnold, General Henry H. "Hap", 54, 111, 112, 119, 121
Assignments. *See* Jobs/utilization
Atlantic coast, 101
Austin, Neva Vredevoogd, 94
Austria, 147
Avenger Field, Texas, 111, 115, 120-21

Bandel, Lieutenant Colonel Betty, 54
Bauer, Marian, 79
Battle of North Atlantic, 97, 107
Bean, Betty, 108
Benefits, military, 4
  AMSC, 127
  ANC, 27
  MCWR, 79
  NNC, 32, 37
  SPAR, 109
  WAC, 48-49
  WASP, 118-21
  WAVES, 59, 71-72
Benevolence, USS, 35
Bengtson, Ida Albertina, 140
Bennington, Audrey, 79, 81, 86

Bennett, Hospital Corpsman Marie, 65, 75
Bernatitus, Lieutenant Ann A., 31, 37
Black women (*see also* Race relations) 4-5, 28,
  146-47
  ANC, 14-15
  Cadet Nurse Corps, 142
  MCWR, 79, 146
  NNC, 32
  SPAR, 146
  WAC, 45, 49-51, 140, 146-47
  WAVES, 72, 146
Blanchfield, Colonel Florence, 28
Blanche F. Sigman, USAHS, 23-24
Bolton Act (Army-Navy Nurses Act). *See*
  Legislation
Bolton, Congresswoman Frances Payne, 127-28
Bombers
  B-17 (Flying Fortress), 111, 116-17
  B-26 (Martin Marauder), 116
  B-29 (Super Fortress), 111, 120
Bonner, Anna, 124
Boosalis, Viola, 16
Bowman Field, Kentucky, 16
Boyce, Colonel Westray Battle, 53, 54
Boyd, Irene, 10
Bramble, USCGC, 109
Bransom, Captain Henry, 80
British Air Transport Auxiliary (ATA), 112
Brownsville, Texas, 117
Bureau of Aeronautics, 57, 60, 62, 65-66
Bureau of Medicine and Surgery, 3, 31, 65, 66, 71,
  75
Bureau of Naval Personnel, 60, 65, 67, 73
Burns, Major Helen, 126

Cadet Nurse Corps, 7, 32, 140-42
Canada, 107
Camp Lejeune, North Carolina, 81-82, 92
Campbell, Marian White, 45
Carpenter, Lieutenant Mary Louise, 24-26
Casualties (deaths), 37, 146
  ANC, 13, 28
  ARC, 133
  NNC, 36-37
  USO, 139

WASP, 121
WAVES, 74
Chatham, Massachusetts, 108
Cherry Point, North Carolina, 85, 88, 91
China-Burma-India Theater (CBI), 13-19, 51,
  127-28, 134
Churchill, Mary, 43
Civil Service, 57, 67, 123, 127, 131
Clark, General Mark, 46, 54
Cleveland, Ohio, 101
Coast Guard Academy, New London,
  Connecticut, 105
Coast Guard Women's Reserve. *See* SPAR
Cobb, Laura M., 30
Cochran, Jacqueline, 111-13, 115-16, 118-21
Coleman, Mary, 136
Commendation letter, 101, 108
Comfort, USS, 13, 129
Conter, Monica E., 10
Continental United States (CONUS), Zone of
  Interior, 9, 98, 127
Corregidor, 11, 27, 31, 103, 124-26
Craig, Major General H. A., 119
Crandall, Lieutenant Elizabeth, 61, 65

D-Day, 34
Daily, Lieutenant Commander Mary, 7, 57, 65
Dallas, Texas, 113
Dauser, Captain Sue S., 31-32, 37
Davis, Lieutenant Colonel Emily C., 54
  Maxine 19
Decorations
  AMSC, 131
  NNC, 31, 37
  SPAR, 103
  WAC, 45, 47, 49, 54
  WAVES, 74
Demarais, Ensign Mary V., note 21, 34
Demobilization, 147-48
  Dietitians, 131
  MCWR, 93-95, 147, 148
  NNC, 31, 37
  Physical therapists, 131
  SPAR, 103, 109, 147, 149
  WAC, 45, 47-48, 53-55

Demobilization (*continued*)
   WASP, 120
   WAVES, 74-75, 147
Dempsey, Dorothy Riley, 101
Dieterle, Lorraine Jacyno, 106-7
Dietitians, 5, 7, 123-32
Directors, 6
Draft, 5, 39, 49, 77, 145, 148
   nurses, 27-28
Durek, Alene, 32
Duties. *See* Jobs/utilization

Eaker, General Ira C., 47, 54
Ede, Doris, 147
Eisenhower, General Dwight D., 46, 47, 54, 138,
   145, 146, 149
El Toro Marine Air Station, California, 88, 90
Ender, Ensign Elizabeth, 67
England. *See* Great Britain
Erickson, Ruth, 29
European Theater of Operations (ETO), 19-20,
   27, 34, 47, 50, 55, 127, 134, 137
Ewa, 91

Ferrying Groups, 113, 115-16
Flight nursing, 16-19, 34-36
Forrestal, Secretary of the Navy James V., 90-91
Fort Des Moines, Iowa, 41-43, 50, 54
Fort Huachuca, Arizona, 14, 15, 45, 49
Fort Oglethorpe, Georgia, 41, 50, 55
Fourteenth Naval District. *See* Hawaii
France, 19, 34, 39, 47, 51, 74, 128, 134, 139, 144,
   146
Frederiksen, Inga, 79

Gaoni, Vida M., 46
Gardiner, Lieutenant Ruth M., 19
George, Major General Harold L., 112
Germany, 2, 17, 19, 26, 39, 47, 109, 124, 128, 130,
   134, 139, 144, 147
G. I. Bill of Rights, 147
Gleason, Dorothy Jeanne, 102
Goodwin, Lieutenant Colonel Katherine R., 54
Gower, Pauline, 112
Grace, Lieutenant Margaret, 14

Grady, Loudene, 92
Gray, Ruth, 136
Great Britain, 2, 19-20, 34, 43, 45, 47, 50-51, 107,
   112, 126-28, 133, 135, 139
Greenland patrol, 97, 107
Guadacanal, 83
Guam, 29-30, 34-35, 128

Hall, Helen, 136
Hallaren, Colonel Mary A., 47, 149
Halsey, Admiral William F., 37, 107
Hamblet, Major Julia E., 80, 93-94
Hamerschlag, Lieutenant (junior grade) Vera,
   107-8
Hancock, Captain Joy Bright, 59-60, 69, 149
Harned, Vivian Reese, 102
Haskell, Lieutenant Ruth, 21
Hawaii (*see also* Overseas deployments)
   ANC, 10
   MCWR, 72-73, 90-91, 146
   NNC, 29
   SPAR, 98, 146
   USO, 139
   WAC, 52
   WAVES, 72-73, 146
Heck, Lieutenant Commander Mary Martha, 34
Henderson Hall, Virginia, 89
Henderson, General Archibald, 89
Henry, Peggy, 136-37
Hensinger, Louise, 92
Hersey, Agnes Rothman, 144
Higbee, Captain Lenah S. (*see also Lenah S.*
   Higbee, USS), 37
Hobby, Colonel Oveta Culp, 6, 9, 40-41, 43-44,
   54, 91
Holcomb, General Thomas, 77-78, 95
Hope, USS, 13
Horton, Captain Mildred McAfee (*see also*
   McAfee, Mildred), 75
Hospital Corps, Navy, 33-35, 66, 68, 75
Houston, Texas, 113-115
Howard, Mary Ferebee, 134-35
Hughes Airport, Texas, 114
Hunter College, New York City, 64-65, 72, 80-82,
   102-3

Italy, 19, 22-24, 34, 39, 46-47, 124, 126, 128, 134, 139

Japan, 2-3, 11, 29-30, 35, 39-40, 53-55, 126, 130, 135, 140, 147
Jefferson, Chief Warrant Officer Alice, 104
Jobs/utilization, 145-46
    ARC, 133-38
    Cadet Nurse Corps, 141-42
    Dietitians, 126-29
    MCWR, 84-88, 91-93, 95
    NNC, 33-35
    Occupational therapists, 125
    Physical therapists, 127-29
    Salvation Army, 139-40
    SPAR, 106-8
    USO, 138-39
    USPHS, 140, 142
    WAC, 43-47, 50-51, 53-55
    WASP, 113, 116-120
    WAVES, 58, 61-62, 64-66, 68-70, 73-75
Johnson, Mary Blakemore, 52

Kendeigh, Ensign Jane, 35-36
Kerensky, Seaman Second Class Elizabeth, 74
Kitchen, Lieutenant Etta Belle, 60
Knox, Frank, 78
Kozak, Lieutenant (junior grade) Stephany J., 34
Kuehlthau, Brunetta A., 124-26

LaFave, Lieutenant Thelma, 19
Lally, Grace, 29
L'Ecuyer, Eleanor C., 100
Legislation, 27, 32-33, 37, 40-41, 48-49, 57-59, 71-73, 91, 97, 105, 109, 119-21, 127-28, 132, 140, 147, 149
    Army-Navy Nurses Act of 1947, 27, 37, 148
    Pay Adjustment Act or 1942, 27, 32
    Women's Armed Services Integration Act of 1948, 55, 81, 95, 109, 149
    Veteran's status for WASP 121
Lejeune, Eugenia D., 86
Lentz, Anne, 78
Lenah S. Higbee, USS, 37
Leone, Lucile Petry, 140

Lindberg, Geraldine D., 130
Link trainers, 66, 73, 74, 86, 104
Little, Zetta, 79
Lockborne AAB, Ohio, 116, 117
Long Beach, California, 113
LORAN, 107-8
Los Alamos, New Mexico, 44-45
Love, Nancy Harkness, 112-113, 116
Lutz, Lieutenant Aleda, 19

MacArthur, General Douglas, 52-54, 125, 146
Mackey, Veronica, 68
Mactan, SS, 133
Mahar, Major Edna, 12
Mainbocher, 60
Manhattan Beach Training Station, New York, 102
Manhattan Project, The, 44-45
Marine Corps Air Station, Mojave, California, 87
Marine Corps Women's Reserve (MCWR), 5, 6, 48, 61-62, 65, 77-95, 97, 108, 119, 146-49
    adjustment, 81-83
    band, 92-93
    black women, 79, 146
    chain of command, 86-88
    demobilization, 93-95, 148
    harassment, 82-83
    jobs, 84-86
    lifestyle, 88-90
    overseas (Hawaii), 90-91
    permanent status, 149
    recruiting, 78-79, 84
    training, 79-81
    uniforms, 81, 83-84
Marshall, General George C., 40, 43, 54
Marshall, Kay, 136
Mather AAB, California, 117
Matsonia, SS, 91
Mauldin, Bill, 22
McAfee, Captain Mildred (see also Horton, Mildred McAfee), 6, 70
    becomes WAVES Director, 58-61
    black women and, 72
    promoted to Captain, 71
    quoted, 63, 70, 75

McClarren, Lucille E., 79
McElroy, Sergeant Major Halbert A., 81
Medals. *See* Decorations
Medical evacuation. *See* Flight nursing
Mediterranean Theater, 19, 127, 137
Mercy, USS, 13
Military Women's Memorial, 150
Missouri, USS, 35, 54, 144
Mobilization, 2-4
  ANC, 2-4, 27
  Dietitians, 123-24
  MCWR, 6, 77-79
  National Guard, 2
  NNC, 2-4, 31-33
  Physical therapists, 123-24
  SPAR, 97-103
  WAC, 39, 49
  WASP, 112-13
  WAVES, 59
Moline, Lieutenant Anna, 24
Moore, Brenda, 51
Morgan, Patricia G., 65
Morris, Gertrude, 42
Motley, Ruby F., 124-26
Mount Holyoke College, Massachusetts, 61, 80-82

National Association for the Advancement of
  Colored People (NAACP), 50
National Catholic Community Service, 138
National Guard, 2
National Jewish Welfare Board, 138
Native American, photo, 90
Naval Air Transport Service (NATS), 62
Navy attack planes, 116
Navy Nurse Corps (NNC), 1-4, 6, 29-37, 144
  demobilization, 147
  status, 147
Navy Women's Reserve. *See* WAVES
New Castle, Delaware, 113
Newfoundland, HMSHS, 22
New Guinea, 11-12, 34, 52, 127, 128, 129, 135-36,
  138, 146, 147
Nimitz, Admiral Chester, W., 37
Normandy, France, 19, 24-27, 134, 146

North Africa, 19-21, 34, 45-46, 127, 131, 134, 137
Northampton, Massachusetts. *See* Smith
  College, 80
Numbers of women, 1, 2, 144
  ANC, 9, 16, 22, 27-28
  ARC, 137
  Cadet Nurses, 142
  Dietitians, 123, 130
  MCWR, 77-79, 84, 93
  NNC, 31-37
  Occupational therapists, 123, 130
  Physical therapists, 123, 130
  SPAR, 98, 103, 106, 109
  WAC, 41, 47-49, 51, 53
  WASP, 121
  WAVES, 58, 60-62, 67, 71-73, 75

Occupation forces, 55, 147
Occupational therapists, 7, 66, 123-32
Osburn, Josephine Clapp, 140
O'Toole, Lieutenant Sarah, 34
Overseas deployments, 144, 146
  ANC, 10-27
  ARC, 133-34
  Dietitians, 123, 126-28
  MCWR, 48, 90-91, 146
  NNC, 29-36
  Physical therapists, 123, 127-28
  SPAR, 48, 98, 109, 146
  USO, 139
  WAC, 45-47, 50-53, 144, 146
  WAVES, 48, 72-73, 146

Pacific coast, 101
Pacific Theater, 127
Pallas Athene, 41, 53
Palm Beach, Florida, 101-4, 106
Palmer, Carroll E., 142
Palmer, Lieutenant Jean, 60
Pardew, Anna Bonner, 124
Parks, Ruth, 9
Pearl Harbor, Hawaii, 2, 3, 9, 10, 29, 34-35, 39, 57,
  91, 97, 112, 124, 133, 140
Pennington, Lieutenant (junior grade) Clyde E.,
  34

Pershing, General John J., 3
Peto, Lieutenant Marjorie, 19-20
Pharmacists, 66
Pharmacist's Mate, 100-4
Philippine Islands, 10-11, 13, 19, 27, 30-31, 34, 52-53, 103, 124-26, 128, 133, 139, 146
Physical therapists, 7, 66, 123-32
Pickens, Lieutenant (junior grade) Harriet, 72
Plummer, Master Sergeant Charlotte, 92
Potter, Helen, 136
Postwar, 143-45
Prisoners of war, 10-11, 29-31, 102, 124-26, 133, 139
Public Health Service. See United States Public Health Service
Pursuit/fighter aircraft, 111, 117
Putney, Dr. Martha, 147

Quinn, First Lieutenant Helena D., 129

Race relations (see also Black women), 4-5, 28, 146-47
    ANC, 14-16, 28
    Cadet Nurse Corps, 142
    MCWR, 5, 79, 146
    NNC, 32
    SPAR, 5, 146
    WAC, 5, 49-51, 146-47
    WAVES, 5, 72, 146
Radio Washington, 73
Ranks/rates
    AMSC, 127
    ANC, 27
    Dietitians, 127-28
    MCWR, 77, 78
    NNC, 32-33, 37
    Physical therapists, 127-28
    SPAR, 98
    WAC, 41-42, 49, 54
    WAVES, 59, 71
Rayburn, First Lieutenant Edna, 129
Recruiting
    ANC, 27-28
    Dietitians, 123
    MCWR, 78-79, 84

    NNC, 31-32, 37
    Physical therapists, 123
    SPAR, 98-102, 108
    WAC, 41, 47, 54
    WASP, 112-13
    WAVES, 58, 60, 63-64, 75
Red Cross. See American Red Cross
Reese-Harned, Vivian, 102
Refuge, USS, 34
Reiper, Rose, 11
Relief, USS, 35
Rescue, USS, 35
Reynard, Lieutenant Elizabeth, 59
Roensch, Eleanor Stone, 44-45
Rogers, Congresswoman Edith Nourse, 40-41, 48
Romulus Air Field, Michigan, 113, 119
Roosevelt, Mrs. Franklin D., 81
Roosevelt, President Franklin Delano, 2, 27, 39, 97, 123, 138-39
Roswell AAB, New Mexico, 116

Salvation Army, 79, 139-40
Saverino, Musician First Class Louis, 92
Schiek, Mary Thomas (later Mary Sargent), 135-36
Schleman, Captain Helen, 98
Segregation. See Race relations
Selective Service and Training Act (see also Legislation), 5
Services of Supply (SOS), 52
Shaw Air Base, South Carolina, 118
Shelly, Commander Mary Jo, 63
Sigman, Lieutenant Blanche Faye, 22-24
Sirmon, Annie Lea, 147
Smallwood, Bonnie, 92-93
Smith College, Massachusetts, 61-62, 80, 105
Smith, Congresswoman (later Senator) Margaret Chase, 101, 132, 149
Smith, Florence Ebersole, 102
Smith, General Holland M., 90
Smith, Lassie Moores, 139
Solace, USS, 29, 35
Southwest Pacific Area (SWPA), 2, 51-53, 134
SPAR, 5-6, 27, 48, 61, 65, 77, 78, 79, 83, 97-110, 119, 146-49

SPAR (*continued*)
  deactivation, 149
  demobilization 108-9
  establishment, 97-98
  jobs, 105-7
  overseas, 98
  recruiting, 99-103, 105
  training, 100-6
  uniforms, 103
SPAR, USCGC, 109-10
Spearfish, USN submarine, 31
Speer, Albert, 144-45
Staats, Lieutenant Mary H., 35
Status, military, 1, 4, 6, 148-49
  AMSC, 7, 148
  ANC, 4, 27, 148
  ARC, 7
  Cadet Nurse Corps, 7
  Dietitians, 7, 127-28
  NNC, 4, 32-33, 37, 148
  MCWR, 145
  Occupational therapists, 7
  Physical therapists, 7, 127-28
  USO, 7
  USPHS, 7
  WAC, 41, 48-49, 54-55
  WASP, 7
Staupers, Mabel Keaton, 15
St. Clair, Ensign Betty, 67
Stone, Ellen, 92-93
Storis, USCGC, 109
Stout, Dottie, 136
Stratemeyer, Major General George, 51
Stratton, Captain Dorothy C., 6, 61, 97-98
Streeter, Colonel Ruth Cheney, 6, 78, 81, 83-84,
    86-87, 91, 93
Strengths. *See* Numbers of women
Stroup, Major Beatrice Hood, xiii
Supply Corps, Navy, 62-63

Taylor, Jane, 79
Torrance, Ensign Elizabeth, note 20, 34
Towle, Colonel Katherine A., 79-81, 93
Training, 148
  ANC, 16-17, 20

Cadet Nurses, 140-42
Dietitians, 24, 124, 132
MCWR, 61, 65, 78-81, 84
NNC, 32-35
Occupational therapists, 124, 132
Physical therapists, 124, 132
SPAR, 61, 65, 100-6, 108
WAC, 41-44, 50, 54
WASP, 113-17, 119-20
WAVES, 59-70, 80, 103
Training aircraft, 111, 114-15
Tranquillity, USS, 35
Traveler's Aid Association, 138
Treadwell, Mattie E., 39
Treasury Department, 97, 109
Truman, President Harry S., 107, 132, 147, 149
Tuomi, Eleanor Nocito, 88

Ukraine, 24-25
Umbach, Lieutenant Edna, 16
United States Public Health Service (USPHS), 7,
    140-2
United Service Organizations (USO), 7, 138-40
University of Iowa, 64
U. S. Air Force (*see also* Army Air Forces), 109,
    121, 148, 149
Utility Aircraft, 111, 114-15
Utilization. *See* Jobs/utilization

Van Gorp, Lieutenant (junior grade) Dymphna,
    34
V-E Day, 54, 130, 144, 147
Veley, Captain Beth, 26-27
Veterans, women as, 143, 150
V-J Day, 54, 93, 102, 130, 139, 144, 147
Vogel, Colonel Emma E., 131

WAAC, 5, 6, 39-50, 57, 77-78, 146
  overseas, 140, 142
  race relations, 140
WAC, 5, 39-55, 79, 108, 119, 128, 131, 144-49
  race relations 146-47
  Regular 145
Waesche, Admiral Russell R., 98
Wainwright, General Jonathan, 11, 37, 107

Waller, Colonel Littleton W. T., 87
War Department, 93, 120
War's end, 93-95, 144
WASP, 6-7, 44, 111-21, 149
  deactivation, 120-21
  duties, 116-20
  origins, 111-13
  status, 7, 149
  training, 113-16
  types of aircraft flown, 111, 114-17, 120
  uniforms, 115-16, 118
Watson, Georgia B., 42-44
WAVES, 5, 6, 27, 48, 57-75, 77, 78, 79, 80, 83, 90-
    91, 97, 103, 105, 107-8, 119, 144, 146-49
  acronym, 59
  benefits, 71
  black women in, 72, 146
  contributions of, 73-74
  deaths of, 74
  demobilization of, 74-75, 147
  discipline, 70-71
  enlisted women's recruitment/training, 62-70
  establishment of, 57-59
  in Hawaii, 73
  marriage/parental policies, 70-71
  officer's procurement-training, 59-62
  overseas, 146
  promotions, 71
  Regular, 149
  uniforms, 60
Weatherford, Lieutenant Wilma, 18

Wedge, Danelia, 79
Weissblatt, Vivian R. (later a Major), 124
Whittaker, Janet, 136
Wilcox, Ella Wheeler, 110
Wild, Gail, 136
Williams, Captain Cornelia, 84
Wills, Ensign Frances, 72
Wilson, Lucy, 11
Wing, Major, 91
Women Airforce Service Pilots. See WASP
Women's Army Auxiliary Corps. See WAAC
Women's Auxiliary Ferrying Squadron (WAFS),
    112-13, 115-16
Women's Armed Services Integration Act of
    1948. See Legislation
Women's Army Corps. See WAC
Women's Flying Training Detachment (WFTD),
    113-15
Women Medical Specialist Corps (WMSC), 7,
    123-32, 148
Women's Reserve (WR) Marine Corps. See
    Marine Corps Women's Reserve
World War I, 1-3, 31, 57, 60, 77, 123

YMCA, 138
YWCA, 138
Yount, General Barton, 113

Zone of Interior. See Continental United States
    (CONUS)